M000050075

Building Globalization

Building Globalization

Transnational Architecture Production in Urban China

XUEFEI REN

THE UNIVERSITY OF CHICAGO PRESS   CHICAGO AND LONDON

XUEFEI REN is assistant professor of sociology and global urban studies at Michigan State University.

The University of Chicago Press, Chicago 60637
The University of Chicago Press, Ltd., London
© 2011 by The University of Chicago
All rights reserved. Published 2011.
Printed in the United States of America
20 19 18 17 16 15 14 13 12 11   1 2 3 4 5

ISBN-13: 978-0-226-70980-2 (cloth)
ISBN-13: 978-0-226-70981-9 (paper)

ISBN-10: 0-226-70980-9 (cloth)
ISBN-10: 0-226-70981-7 (paper)

Library of Congress Cataloging-in-Publication Data

Ren, Xuefei.
  Building globalization : transnational architecture production in urban China / Xuefei Ren.
     p. cm.
  Includes bibliographical references and index.
  ISBN-13: 978-0-226-70980-2 (cloth : alk. paper)
  ISBN-10: 0-226-70980-9 (cloth : alk. paper)
  ISBN-13: 978-0-226-70981-9 (pbk. : alk. paper)
  ISBN-10: 0-226-70981-7 (pbk. : alk. paper) 1. Architecture and globalization—China.
2. Urban renewal—China. 3. City planning—China. I. Title.
  NA2543.G46R46 2011
  307.1'2160951090511—dc22

                                                        2010032190

♾ The paper used in this publication meets the minimum requirements of the American National Standard for Information Sciences—Permanence of Paper for Printed Library Materials, ANSI Z39.48-1992.

FOR MY PARENTS

Contents

List of Illustrations   ix

Preface: Up in Flames   xi

Acknowledgments   xiii

Abbreviations   xvii

Map of China   xviii

CHAPTER 1.   Space, Capital, and Global Cities:
An Introduction   1
- Transnational Architectural Production   6
- Building China's Global Cities   10
- The Study   13
- Organization of the Book   16

CHAPTER 2.   Transnational Architectural Production:
Firms, Cities, Trends   19
- World City Networks   21
- The Power of Large   24
- The Power of Small   33
- A Typology of Cities   37
- Locating Transnational Architectural Production
in China   38
- Ordos 100   58

CHAPTER 3.   Architecture, Media, and Real Estate Speculation   60
- From Peking to Beijing: A Genealogy of Downtowns   61
- Architectural Spectacles: From SOHO NewTown to the
Commune to Jianwai SOHO   71

- Public Spectacles and Place Making   79
- SOHO Xiaobao: From Sales Brochures to a Literary Magazine   84
- Developers and Policy Making   86
- The Art of Sales, the Game of Survival   91
- The Divided City   96
- Shifting Centers, Shifting Powers   97

CHAPTER 4.   History, Cosmopolitanism, and Preservation   99
- Deciphering Preservation in Urban China   102
- From *Chai* (Demolition) to *Bao* (Preservation)   104
- Xintiandi: New Heaven and Earth   110
- Displacement, Relocation, and Compensation   124
- Beijing Preservation   132
- The New "Old" Chinese City   136

CHAPTER 5.   Olympic Spectacles, Critical Architecture, and New State Spaces   140
- Olympic Beijing   142
- A National Bid for the Olympics   144
- Going for Global Architecture   148
- The Bird's Nest Controversy   152
- Critical Architecture: A Debate   159
- Architecture, State, and Political Change   164

CHAPTER 6.   The Power of Symbol   167
- Symbolic Spaces   167
- Symbolic Capital and Its Transformations   169
- Symbolic Power: Repositioning of Territorial Elites   172
- An Urban Revolution, from Above and Below   176

Appendix: A Methodological Note on Network Analysis   179

Notes   189

Bibliography   201

Index   213

Illustrations

TABLES

Table 2.1   Projects by SOM, 1936–2008 / 26

Table 2.2   City locations of major projects designed by SOM, 2000–2008 / 26

Table 2.3   National origins of the top fifty architecture firms of 2007 / 27

Table 2.4   Cities with the largest number of branch offices of the top hundred architecture firms / 28

Table 2.5   Centrality scores and rankings for the top fifty cities / 30

Table 2.6   Rankings of cities in previous studies / 32

Table 2.7   Boutique architectural firms' consumption and production cities: A comparison / 35

Table 2.8   Select list of megaprojects designed by international architecture firms in Beijing and Shanghai, 1998–2008 / 52

Table 4.1   Demolition and relocation of residents in Shanghai, 1995–2008 / 104

Table 4.2   The twelve historical and cultural heritage areas of 2003, Shanghai / 109

Table A.1   Correlations of different centrality measures / 180

Table A.2   Fifty largest architecture firms by country in the *BD* survey, 2007 / 180

Table A.3   Select list of fifty boutique architecture firms by city location / 181

Table A.4   OMA's global architectural team working on the CCTV Project, Beijing / 182

Table A.5   List of participating architects for Ordos 100 project, Inner
            Mongolia, China / 185

FIGURES

Figure 1.1   The Commune by the Great Wall, Beijing / 2

Figure 1.2   Shangdu SOHO, designed by Peter Davidson, Beijing / 3

Figure 1.3   The National Center for the Performing Arts, designed by
             Paul Andreu, Beijing / 4

Figure 1.4   The China Central Television Headquarters, designed by
             Office for Metropolitan Architecture, Beijing / 5

Figure 2.1   The architecture branch office network of 198 world
             cities / 29

Figure 3.1   The historical center of Beijing / 63

Figure 3.2   Map of Beijing / 67

Figure 3.3   Central business district, Beijing, 2009 / 70

Figure 3.4   SOHO NewTown, Beijing / 72

Figure 3.5   Jianwai SOHO, Beijing / 77

Figure 3.6   Performance art project at Jianwai SOHO, 2005 / 80

Figure 3.7   Migrant workers waiting to be taken to a cinema, Beijing,
             2005 / 82

Figure 4.1   "Chai," the demolition sign, Shanghai / 100

Figure 4.2   Map of Shanghai / 108

Figure 4.3   Shikumen houses used by multiple families / 111

Figure 4.4   Taipingqiao Park built on former neighborhoods / 115

Figure 4.5   Renovated shikumen building as Starbucks / 116

Figure 4.6   The neighborhood near Xintiandi being demolished,
             2006 / 127

Figure 4.7   Hutongs being demolished, Beijing, 2008 / 133

Figure 5.1   The Bird's Nest, Beijing, August 2008 / 141

Figure 5.2   Jianguomen Boulevard, central business district, Beijing,
             August 2008 / 143

Preface

Up in Flames

On the evening of February 8, 2009, the last day of the Chinese Lunar New Year, the unfinished CCTV (China Central Television) complex in Beijing erupted in a spectacular fire. The fire, caused by illegal fireworks set off by CCTV's own employees to celebrate the new year, engulfed every floor of the five-star Mandarin Oriental Hotel, a fifteen-hundred-seat theater, and state-of-the-art recording studios housed in the complex. The CCTV headquarters is the most controversial development among all the megaprojects built in Beijing in the pre-Olympic years, not only for its astronomical construction cost but also for its potent symbolism. With its striking design by OMA (Office for Metropolitan Architecture), a renowned European architecture firm, the project clearly signifies the financial and political prowess of China Central Television—the most powerful broadcasting network in China and the propaganda hub of the Chinese communist party-state. Architectural marvels such as the CCTV building indicate a clear transformation of the Chinese party-state, which has become a visible force of architectural globalization by financing large-scale iconic projects.

The image of the CCTV complex ablaze is no less spectacular than the iconic architecture itself. Soon after the fire broke out, thousands of residents hurried to the site to take photos of the fire with cell phones and cameras from all possible angles. Major media networks, including the BBC and CNN, also rushed to the site to record the spectacle. Local celebrities, from the real estate tycoon Pan Shiyi to iconoclast artist Ai Wei Wei, competed to post photos of the fire on their blogs and claimed, "I was there—at the CCTV fire!" Within less than an hour, news of the CCTV fire was spread via Twitter all over the world, and images and video clips of the blaze were already on YouTube.

In the meantime, the Chinese government issued a censorship notice to various news sources and websites in an attempt to control the coverage of the fire. The censorship notice specifically ordered news outlets not to post any photo images, not to report the incident in detail, and only to publish the official report of the fire from the state-controlled Xinhua news service. As a result of this deliberate government censorship, television coverage of the fire was nonexistent in China, and major domestic websites pulled off the fire photos they had posted. But ironically, some Internet users managed to post the original government censorship notice and various revised photos mocking the CCTV fire on the Web.[1] The fire was no minor loss, but little sympathy for the tragedy could be found in the online postings and commentaries. On the contrary, many saw the fire as a well-deserved punishment for the extravagant government expenditure of public money on the CCTV project.

If the Olympics opening ceremony staged in the National Stadium in August 2008 was a bright spectacle symbolizing the ascendance of China as a new power on the world stage, then the CCTV fire six months later was a dark spectacle marking a turning point of China's urban construction boom. Iron fences have replaced the Olympics billboards of a year ago in an attempt to hide the charred remains of the building. But residents, tourists, architecture students, and other passersby come to the site on a regular basis, registering with cameras the damaged architectural masterpiece. In a strange way, the burned CCTV tower, peeking from behind the iron fences, has also brought a certain kind of relief to the city and its residents, suggesting the end of spectacles, the fragility of architecture, and the return of normality and, possibly, ordinariness too.

This book tells a story of China's urban transformations through the lens of the architectural metamorphoses in Chinese cities. The main bulk of fieldwork was conducted in Beijing and Shanghai between 2004 and 2008—an extraordinary time period of massive urban renewal and destruction. The events that happened and urban megaprojects constructed during this period have in many ways fundamentally changed the social and spatial organization of Chinese cities and urban life. By zooming in on the social worlds of both power brokers—those who have great influence on reshaping Chinese cities—and ordinary urban citizens, this book provides an account of how Chinese cities were made, remade, and unmade in the first decade of the twenty-first century.

Acknowledgments

In 1998 I left China for Japan to pursue my postgraduate study in sociology and urban planning. At Nagoya University and Tokyo Metropolitan University, I had the good fortune to work with Yasushi Matsumoto, one of the finest urban scholars in Japan. It was during my years in Japan and under the guidance of Matsumoto that I began to embark on urban research. My general intellectual thirst to make sense of the urban crystallized into concrete research questions and projects once I began my doctoral study in Chicago in 2001. Here again I was extremely fortunate to work with many inspiring professors and fellow graduate students. Saskia Sassen introduced me to many key institutions around the world that were crucial for this research. Her sharp, concise, and humorous comments were especially illuminating at times when I was overwhelmed by fieldwork encounters. Input and feedback from William Parish, Dingxin Zhao, and Anthony King (SUNY–Binghamton) were also crucial in shaping the contours of the final book. King's writings on spaces of globalization inspired me to choose transnational architectural production as a topic in the first place.

I must also thank the University of Chicago for its institutional support. It was a great privilege to spend six years in such an intellectually stimulating environment as Hyde Park. The numerous workshops at the university provided good venues for me to present my work in progress. I would like to thank the participants at the Workshops on East Asia, Built Environment, Culture of Globalization, and Urban Structure and Processes. The informal study group of Chinese sociology Ph.D. students was a major source of support, friendship, and inspiration. Many other graduate students and faculty also read my draft chapters and provided insightful feedback for revisions. My classes at the Graham School of General Studies in

2006 and 2007 offered great opportunities to practice communicating my ideas in jargon-free language. The Division of Social Sciences and the Center for East Asian Studies at the University of Chicago provided crucial funding for dissertation fieldwork and writing.

When I left China in 1998, most Chinese cities were still in the stage of taking off—although the dawn of a new era could be clearly felt in the air, the pace of urban redevelopment was still relatively slow. But when I returned to China in 2004 to begin fieldwork, I found myself in the middle of an urban construction boom. My rediscovery of urban China would have been very different without the many people I got to know during my fieldwork. They generously took the time to share with me their views, critiques, and dreams about Chinese cities. Xu Yang at SOHO China introduced me to many key figures in the real estate and media sectors in Beijing. Developer Pan Shiyi at SOHO China and artist Ai Wei Wei showed me how real estate, art, and entertainment can be creatively mixed. The creative works of Neville Mars, Bert de Muynck, Monica Carrico, and many other young European architects based in China inspired me to dig harder and deeper into the city-making exercise in China. In Shanghai, developer Vincent Lo, architect Ben Wood, Luwan district government official Lu Zhiqin, and residents in the Xintiandi area showed me the delicate power balance in the property development process. In both cities, I had easy access to a large number of architects from different backgrounds working in various types of firms. Their views on urban China greatly informed the analyses presented here. My academic colleagues at Chinese universities connected me to many other urban scholars in China. Special thanks go to Zheng Shiling and Zhu Dajian at Tongji University, Yu Hai at Fudan University, Cheng Tongshun at Nankai University, Feng Shizheng and Xia Jianzhong at Renmin University, and Wang Tianfu and Xiao Lin at Tsinghua University.

Much of this manuscript was written in the bucolic confines of the Michigan State University (MSU) campus. After leaving Chicago, I was fortunate to start my first job in the Department of Sociology and Global Urban Studies at MSU. It would not have been possible to complete this book without the generous IRGP grant from MSU that provided crucial funding to enable follow-up fieldwork and concentrated writing in 2008 and 2009. Special thanks go to Jan Bokermeier, Steve Gold, and Laura Reese. My colleagues at MSU—Peilei Fan, Guo Chen, Alesia Montgomery, Larry Busch, Zhenmei Zhang, and Carl Taylor, among many others in sociology, geography, and urban planning—also provided good vibes and collegial support. Xueshi Li and Minting Ye are excellent research assistants who helped update some of the data used in the book. The interdisciplinary Global Urban Studies Program provided continuous intellectual stimulus.

I have also greatly benefited from feedback from organizers and participants at conferences at which I presented my work, including the American Sociological Association, the Midwest Sociology Association, the Association of American Geographers, the Urban Affairs Association, the Association of Collegiate Schools of Planning, the Association of European Schools of Planning, the American Anthropology Association, and the Research Committee 21 (Urban and Regional Development) of the International Sociology Association. Many colleagues and friends have kindly invited me to present my work at their institutions. I presented various chapters of this book at the University of Toronto, the University of Michigan, Northwestern University, Rikkyo University (Japan), Hong Kong Baptist University, Ritsumeikan Asia Pacific University (Japan), University of California–Berkeley, Bowdoin College, and the New School of Social Research. Special thanks go to Mary Gallagher, Adrian Blackwell, Tong Lam, Wendy Griswold, Danching Ruan, Yasushi Matsumoto, and Eiko Ikegami. Many helpful comments from the diverse audiences at these presentations were incorporated in the final manuscript.

Many of the ideas in the book were inspired by conversations and e-mail exchanges with my urban colleagues around the world. I would like to thank specially Fulong Wu, Neil Brenner, Laurence J. C. Ma, Kevin Cox, Leslie Sklair, Tony Orum, Deborah Davis, Sophie Body-Gendrot, James Farrer, Andrew Field, Duanfang Lu, Liza Weinstein, Xiangming Chen, Gerardo del Cerro, Jun Jiang, Ning Ou, Meng Sun, Yue Zhang, Tingwei Zhang, Tan Kok Meng, Zhiyuan Yu, Jingsheng Zhu, and Pu Miao. Fulong Wu and Neil Brenner kindly read the whole manuscript on short notice at the final revision stage.

Chapters 4 and 5 were originally published in *City and Community* and the *Journal of Urban Affairs*. Both chapters have been rewritten and substantiated with new fieldwork materials for inclusion in this book. The editors and anonymous reviewers at these journals offered insightful suggestions.

I would also like to thank my editors at the University of Chicago Press, Doug Mitchell and Tim McGovern, for their confidence in this book and their support during the review and production process. Rachel Kamins, former copyeditor for the *American Journal of Sociology*, offered much-needed help with proofreading and copyediting. Ellen White at Michigan

State University and Andrew Clark at MAS Studio in Chicago helped make the maps in the book.

The journey of making this book would have been unimaginable without friends and family. I will always be grateful to Ronen Steinberg, who read and edited every chapter of this manuscript more than once. Without his wit, love, and laughter, this journey would have been a different one. Jingsheng Zhu and Yu Liu in Hyde Park are great hosts during my frequent weekend trips to Chicago. Neil Brenner has helped me discover the joy of running and offers excellent advice to stay injury-free. My sister Yunfei always brings balance to my life by not taking me too seriously. Finally, the love and support from my parents over the years made it possible for me to study and travel the world. Their life philosophy and resilience showed me the strength of the generation of the Cultural Revolution.

Abbreviations

AIA	American Institute of Architects
BD	*Building and Design*
BIAD	Beijing Institute of Architecture Design
BMPC	Beijing Municipal Planning Commission
BOBICO	Beijing Olympic Games Bid Committee
BOCOG	Beijing Organizing Committee for the Olympic Games
CAJ	China Academic Journals database
CBD	Central Business District
CCP	Chinese Communist Party
CCTV	China Central Television
CITIC	China International Trust and Investment Corporation
ENR	*Engineering News Record*
FDI	Foreign Direct Investment
GATS	General Agreement for Trade in Services
GaWC	Globalization and World Cities Research Group
IOC	International Olympic Committee
OMA	Office for Metropolitan Architecture
RIBA	Royal Institute of British Architects
SEZ	Special Economic Zone
SOE	State-Owned Enterprise
SOM	Skidmore, Owings & Merrill LLP
WTO	World Trade Organization

Chinese personal names appearing in the book follow last-name-first order.

FRONTISPIECE. Map of China

CHAPTER ONE

Space, Capital, and Global Cities: An Introduction

On the northern outskirts of Beijing, a cluster of twelve newly built, ultramodern luxury villas is hidden in the rolling mountains near the Great Wall. This place is called the Commune by the Great Wall. Although the name is borrowed from "people's commune"—a collective farming system established during the socialist period in rural China—the place evokes no memories of socialist communes. With each house designed by a prominent architect, the Commune by the Great Wall is the most upscale resort hotel in the country (fig. 1.1). It regularly hosts celebrities, business executives, and multinational corporations for company events. The main villa is the private clubhouse of the development company SOHO China, a sophisticated real estate firm well known for its extensive use of avant-garde architecture to brand its projects.

On a hot summer day in 2004, the clubhouse was packed with local celebrities, business executives, foreign expatriates, and journalists. I was among the five hundred guests invited to the gala evening celebrating the opening of the company's next megaproject—Shangdu SOHO, a high-profile mixed-use development in the central business district in Beijing (fig. 1.2). Nothing about the opening ceremony resembled a promotional event by a real estate company. Following an exotic flamenco dance performance, the developer Pan Shiyi introduced the Australian architect Peter Davidson. As the designer of Federation Square in Melbourne, Davidson is known for creating bold design images through the use of abstract geometric forms. In a talk delivered in English about his conceptualization process, Davidson made frequent references to postmodern architectural theory. A few times during the talk, the translator could not find the right

FIGURE 1.1. The Commune by the Great Wall, Beijing. Photograph courtesy of SOHO China.

Chinese words for his architectural jargon. It was unclear how many in the audience actually understood what the architect was trying to communicate. But it didn't matter much to the host, since the sole purpose of the event was to let people know that this was yet another project from SOHO China designed by a prominent international architect.

A preference for international architects is evident not only in commercial developments but also in large-scale public projects. In the past few years, the city government of Beijing has commissioned international architecture firms to design a number of high-profile public projects, including the National Center for the Performing Arts, designed by Paul Andreu (fig. 1.3), the CCTV headquarters by OMA (fig. 1.4), the National Olympic Stadium, or "Bird's Nest," by Swiss architects Jacques Herzog and Pierre de Meuron, and Terminal 3 of Beijing International Airport, by Norman Foster. These signature projects have transformed the image of Beijing from that of a dusty postsocialist city into that of a global metropolis. Other cities across the country have imitated the practice of organizing design competitions and inviting international architects to design public buildings. As a result, ironically, many organizations and branches of the Chinese communist party-state are increasingly accommodated in buildings designed by cutting-edge international architects.

To a large degree, market logic explains the search for international architects by private developers and national and local governments in China. For private developers, cutting-edge architectural design, especially by well-known international architects, is a marketing tool to brand

FIGURE I.2. Shangdu SOHO, designed by Peter Davidson, Beijing. Photograph courtesy of SOHO China.

FIGURE 1.3. The National Center for the Performing Arts, designed by Paul Andreu, Beijing. Photograph by the author.

and sell their projects. By associating themselves with international design firms, local developers can create a public image as sophisticated patrons of architecture rather than profit-driven speculators, thus differentiating their projects in the crowded property market. For investors, a property associated with a prominent international architect is an indisputable status symbol; and more important, investing in a "signature building" can reduce risks and yield a higher financial return. But market logic alone cannot fully explain the search for international architects by China's new urban elites. The state-sponsored megaprojects, such as the Olympic Stadium, require tremendous resources and cannot be justified in market terms. In spite of the controversies they have generated—a topic I will turn to later—the Chinese state has backed these projects both financially and politically. Under the spotlight of the 2008 Olympics, the Chinese government staged a spectacle in the Bird's Nest to demonstrate the country's rise as a geopolitical power. The search for international architects, therefore, has to be understood within a broader conception of power, one that goes beyond pure market logic.

Chinese cities are not alone in their pursuit of prominent international architects for city branding and promotion. From Bilbao to Chicago, urban governments have competed with one another to use prestigious international architects to put their cities on the map.[1] These projects represent a fundamental change in the way urban space is produced today. In the age of globalization, urban space is increasingly shaped by transnational articulations. Transnational architectural production has become a major mode of spatial production, characterized by the involvement of a wide spectrum of actors—architects, developers, investors, media networks, and state bureaucrats—in the deterritorialized production, consumption, and interpretation of urban space.

China provides a privileged site for studying transnational architectural production, because of the scale and speed of urban construction currently taking place in Chinese cities. This book examines the role of transnational architectural production in the making of China's global cities. It explores the economic, political, and cultural logics that underlie the search for international architects by the governing urban elites in China.

FIGURE 1.4. The China Central Television Headquarters, designed by Office for Metropolitan Architecture, Beijing. Photograph by the author.

Based on fieldwork in Beijing and Shanghai conducted from 2004 to 2008, the book examines how the symbolic capital of architectural design is transformed into economic, political, and cultural capital by various local and translocal actors. It tells a story of China's urban revolution through the lens of the architectural metamorphoses in Chinese cities.

Transnational Architectural Production

By "transnational architectural production," I refer to the increasing participation of transnational agents in the consumption, production, and interpretation of architecture and buildings. In a globalized world, the forces that help produce a building often operate beyond national boundaries, as seen in the circulation of investment capital, the movements of built-environment professionals, and the diffusion of new design technologies. It has also become more common than before for a place to be consumed not only locally, by residents and visitors—through being there and experiencing it—but also globally, by a wider audience of spectators who watch the images of places, buildings, and architecture circulate in global telecommunication networks. Architecture and buildings are also subject to multiple—and often contradictory—interpretations and are invested with different meanings by both local and translocal actors. These competing interpretations form a critical element of transnational architectural production.

What are the socioeconomic and technological conditions that have enabled this process? Scattered practices of transnational architectural production can be found throughout history. However, the scale of such production has reached an unprecedented level in the most recent phase of globalization, since the 1970s. Globalized architectural production has matured as a major mode of spatial articulation in the context of broader structural and regulatory changes.

Here I single out four conditions of possibility that have enabled the full-fledged globalization of architectural practices: the integration of the global economy and the liberalization of trade in services, the development of telecommunication networks, the ascending importance of the symbolic economy in postindustrial cities, and the rescaling of state power at the metropolitan level.

First, the free movement of multinational capital provides financial resources for high-profile architectural projects in global cities, where the return on investment is the highest. Most urban megaprojects across the world are financed by multinational capital from a variety of sources. In its three decades of market reform, China has emerged as a new economic powerhouse and has become a major destination for foreign direct investment (FDI). Its continued economic growth has been accompanied by a construction boom, with urban areas expanding at an unprecedented speed. As host cities of the 2008 Olympics and the 2010 World Expo, Beijing and Shanghai have witnessed the construction of a large number of high-profile architectural projects, many of which were financed by domestic and international investment capital. China's current construction boom and rapid urbanization have created a huge demand for architects and planners, which cannot be met by local design workforces alone. A substantial gap has thus been created between the demand and the supply of architectural design labor, in spite of the quickly expanding architecture programs in Chinese universities that put tens of thousands of new graduates on the market every year.

The shortage of architectural design labor is eased by the liberalization of trade in services, which has greatly reduced barriers to the production and consumption of architectural services across national boundaries. Both goods and services are now distributed and consumed on an increasingly transnational scale. The production of services has become more flexible and spatially dispersed, to take full advantage of the new market and cheaper labor in various regions. The World Trade Organization (WTO) includes engineering and architectural design in the category of tertiary services, together with other intangible business services such as finance, insurance, and consulting. In 1993, the WTO member countries signed the GATS (General Agreement for Trade in Services), which became operative in 1995. The GATS framework suggests that the likely shortage of local professional knowledge can be corrected by the invisible hand of the market through the supply of international services.[2] After China's accession to the WTO in 2001, it gradually opened its construction market to international architecture firms, while reserving some restrictions such as requiring foreign firms to partner with local firms. By the end of 2006, China had lifted most restrictions and allowed foreign-owned professional design firms to practice independently. The domestic construction and design market thus became immediately accessible to international architecture firms. Transnational architectural production taking place in China has to be understood within this larger context of the deregulation and liberalization of trade in services led by the GATS and the WTO.

Second, the innovation in telecommunication technologies has liberated architectural production from territorial domains, as graphic drawings can be transferred instantly between design centers and construction sites across the globe. Architecture used to be a local employment industry, spatially determined as a service to nearby building construction. Architects and construction managers had to inhabit the same production space, to allow design drawings to be exchanged in a reasonable amount of time.[3] However, the changing technological context has redefined how architecture can be produced. Enhanced global connectivity, transmission speed, and network capacity have made it possible to transfer large design drawings instantly, thus providing a technological infrastructure for transnational architectural production. Physical proximity between design and construction has been made less relevant. The ability to transmit design drawings quickly across space has dispersed the production of architectural services spatially according to relative advantages.[4] Architectural production can now move to where the market and cheaper labor are located. China has become the destination for international architects precisely because it combines the advantage of having a strong construction market and a cheaper design workforce. International architecture firms can now first produce conceptual designs in their home offices and then transfer them to local project offices in China. Local architects can quickly translate the conceptual designs to technical drawings in compliance with local construction codes and regulations. Transnational architectural production therefore exemplifies the new international division of labor and flexible production, utilizing the relative advantages of different regions for capital accumulation.

Technology and digitization have facilitated architectural globalization and helped create the genre of signature buildings. From Frank Gehry's Guggenheim Museum in Bilbao to OMA's CCTV headquarters in Beijing, with the aid of computers and advanced modeling, architects have turned previously unbuildable structures into reality. The global telecommunication network has also changed the way architecture is consumed. As images of signature buildings are commonly circulated through cell phones, e-mails, and the Internet, the consumption of urban space is increasingly taking place on a transnational scale. In the process, the visual impact of architecture has become paramount, and the image of a building is often all that matters for its visual consumers across the globe. The technological context has therefore provided a crucial condition for transnational architectural production, by changing the ways in which architecture is produced and consumed.

Third, transnational architectural production has to be situated in the context of postindustrial cities, where architectural projects have become an instrument for place promotion and urban revitalization. Following the shift from the Fordist to the post-Fordist mode of production, Western cities have changed from manufacturing and administration centers into postindustrial sites with strong business services and consumption and entertainment functions.[5] Broader socioeconomic forces at the global, national, and urban levels are intertwined, working together to reshape the urban spaces of postindustrial cities. In the process, old urban forms have been rehabilitated to adapt to new uses, and new types of urban spaces are being created. Architectural megaprojects are examples of the new urban spaces produced in today's postindustrial cities. Urban governments compete with one another to construct high-profile architectural projects in an attempt to reorient the image of their cities and attract international investment and tourism.

Although the larger Shanghai and Beijing metropolitan areas are not yet postindustrial, deindustrialization processes have been clearly taking place in the inner-city districts. There, service industries have replaced manufacturing, and interurban competition has driven local government officials to use global architecture for place making. After Shanghai built a state-of-the-art international airport, an upscale opera house, and its flagship Pudong financial district—all from designs and master plans by international firms—Beijing followed suit and commissioned international architects to design several architectural monuments for the Olympics. These practices were also followed by Guangzhou, a megacity in the south, which invited Zaha Hadid—a regular presence in the international circuit of elite architects—to design an opera house and a stadium. The symbolic capital of architectural design has thus become an important impetus for economic development of Chinese cities in the context of deindustrialization and interurban competition.[6]

Last, because transnational architectural production mostly takes place in global cities or global city regions, it is inseparable from the larger process of state rescaling, in which state power, authority, and resources converge largely at the metropolitan level. Intercity competition for investment capital has intensified to such a degree that state power has had to be redirected to the urban level to enhance cities' competitive advantages. In response to broader structural changes since the 1970s, such as deindustrialization and the retrenchment of the welfare state, the economic contexts of Western cities have changed and major metropolitan regions have had to adopt entrepreneurial policies to attract capital investment. Although administrative boundaries remain fixed, changes in state practices and regulatory policies have reconstituted the meanings of territorial divisions and intergovernmental relations. There has been a reshuffling of state power and a circulation of resources between different geopolitical scales, and urban regions have become key institutional sites of state power reconfiguration.[7]

As in Western cities, the reconfiguration of state power has been particularly consequential for the transnational architectural production and urban changes taking place in Chinese cities.[8] As the urban scale interacts more smoothly than the national scale with the global economy, the Chinese central government has gradually converged power, authority, and resources in metropolitan governments since the 1980s. Like postindustrial Western cities, Chinese cities have adopted entrepreneurial strategies of urban governance. But in contrast to Western Europe and the United States, the rescaling of the Chinese state has been a centrally directed program devised by the national government, instead of a response to postindustrial transitions. The metropolitan governments, with power scaled down from the central government and scaled up from villages and townships, largely account for the "Chinese speed" of urban development—the vast residential displacement, massive demolition and urban renewal, and fast planning and implementation of architectural megaprojects. The state is a crucial actor and an enabler for transnational architectural production, by regulating, commissioning, and sponsoring architectural projects.

These broader structural and regulatory forces have made conditions ripe for the full-fledged globalization of architectural production. Transnational architectural production can be observed in smaller and marginal cities. But it is in the global or rapidly globalizing cities where we observe the greatest variety and intensity in the dynamics of transnational architectural production. This book uses the rapidly metamorphosing Beijing and Shanghai as empirical sites to examine the role of transnational architectural production in building global cities.

Building China's Global Cities

In the early 1980s appeared the first research concerning the emergence of a new type of city—the global city.[9] The original theoretical articulation by John Friedmann and Saskia Sassen attributes the formation of global

cities to structural changes in the world economy.[10] In Sassen's formulation, for example, one key dynamic is the decentralization of manufacturing jobs and service outlets, which has brought about a reconcentration
and expansion of economic command-and-control functions.[11] Global
cities are thus strategic nodes in the world economy because of their concentration of specialized producer services firms. Urban researchers have
conducted individual case studies, historical and comparative analyses,
and relational network analyses to examine the changing power relationship in the global urban hierarchy and the different pathways of global
city formation.[12] It is widely agreed that global city formation is a long
and historically accumulated process abundant with uncertainties and
contingencies, and that economic polarization and spatial segregation are
universally observed negative consequences in global cities.

Policy makers and academics in China got hold of the concept of global
cities in the mid-1990s, when government officials started to speak of
building China's "international metropolises" (*guojihua dadushi*). Major policy and academic journals started in this period to publish articles
discussing how to develop international metropolises in China. A recent
title keyword search on the term "international metropolis" in the China
Academic Journals (CAJ) database yielded 14 results among publications
before 1993. The number of hits jumped to 68 in publications between
1994 and 1997, sharply declined to 23 in the period from 1998 to 2002
(during the aftermath of the Asian financial crisis), and bounced back to
85 in the period from 2003 to 2007.[13] Earlier publications mostly used the
term "international metropolis," while later ones adopted the concepts
of "global cities" (*quanqiuhua chengshi*). The frequent use of the term
"global cities" in the policy debate indicates the desire of the central and
local governments to transform large Chinese cities in order to tap into
international investment and to promote urban growth.

In the early discourse on global cities, government officials and academics argued that China needed to develop its own global cities in order
to be "integrated into the world" (*yuguoji jiegui*). Yan Xiaopei, then a geography professor at Sun Yat-Sen University and currently the vice mayor
of Shenzhen—a booming city of nine million in the south—wrote in a
1994 article that building global cities was integral to China's modernization project.[14] In spite of the policy of "strictly controlling the growth of
large cities, while developing medium and small-sized cities," proposed by
the central government in 1990, the latter half of the 1990s saw a surge of
global city discourse and policy initiatives. Local governments competed

with one another and declared their intention to remake themselves into global cities. By the end of the 1990s, more than forty-three Chinese cities had announced plans to become global cities; this group included not only booming commercial centers such as Beijing and Shanghai but also small trading posts such as Manzhouli and Heihe on the northern border with Russia.[15] Government officials and academics argued that only by developing global cities could China effectively tap into international investment, attract multinational firms, and realize its economic takeoff. They also identified the deficiencies of Chinese commercial capitals as compared with other established global cities, such as low levels of productivity and economic output, underdeveloped tertiary industry, the high percentage of manufacturing in the urban economy, and, most important, the lack of infrastructure and architectural projects that could change the image of postsocialist Chinese cities.

The Asian financial crisis in 1997 reoriented the global city discourse in two different directions. On the one hand, opponents began to question some municipalities' unrealistic goals of becoming global cities. These critics pointed out that governments should objectively evaluate their conditions and that not every Chinese city could or had to become a global city. Unrealistic claims of building global cities led to overinvestment in face-lifting infrastructural projects and the neglect of many urgent needs of ordinary citizens, such as affordable housing and other social welfare services. On the other hand, advocates argued that large commercial centers such as Beijing and Shanghai had real potential to become China's global cities and should be given policy priority. They argued that an economic superpower without global cities could only serve the interests of foreign capital; that only by developing its own global cities could China become a real economic power; and, moreover, that to avoid takeover by multinational firms, the central government should have ultimate control over its global cities.[16] As more research and publications on global cities were introduced to China, "global city" became a buzzword used in the official discourse of the Shanghai and Beijing city governments in articulating their ambitions.

The image being invoked in the global city discourse is of a city with skyscraper buildings, impeccably modern infrastructure, and a large number of specialized business services firms. Two features characterizing the specificities of Chinese global cities can be identified from this discourse. The first is the emphasis on infrastructure, signature buildings, and the built environment—namely, on the *visual image* of a global city. In other

words, for Beijing and Shanghai to become truly global cities, policy makers believe that these cities have to first adopt a "global city look" by constructing state-of-the-art infrastructure and flagship architectural projects.
They argue that if the government took the lead in "building the stage"
(a metaphor for developing infrastructure and remaking built environments), then "the performers" (referring to foreign investors and companies) would come.[17] This policy orientation has led to a rush of building
expressways, bridges, airports, and skyscrapers in many large and small
cities across the country.

The second signal feature of the global city discourse in China is its
emphasis on the role of the state in directing the development of global
cities. The project of global city building in China is essentially a state
project. The state regulates the magnitude and pace of market-driven urban development by legal and administrative means. Meanwhile, as an
economic actor, the state also actively participates in the race of urban
development, through its agencies such as state-owned enterprises (SOEs)
and quasi-SOEs. This political logic produces certain practices peculiar
to global city building in China—practices that are centered on urban
property development because all land belongs to the state and the state
has more control in the property sector than in others. Thus, the two em-
phases in the global city discourse—the visual image of a city and the role
of the state—reinforce one another, and together they explain why, in the
Chinese case, construction of architectural megaprojects has become a
core strategy in the state project of building global cities.

The Study

This book is situated within the larger literature on globalization and
urban change. Previous research has approached global city formation by
examining the economic functions of global cities, such as to serve as the
command-and-control centers of the world economy. Recent years have
also seen the publication of a considerable number of studies on globalization and the transformation of Chinese cities. Most studies in this
literature have examined urban changes in China from an institutional
perspective, by analyzing the mechanisms and implications of land, housing, and other reforms.[18] This book diverges from the functional approach
of global city studies and the institutional approach of urban China studies
by studying urban social change in contemporary China through the lens of

architectural production. I seek to understand the rationales and logics underlying the search for international architects among China's urban elites and examine to what extent the symbolic articulation of urban space contributes to capital accumulation in globalizing Chinese cities. Specifically, I examine why private developers and government organizations show such clear preference for international architects, how connections are forged between international architects and local urban elites, and how the flow of architectural design, deterritorialized from its original local and national settings, is reinterpreted in the new Chinese cities. Taken together, these questions lead to an investigation of the role of transnational architectural production in the making of global cities.

A large number of urban China studies have so far focused on a single Chinese city—Shanghai.[19] Since the beginning of the twentieth century, Shanghai has experienced several phases of transformation: from a semicolonial Chinese city to a socialist city, and then to a globalizing city emerging out of the neoliberal reform of the 1980s. The drastic urban changes unfolding in the city account for the vast scholarly interest in the urban experience of Shanghai, and the city has always had a unique presence in the debates concerning the nature of modernity, metropolises, and globalization. However, the proliferation of studies on Shanghai has also led to a tendency to generalize theoretical insights drawn from Shanghai and apply them to all other Chinese cities. Meanwhile, the diverse urban experiences of other Chinese cities remain largely unexplored.[20] This book addresses the current imbalance in the literature by including Beijing as a site as well. The two cities differ greatly in the composition of their urban economy, their structures of governance, the historical layers of their built environment, and their legacies of past urban planning. Moreover, the status of Beijing as the capital of China has also brought its own complexities. By taking into account these variations, this study examines how the process of transnational architectural production is filtered through local urban contexts and leads to different outcomes.

Chinese cities represent privileged sites in which to undertake the investigation of transnational architectural production. In its sheer pace and magnitude, the urban construction currently taking place in China amounts to a natural experiment of "building globalization." I focus on three projects as concrete sites for investigation—Jianwai SOHO, a privately funded mixed-use commercial development in the central business district (CBD) in Beijing; Xintiandi, a preservation-based redevelopment project in inner-city Shanghai; and the National Olympic Stadium in the

Olympic Park in Beijing. I selected projects with different ownerships, locations, and functions in order to examine the variety of projects commissioned to international architects. Moreover, as the purpose of the study is to examine the role of high-profile architectural megaprojects in the making of global cities, all of the selected cases are large-scale, flagship projects widely publicized in the media.

The ethnographic fieldwork was carried out over repeated visits to China between 2004 and 2008. I conducted over a hundred in-depth interviews with developers, architects, urban planners, government officials, and local residents, as well as journalists, academics, and artists who were either directly involved in the three projects or knowledgeable about them. In addition to these interviews, I spent some time in a few architectural design offices to observe how international architects collaborate with local architects. I frequently visited the three projects and observed how these newly created spaces were consumed, interpreted, and reproduced on an everyday basis by a variety of city users.

The case studies on Beijing and Shanghai are relation-based investigations of transnational networks that operate both within and beyond these two sites. During my fieldwork I paid particular attention to the transnational linkages forged among different actors, including developers, investors, municipal and district officials, local design institutes, architects, journalists, neighborhood residents, artists, and academics. The intricate personal and institutional networks linking these actors operate both within local contexts and across city and national boundaries. Some actors in the networks are more locally confined owing to the limited resources at their disposal, but others are less restricted. This network-based investigation has given me several important insights. For example, the privileged status of international architects in China has to be partly attributed to their "bridging" position in this transnational network of architectural production, bringing new design concepts, technical expertise, and institutional resources from abroad to China.

I complement the case studies with a quantitative assessment of the globalization of architectural production. With statistics compiled from various trade publications, I examine the geography of the globalization of architectural practices by focusing on two types of firms—large commercial firms with multiple branch offices and small boutique firms, often based in a single location. The quantitative data can map the structure of the global network of architectural production and consumption and identify where Beijing and Shanghai are positioned in this network. In

addition to the fieldwork data and network data, I have also used data
from sources such as government statistics, reports released by private
development companies, trade publications of the real estate and architectural design industries, promotional brochures, and architectural design
drawings and briefs, as well as online postings by developers, architects,
and critics on architecture and real estate blogs.

Organization of the Book

The subsequent chapters are organized thematically. Chapter 2 maps the
contemporary geography of architectural production by analyzing the
location data of offices of leading architecture firms. I discuss the two
different geographies produced by large and small firms. Cities such as
Basel, Rotterdam, and Tokyo, where many small but highly innovative
firms are based, are production centers in the global network of architectural design, while cities such as Shanghai, Dubai, and Beijing, where
the construction market is, are consumption centers. The increasing separation, or disjuncture, between where the initial design is conceived and
where it is consumed is reshaping the landscape of architectural practices.
The change is seen in the modification of design approaches on the part
of architects to minimize uncertainty in the process of construction, over
which they often have little control; in the emergence of a new stratum of
brokers capable of bridging the cultural gap; and in the cross-fertilization
of new design ideas and concepts in the process of collaboration.

Chapter 2 also provides a historical analysis of transnational architectural practices in China and examines the role of the state in regulating and
facilitating architectural production. In the period from the 1860s to 1949,
architectural transplantation was largely a colonial articulation—a one-
way exportation of architectural design from the West to foreign concessions in port cities such as Shanghai. In the next period, from 1949 to 1978,
major architectural projects, such as the Ten Great Buildings constructed
in Beijing in 1950, were part of a national project by the communist regime
to represent the new socialist order. The Soviet Union replaced the capitalist West as the main source of influences on architecture in mainland
China. In the transitional '80s, Western architectural theories flooded in
with the initiation of the Open Door policy, and international architects
were invited to work on building projects that clearly targeted foreign investment and tourism. Architectural production entered a transnational

era in the 1990s, with the breakdown of previous trade barriers and the integration of the international design and labor market. The Chinese state, in this post-1990s period, has become a major sponsor for large-scale iconic architectural projects.

In chapter 3, I examine how signature design from international architects is employed by local private developers as a branding tool to market their properties. The market economy in China has opened up space for a new generation of entrepreneurs. With case studies of megaprojects developed by SOHO China, a private real estate company based in Beijing, this chapter examines how the new entrepreneurs have used architecture, mostly from international designers, to create their niche in the competitive property market. Based on field interviews and participant observation, this chapter shows how the developers have turned their megaprojects, one after another, into publicity extravaganzas, where talks and panel discussions on architectural design have replaced conventional means of advertising. In the process, local developers have accumulated economic, political, and cultural capital by associating themselves with avant-garde architecture. This chapter also investigates the close connection between the media and real estate speculation by examining how a small circle of powerful developers have used the media to influence national policy making.

Chapter 4 examines transnational architectural production in the arena of historical preservation through a case study of Xintiandi in Shanghai, where two blocks of *shikumen* houses, Shanghainese tenements built by Western landlords for Chinese tenants in the colonial period, were turned into a chic entertainment quarter by international developers and architectural firms with support from local governments. The history of shikumen as dwellings of lower-middle-class tenants throughout the twentieth century has been carefully erased. Instead, by emphasizing international linkages such as the houses' Western-influenced architectural features, developers and international architectural firms have repackaged shikumen into a symbol of Shanghai's cosmopolitan past and used it to project an even brighter global future.

Chapter 5 examines the relationship between architecture and nation building in the age of globalization, through a case study of the construction of the National Olympic Stadium in Beijing. Market logic alone cannot fully explain the massive architectural projects constructed for the 2008 Olympics. In the case of the National Stadium, the Chinese state exploited the symbolic capital of architectural design to narrate national ambitions; in the process, global architecture became national expression. I analyze the debate about design revisions of the stadium between cultural liberals and conservatives. Rather than aesthetics, government accountability, and the nationality of the architects, the debate is more about what it means to be "contemporary Chinese." The debate over the Bird's Nest and other foreign-designed high-profile projects mostly took place between 1998 and 2004, and they served as a harbinger for the later development of architectural criticism. At the end of chapter 5, I discuss what "critical architecture" means and how it can be achieved in the Chinese context—a debate initiated by architectural historian Zhu Jianfei that had widespread repercussions in the architectural community.

The book concludes by questioning the extent to which the articulation of the urban built environment has contributed to the making of global cities. Transnational architectural production has become a major force of capital accumulation in the process of making global cities. Signature designs from internationally renowned architects function as symbolic capital, which is transformed into economic, political, and cultural capital by various actors in this process. Elite international architects are sought after by local private developers as a branding strategy to differentiate their properties, by city officials as a way of promoting their political careers, and by the Chinese state to articulate national ambitions. The concluding chapter also provides a substantial discussion on the repositioning of territorial elites in globalizing Chinese cities, identifying five major groups among the new power elites: domestic entrepreneurs, new property owners, international investors, globalizing state bureaucrats, and transnational cultural professionals. The rise of the new power elite is accompanied by the further marginalization of the dispossessed—such as rural migrants and the urban poor. Transnational architectural production, with its dynamics and the diverse actors involved, therefore, offers an illuminating site in which to investigate globalized and capitalist urbanization.

Transnational Architectural Production: Firms, Cities, Trends

A recent issue of *Domus* magazine featured an advertisement for SOM (Skidmore, Owings & Merrill), the prototype of corporate architecture firms. Headquartered in Chicago, SOM boasts eight branch offices in North America, Europe, and Asia. In large, bold letters, the advertisement gave an impressive list of statistics—in 2008, SOM's nine offices employed a total of 1,521 employees from eighty countries, currently working on projects in fourteen countries, and since 1936, the company had built more than ten thousand projects over 92.9 million square meters.[1] On the other end of the spectrum of competitive architectural practices are small boutique firms, some led by prominent architects, characterized by their mobility, flexibility, and strong project-delivery capacity. Small firms often lack a global network of branch offices and a large employment base, but they can nevertheless powerfully compete with large firms on the strength of their progressive thinking, innovative ideas, and, in some cases, brand associations with celebrity architects. They exemplify a different form of power, that is, the power of small—the small firm size enables flexibility in assembling resources and the formation of strategic alliances in such firms' global operation. The leading architecture firms, large and small, have formed a seamless global network of architectural production, providing design expertise to private and public clients in all corners of the world. The global expansion of the leading architecture firms has had a great impact on the built environments of world cities, and in the formation of this globalized architectural production network, a number of cities have emerged as strategic nodes—consumption or production sites where architecture firms launch their global operations.

This chapter examines how the different strategies and practices of architecture firms have produced variegated geographies of global architectural production. The first part of the chapter will locate world cities within the transnational network of architectural production and examine the meaning of "power" in the global city network of architectural design. I propose a typology by distinguishing two major types of powerful cities: consumption cities and production cities. Cities such as Beijing, Shanghai, Dubai, and Abu Dhabi are powerful *consumption sites* with active construction markets and a great number of international architecture offices. But they have yet to develop an institutional infrastructure, an ecological system of architecture schools, publications, critics, and exhibition spaces that is necessary for continuous design innovation. Cities such as Tokyo, Rotterdam, Basel, and a number of other European cities are *production sites* in the network, with a less active real estate sector but many small boutique design firms, such as SANAA (founded by Kazuyo Seijima and Ryue Nishizawa) in Tokyo, OMA in Rotterdam, and Herzog & de Meuron in Basel. Highly innovative design concepts and ideas are first conceived in these cities and then translated into design drawings and used to guide construction in consumption cities. The distinction between production and consumption cities is not rigid, and not every city can neatly fit in one of the two categories, but the typology is useful for conceptualizing the different roles that major cities play in the global network of architectural production. A separation, or disjuncture, between where architectural design is first conceived and where it is eventually consumed characterizes the current state of architectural globalization and, at the same time, also raises new challenges and possibilities for the architectural profession.

The second half of the chapter will contextualize transnational architectural production in China and highlight the different roles played by the state in regulating and facilitating architectural flows in different historical periods. In the pre-1949 era, scattered practices of transnational architectural production could be observed in a few large cities such as Shanghai, Beijing, and Nanjing, where private architecture firms—both foreign and Chinese—flourished, if only briefly, until the outbreak of World War II. From 1949 to 1978, through the three decades of the socialist period, architectural practices in mainland China were largely insulated from the world. Private architecture firms disappeared altogether, and state-owned design institutes were established by the government to fill the void. These institutes churned out standardized design solutions for housing and public buildings across the country and produced the homogeneous socialist urban landscape. In the thirty years of market reform since 1978, state-owned design institutes have gone through rapid privatization and re-structuring, and they are joined by international design firms and private Chinese architecture firms, together constituting the three major play-ers in the marketplace. State-owned design institutes still claim the lion's share of the market, but international firms and private Chinese firms are quickly catching up. International firms, especially, have dominated the high-end portion of the design market and landed commissions for the highest-visibility trophy projects. The role of the state has also changed through different periods, and in the contemporary period, the Chinese state has become the main enabler of transnational architectural produc-tion by sponsoring, facilitating, and regulating architectural megaprojects. The chapter will end with the episode of the recent Ordos 100 project (2008–10): artist Ai Wei Wei and architects Jacques Herzog and Pierre de Meuron invited one hundred international architects to Ordos, a mining town in the province of Inner Mongolia, to design one hundred private villas, cultural museums, and government buildings for a local developer. The case of Ordos 100 illustrates the power of architectural consumption cities in the global architectural production chain. By tracing transnational architectural production from the 1850s to the 2000s, and from Beijing and Shanghai to Ordos, this chapter shows that urban China has become fer-tile ground and strategic terrain in the globalization of architecture.

World City Networks

One of the central topics in urban studies is intercity connectivity, that is, the various kinds of global flows that weave world cities together into a world city network. This relational or network mode of studying cities developed from the world system perspective.[2] World system scholars view the socioeconomic conditions of a country as a function of its position in a world system of nation-states. According to Immanuel Wallerstein, the world system has a core, a semiperiphery, and a periphery, with a small number of advanced economies positioned in the core and the major-ity of developing and underdeveloped economies at the semiperiphery and periphery. This world system paradigm has gradually receded in the social sciences, as global economic transactions have increasingly taken place on geopolitical scales other than that of the nation-state, such as between major cities, global trading blocks, and free-trade zones. The new conditions of the world economy have presented problems for the world system perspective, which mainly focuses on interstate relations. World city network studies were launched against the statecentric view and posit that the nation-state is no longer a meaningful unit of analysis for studying global political-economic dynamics. As global flows are often articulated on the urban scale, cities, instead of nation-states, should be the primary scale for analysis.[3] Moreover, it is no longer sufficient to study *intrinsic* structures within cities; instead, more attention should be paid to the *extrinsic* relations among cities and to how they are related to one another, because "cities are reproduced by what flows through them rather than what is fixed within them."[4]

World cities are increasingly linked with each other by the transnational flow of capital, information, and human resources, and global economic integration has produced centers and margins in the world city system. Urban researchers have especially focused on the cities occupying central positions in the global city network, such as New York, London, and Tokyo. In an 1986 article, John Friedmann identified a number of socioeconomic processes commonly observed in global cities, such as their command-and-control functions, their role as destinations for immigrants, and the polarization of their urban labor markets.[5] Saskia Sassen further focuses on global city formation and stresses the role of specialized firms that provide producer services, such as law, finance, accounting, and advertising, arguing that the concentration of a large number of such specialized producer services firms has turned certain cities into the command-and-control centers of the world economy.[6] These powerful global cities are major articulators of regional, national, and global economies, and they are increasingly linked with one another by intercity flows.

Although some theoretical foundations were laid in the beginning stage of world city network research, the field had a slow takeoff because of the lack of data that could capture intercity connectivity. Most data on trade, investment, immigration, and other types of flows were collected at the country level instead of the city level. For example, researchers can easily get data on foreign direct investment (FDI) from one country to another, but it would be difficult to get the same data on FDI from one city to another. In many of the early studies, no relational data were used to capture intercity flows. This scarcity of city-level data was often called the "dirty little secret" of global city research.[7]

The scarcity of city-pair data has gradually been remedied since the mid-1990s. The GaWC (Globalization and World Cities) research group, based at Loughborough University in the UK, has conducted quantitative studies using branch office networks as measures of intercity connectivity. Compared with immigration and trade data, data on branch office locations of business firms are easier to collect. In addition, the use of data on branch office locations is well grounded in the theoretical literature that has specified the role of producer services firms in global city formation.[8] For example, if a leading law firm has branch offices in New York, London, Dubai, and Hong Kong, then it is assumed that there are various types of intercity flows (personnel, information, finance, etc.) circulating among the branch offices, which constitute ties or connections among the cities. Peter Taylor, the leading geographer of the GaWC research group, labeled this approach the "corporate organization solution" to studying the world city network.[9]

Researchers have used branch office data to empirically test world city hypotheses and identify the structure of the world city network. For example, J. V. Beaverstock, R. G. Smith, and P. J. Taylor constructed a roster of fifty-five cities by calculating the number of branch offices of leading accountancy, advertising, banking/finance, and law firms in individual cities.[10] Taylor used principal component analysis to examine data on the office locations of one hundred business services firms and identified a set of "articulator cities" and "primary field cities" as places most closely connected to other cities.[11] Arthur S. Alderson and Jason Beckfield applied network analysis to data on the headquarters and subsidiaries of the Fortune Global 500 enterprises and found that the world city network approximated an idealized core-periphery structure.[12] The core of the world city network is made up of seven blocks of cities occupying a primary position in the network. The most active of these blocks is the group formed by the four most powerful cities—New York, London, Tokyo, and Paris.

In addition to branch offices, the other frequently used source of information is air travel, as city-pair data on air traffic are relatively available.[13] Researchers have studied the structure of the world city network by examining how individual cities are interconnected in the worldwide web of air traffic. For example, David A. Smith and Michael Timberlake applied network analysis techniques to data on airline passenger travel between world cities in multiple time periods between 1985 and 1997 and identified London, Frankfurt, New York, Tokyo, Amsterdam, and Zurich as the structurally dominant global cities.[14] They also located a tier of "gateway cities," such as Miami, Los Angeles, Hong Kong, and Singapore, which seem to link different time zones. They concluded that the top tier of global cities had grown to include more cities over the years from 1985 to 1997 and that several cities in East Asia had risen to global city status over time.

The world city network studies are based on the assumption that socio-economic processes taking place within individual cities need to be understood in terms of their relations to other cities, in the form of branch office connections, airline travel, and other flows. Adopting this relational way of thinking, the next section will map the geography of global operations of large architecture firms by examining their branch office locations. Specifically, I will examine where contemporary Chinese cities, such as Beijing and Shanghai, are positioned in the global network of architectural production in relation to other major cities.

The Power of Large

Large firms with multiple branch offices dominate the architecture profession in terms of design revenues, project delivery, and international outreach, in spite of the fact that the majority of architecture firms are smaller practices with fewer than fifty staff and no branch offices. According to a 2006 AIA (American Institute of Architecture) survey, architecture firms with fifty or more employees accounted for less than 4 percent of all architecture firm offices but almost 42 percent of all staff at architecture firms and almost 52 percent of all billings. The AIA survey also suggests a continued increase in productivity at larger architecture firms. By accounting for a larger share of billings than of payroll, the typical employee at a larger firm is generating more revenue on average than a typical employee at a smaller one. Large firms continue to offer a broad range of design-related services, from interior design and landscape architecture to construction management and design-and-build, and they have shown no signs of cutting back this variety of offerings. As generalist "supermarket-style" operations, these large firms can cater to the trend toward larger and more complex projects and clients that want single-source delivery.

Large architecture firms from the United States and Europe have rapidly expanded their overseas markets. According to a 2008 *Engineering News Record* (*ENR*) survey, for US design firms, revenue from outside the United States grew to $19.7 billion, which was a 32 percent increase over the previous year.[15] Regions with booming property development and large-scale infrastructure construction have attracted a large number of architecture firms. Over the past few decades, large architecture firms have followed the shifts of the construction market from the Middle East in the 1970s to Southeast Asia in the 1980s and to China in the late 1990s. Top design firms are diversifying their portfolios in order to remain stable especially in uncertain economic times, and for many US firms, "keeping revenue rolling means going abroad to hot markets such as the Middle East, India, and China."[16] One of the top one hundred US design firms, HOK, reported that in 2007, for the first time in its history, international work represented more than 40 percent of its annual revenue.[17]

The example of SOM, mentioned at the beginning of this chapter, can offer some good illustrations of how large architecture firms have quickly globalized in terms of branch office expansion and project delivery. Table 2.1 shows the fast international expansion of SOM, with projects outside North America accounting for 49 percent of the total. Asia and the Middle East are fast-growing international markets for SOM, with 22 percent and 7 percent of the firm's total projects between 2000 and 2008 built in these two regions, respectively. China features heavily in SOM's portfolio—in the period between 2000 and 2008, SOM built 29 megaprojects in Chinese cities, which accounted for 13 percent of the firm's total projects in that period. Table 2.2 gives a list of major cities where SOM has built the most projects. New York and London, two top-tier global cities, are major markets for SOM; Chicago, owing to its headquarters status, also hosts a large concentration of SOM's projects. However, in the list, US cities are fewer in number than Asian, Middle Eastern, and European cities. These statistics demonstrate the enormous capacity for project delivery of large commercial architecture firms and show strong evidence that Asia and Middle Eastern Gulf cities are strong emerging markets for these large firms.

While it is impossible to assess the increase in international commissions, the response of the architecture profession to globalization is clearly illustrated by the rising number of branch offices opened in various global regions. Establishing branch offices is a major strategy for design firms to explore new markets, reach new clients, and supervise building construction. According to a 2009 survey by *Building and Design* (*BD*) magazine, the fifty largest architecture firms in the world have 516 offices in 198 cities.[18] This implies that each of the top fifty firms has, on average, ten offices worldwide. The number is remarkably high considering the fact that the vast majority of architecture firms are led by sole practitioners in one office location.

TABLE 2.1 **Projects by SOM, 1936–2008**

	1936–1999		2000–2008	
Region	No. of projects	Percent of total	No. of projects	Percent of total
Asia	6	8	50	22
Middle East	0	0	15	7
Europe	11	15	43	19
North America	58	77	117	51
Others (Africa, Latin America, Australia)	0	0	4	2
Total	75	100	229	100

Source: http://www.som.com.

The list of the fifty largest architecture firms is dominated by American and European firms (see table A.2). Table 2.3 shows the national origins of the top fifty firms. American and British firms account for 68 percent of the list. Together with other European firms and Australian firms, these Western firms represent 88 percent of the top fifty list. Table 2.4 is a list of the cities with the largest number of branch offices. Shanghai ranks first, with 24 offices, followed by London, with 22. Major American cities also

TABLE 2.2 **City locations of major projects designed by SOM, 2000–2008**

City	Number of projects
New York	25
Chicago	21
London	17
San Francisco	9
Beijing	6
Shanghai	6
Hyderabad	5
Newark, NJ	5
Dubai	4
Moscow	4
Dublin	4
Doha	3
Mumbai	3
Hong Kong	3
Nanjing	3
Seoul	3
Washington DC	3
Detroit	3
Los Angeles	3
Total	130

Source: http://www.som.com.

rank high in the list, including Washington DC (17 offices), New York (15), Los Angeles (12), and San Francisco (12). Other emerging markets such as Dubai (19 offices), Beijing (15), and Abu Dhabi (10) have also attracted a significant number of design firms to establish branch offices. Although Beijing and Shanghai boast a total of 39 international design offices, no firms from mainland China appear in the list of the top one hundred design firms.[19] The two Chinese entries are registered in Hong Kong, the former British colony (Palmer & Turner Architects and Engineers, and Leigh & Orange), demonstrating how postcolonial connections are manifested in commercial architectural practices.

Below, I present a network analysis of the branch offices of the top fifty design firms, the goal of which is to identify the positions of world cities in this network of architectural design formed by the globalization strategies of corporate architecture firms. The data required for network analysis are relational data composed of nodes and ties; in the case of the global network of architectural production, cities are the nodes and branch office connections constitute ties (see the methodology note in the appendix). The final dataset includes the 516 branch offices of the top fifty firms located in 198 world cities. Figure 2.1 is the overall network of 198 cities as generated by the network analysis program UCINET 6.0.[20] Specifically, I used three centrality measures—degree centrality, closeness centrality, and betweenness centrality—in order to examine which cities occupy central positions in this global network of architectural design.

Degree centrality is measured by the number of ties connecting a city to other cities and is calculated by dividing the actual number of ties

TABLE 2.3 **National origins of the top fifty architecture firms of 2007**

Country	Number of firms	Percent of total
US	23	46
UK	11	22
France	1	2
Denmark	1	2
Germany	1	2
Sweden	1	2
The Netherlands	1	2
Australia	5	10
Japan	3	6
Hong Kong	2	4
UAE	1	2
Total	50	100

Source: *BD* World Architecture Survey, 2007.
Note: The list does not include BDP International and Atkins, two generalist consulting firms that do not list architectural design as their main activity.

TABLE 2.4 **Cities with the largest number of branch offices of the top hundred architecture firms**

Rank	City	Number of branch offices
1	Shanghai	24
2	London	22
3	Dubai	19
4	Washington DC	17
5	Beijing	15
5	New York	15
7	Hong Kong	12
7	Los Angeles	12
7	San Francisco	12
10	Abu Dhabi	10
10	Chicago	10
12	Seattle	9
12	Singapore	9
14	Atlanta	8
14	Dallas	8

Note: The list does not include BDP International and Atkins, two generalist consulting firms that do not list architectural design as their main activity.

connecting a city to others by the maximum possible number of ties. It identifies as powerful those cities with the largest number of ties connecting them to others. In the first column in table 2.5, Shanghai ranks at the top with the highest degree centrality score, followed by London. Dubai and Beijing, cities with strong property construction markets, also rank among the top five. The major American cities Washington DC, Los Angeles, and San Francisco rank among the top ten, which can be explained by the fact that twenty-three out of the top fifty firms are American firms, which tend to have branch offices in major American cities.

Closeness centrality is measured by the distance between a city and other cities in the network. It identifies as powerful those cities with the shortest paths to others in the network. In the second column in table 2.5, the pattern of closeness centrality is similar to that identified for degree centrality. London ranks at the top, which means that London is the shortest distance from other cities and therefore is the best-connected city in the global design network. Shanghai, Dubai, Beijing, and Abu Dhabi, all cities with strong construction markets, rank among the top ten, which suggests that these new globalizing cities are now well integrated into the global network of architectural design. The major American cities Washington DC, New York, and Los Angeles are also close in rank to other cities among the top ten.

Betweenness centrality is measured as the degree to which a city stands between other pairs of cities. It identifies as powerful those cities that lie on the paths connecting other cities. Cities with higher betweenness have greater power in the sense that they can serve as brokers, controlling the flow of information through the network. As shown in the third column in table 2.5, the cities in the top ten in terms of betweenness centrality are slightly different from the top ten for degree centrality and closeness centrality. For example, only two firms have offices in Stockholm, and six firms have offices in Warsaw. Thus, measured in terms of degree centrality, these cities rank far down the hierarchy—both are out of the top fifty. However, the firms with offices in Stockholm and Warsaw also have offices in other marginal cities in Sweden and Eastern Europe. Therefore, the high betweenness scores of Stockholm (3rd) and Warsaw (7th) can be explained by the fact that they stand on the paths between these marginal northern and Eastern European cities and other cities in the network. Their scores do not represent power or centrality in the sense of having more connections with other cities. Other entries among the top ten include the familiar names, with London ranked at the top, followed by Chinese and Middle Eastern cities as well as major American cities. Hong Kong and Singapore, two Southeast Asian cities, appear near the top for all of the three centrality measures, which indicates central positions for Hong Kong and Singapore in the network.

Two major findings can be drawn from the network analysis. First, the

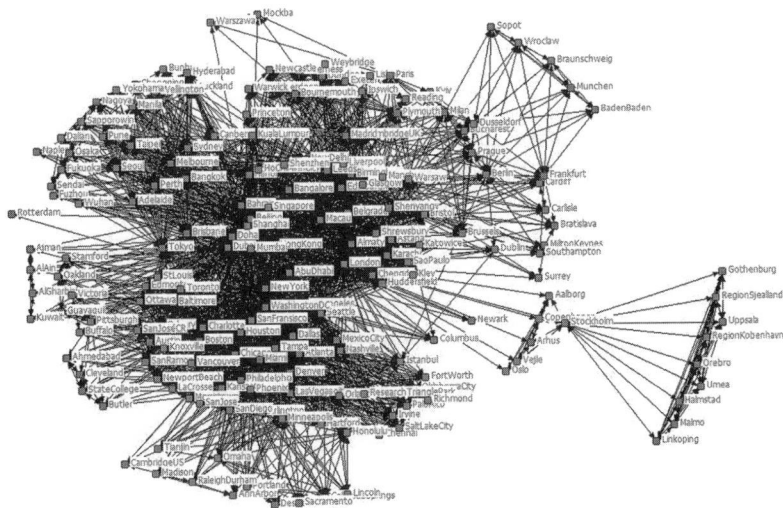

FIGURE 2.1. The architecture branch office network of 198 world cities.

TABLE 2.5 **Centrality scores and rankings for the top fifty cities**

Rank	City	Degree centrality	Rank	City	Closeness centrality	Rank	City	Betweenness centrality
1	Shanghai	329	1	London	259	1	London	4599.72
2	London	287	2	Shanghai	266	2	Shanghai	1951.77
3	Dubai	252	3	Dubai	284	3	Stockholm	1692
4	Washington DC	242	4	Beijing	285	4	Beijing	1353.36
5	Beijing	216	5	Washington DC	293	5	Dubai	1214.79
6	New York	207	6	New York	305	6	Washington DC	946.09
7	Los Angeles	198	7	Los Angeles	309	7	Warsaw	777.37
8	Hong Kong	173	8	Singapore	310	8	New York	583.76
9	San Francisco	165	9	Hong Kong	311	9	Hong Kong	558.01
10	Singapore	155	10	Abu Dhabi	318	10	Abu Dhabi	525.31
11	Chicago	143	11	Seattle	324	11	Singapore	446.71
12	Dallas	134	12	Mumbai	325	12	Los Angeles	424.39
13	Abu Dhabi	133	13	San Francisco	332	13	Seattle	376.71
14	Seattle	127	14	Phoenix	339	14	San Francisco	304.24
15	Atlanta	123	14	Manchester	339	15	Chicago	275.16
16	Phoenix	115	16	Chicago	340	16	Phoenix	271.7
17	Denver	107	17	Warsaw	341	17	Mumbai	239.68
18	Miami	104	18	New Delhi	342	18	Moscow	197.66
19	Mumbai	99	19	Denver	343	19	Tokyo	196.03
20	Manchester	93	20	Edinburgh	344	20	Philadelphia	191.72
20	Warsaw	93	20	Dallas	344	21	Manchester	183.59
22	Edinburgh	91	22	Moscow	345	22	Denver	163.50
23	Houston	89	23	Birmingham, UK	346	23	Berlin	158.97
24	Boston	88	24	Atlanta	347	24	New Delhi	153.17
25	Moscow	87	25	Glasgow	348	25	Brisbane	123.76

Rank	City	Value	Rank	City	Value	Rank	City	Value
26	Tampa	86	25	Bangalore	348	26	Dusseldorf	123.53
27	Brisbane	85	25	Miami	348	27	Miami	118.38
28	Glasgow	83	25	Liverpool	348	28	Edinburgh	116.21
29	Birmingham, UK	80	29	Bahrain	350	29	Bahrain	111.18
29	Tokyo	80	30	Leeds	352	30	Bristol, UK	108.05
31	Liverpool	73	32	Tokyo	352	31	Madrid	102.57
31	Charlotte	73	32	Ho Chi Minh City	354	32	Ho Chi Minh City	99.02
33	New Delhi	72	32	Doha	354	32	Hanoi	99.02
34	Las Vegas	70	32	Hanoi	354	34	Birmingham, UK	95.2
35	Bahrain	68	32	Tampa	354	35	Doha	94.11
36	Bangalore	67	36	Shenzhen	355	36	Dallas	92.28
37	Bangkok	62	36	Bristol, UK	355	37	Minneapolis	91.61
38	Leeds	61	38	Brisbane	356	38	Las Vegas	83.96
38	Detroit	61	38	Boston	356	39	Boston	83.06
38	Vancouver	61	38	Houston	356	40	Glasgow	82.83
38	Hanoi	61	41	Las Vegas	357	41	Kansas City	75.212
38	Minneapolis	61	42	Charlotte	360	42	Atlanta	73.89
43	Orlando	60	43	Macau	361	43	Bangalore	71.38
43	Doha	60	44	Detroit	362	44	Orlando	67.96
45	Mexico City	59	45	Shrewsbury, UK	364	45	Charlotte	65.79
46	Melbourne	57	45	Katowice	364	46	Detroit	57.02
47	Bristol, UK	54	45	Kiev	364	47	Frankfurt	55.01
47	Toronto	54	45	Belgrade	364	48	Liverpool	54.94
49	Ho Chi Minh City	52	45	Chengdu	364	49	Shenzhen	50.85
50	Perth	51	45	Almaty	364	50	Bangkok	49.21

TABLE 2.6 **Rankings of cities in previous studies**

Friedmann (1995)	Beaverstock et al. (1999)	Alderson and Beckfield (2004)
Global financial articulations: London, New York, Tokyo	Alpha world cities: a. London, Paris, New York, Tokyo b. Chicago, Frankfurt, Hong Kong, Los Angeles, Milan, Singapore	Top global cities: London, New York, Paris, Tokyo
Multinational articulations: Miami, Los Angeles, Frankfurt, Amsterdam, Singapore	Beta world cities: a. San Francisco, Sydney, Toronto, Zurich b. Brussels, Madrid, Mexico City, Sao Paulo c. Moscow, Seoul	Other top ten cities: Düsseldorf, Amsterdam, Zurich, Munich, Osaka, San Francisco
Important national articulations: Paris, Zurich, Madrid, Mexico City, Sao Paulo, Seoul, Sydney	Gamma world cities: a. Amsterdam, Boston, Caracas, Dallas, Düsseldorf, Geneva, Houston, Jakarta, Johannesburg, Melbourne, Osaka, Prague, Santiago, Taipei, Washington b. Bangkok, Beijing, Rome, Stockholm, Warsaw c. Atlanta, Barcelona, Berlin, Buenos Aires, Budapest, Copenhagen, Hamburg, Istanbul, Kuala Lumpur, Manila, Miami, Minneapolis, Montreal, Munich, Shanghai	Other top twenty cities: Frankfurt, Vevey, Chicago, Stockholm, Dallas, Detroit, Utrecht, Toronto, St. Louis, Basel

global urban hierarchy in the field of architectural design differs from that in other fields (table 2.6). Previous studies show that New York, London, Tokyo, Paris, and a few other cities occupy the top of the urban hierarchy in the field of producer services, such as finance, law, and accounting. However, in the field of architectural design, out of this group only London and New York remain among the top ten. London has the highest score on two of the three measures of centrality. New York also appears in the top ten for all three centrality measures. This confirms the eminent status of London and New York as global design centers. Tokyo and Paris, two cities that are well established in business services, drop to a lower status in the design field. The lower status of Tokyo can be explained by the location strategies of large Japanese architecture firms, which maintain offices mainly within Japan or East Asia and have not yet reached out to international markets. Paris is undoubtedly one of the major production sites of innovative architectural design. However, many leading French design firms are smaller practices, in contrast to corporate American firms, and therefore have a weaker presence in the top fifty list. Major American cities, such as Washington DC, Chicago, and San Francisco, occupy more central positions in the network of architectural design than in other business services networks. This again indicates the dominance of American firms in the top fifty list.

Second, Chinese and Middle Eastern cities are near the top of the city rankings for all three centrality measures, and Shanghai, Beijing, Dubai, and Abu Dhabi occupy central positions in this network of branch offices of large design firms. Shanghai and Dubai, in particular, have surpassed major American cities such as New York and Washington DC in terms of connectivity with other cities in the network. The high rankings of these Chinese and Middle Eastern cities clearly reflect the resource- or market-oriented nature of architectural production. The central positions of these market-oriented cities might be just a temporary trend, lasting until the construction boom recedes and international architectural offices leave. However, it is also possible that local firms in these cities will quickly catch up, and eventually these cities will become new global design centers providing services for other markets. Follow-up analyses at multiple time intervals will be needed to trace future trends.

In general, these findings demonstrate the dynamic nature of the world city system. The structure of the world city system varies from industry to industry and fluctuates as global urban competition intensifies. In the network of cities produced by the branch office ties of large architecture firms, three groups of cities are competing for the core positions: (1) London and major American cities, (2) Chinese and Middle Eastern cities, and (3) Southeast Asian cities such as Hong Kong and Singapore. Each of these three sets of cities has a large number of branch offices, which closely connect them with one another and with other, more marginal cities in the network. The network analysis presented in this section has examined the branch office location patterns only of the largest design firms. The next section will examine the geography of small boutique design firms, with an entirely different group of cities positioned at the center of the network of architectural production.

The Power of Small

As many have noted, the architectural design industry has a distinctive star system.[21] "Global architects" build their fame on the basis of public, professional, and commercial recognition.[22] Prestigious boutique design firms, often led by a global architect based in one location, have enormous cultural power and capacity for project delivery. In spite of their compact size, their brand recognition enables them to attract creative talent, assemble a flexible workforce, and deliver projects on the global scale. Many of these boutique firms are unlikely to appear in any major industry surveys based on financial power and employment base, but their work is frequently introduced in major architecture publications. I created a list of fifty small boutique firms or architects that frequently appeared in the magazines *Domus* and *Architectural Review* in 2007 and 2008 (see table A.3).[23] The exercise by no means intends to provide an exhaustive survey of small boutique firms; rather, the purpose here is to construct a sample of well-recognized small firms in order to examine the geography of their office locations, which, as I will show, reveals that cities in the network of transnational architectural production can be powerful in ways other than those identified in the previous section.

With a few overlaps, such as Foster & Partners, Herzog & de Meuron, and OMA, the list of small boutique firms largely diverges from the list of the fifty largest architecture firms as analyzed in the previous section. The city locations of these small but highly innovative firms indicate a different geography of power and centrality from that created by large firms. First, we find that Tokyo, along with New York and London—the two cities with a concentration of large firms as well—are the basing points for many of these boutique firms (see table 2.7). Especially noteworthy here is the frequent appearance of innovative Japanese firms, such as SANAA, in major architecture magazines.[24] The professional recognition of many Tokyo-based design firms indicates the disjuncture between architectural production and architectural consumption. It seems that Tokyo, with a saturated real estate market, nevertheless functions as a strategic node of design production and innovation. The second noticeable feature is the lack of Asian cities other than Tokyo and of cities in the Middle East among the locations of boutique firms. Beijing, Shanghai, Hong Kong, Dubai, Abu Dhabi, and other cities in those regions that boast a large number of branch offices of large architecture firms do not appear anywhere in the list of top city locations for boutique firms. This again testifies to the divergence between the production and consumption of architectural design; cities with robust construction markets, as mentioned above, have yet to become equally competitive production sites of innovative architectural design. Last, we see the strong presence of Western European

TABLE 2.7 **Boutique architectural firms' consumption and production cities: A comparison**

Consumption cities		Production cities	
Rank	City	Rank	City
I	Shanghai	I	Tokyo
2	London	2	New York
3	Dubai	3	London
4	Washington DC	4	Berlin
5	Beijing	5	Los Angeles
6	New York	6	Madrid
7	Los Angeles	7	Paris
8	Hong Kong	8	Oslo
9	San Francisco	9	Amsterdam
10	Singapore	10	Basel
11	Chicago	11	Dublin
12	Dallas	12	Genoa
13	Abu Dhabi	13	Haldenstein
14	Seattle	14	Cologne
15	Atlanta	15	Lisbon
16	Phoenix	16	Ljubljana
17	Denver	17	Osaka
18	Miami	18	Philadelphia
19	Mumbai	19	Rotterdam
20	Manchester	20	Sao Paulo

cities among the basing points for boutique firms. In addition to Tokyo, New York, and London, the network of Western European cities forms another center for innovative architectural production.

The global firm OMA offers a good illustration of boutique design firms' flexibility in project delivery and their capacity for networking and mobilizing resources. From 1978 to 1999, most of the projects built by OMA were in Europe (twenty-four projects in total), with only three projects in Asia (in Japan and Korea). However, OMA has quickly expanded its international market since 2000, providing architectural design services for projects in Asia, the Middle East, and North America. According to the statistics provided on OMA's website, from 2000 to 2008, OMA delivered sixty-nine projects in thirty-six cities in twenty-one countries. These projects range widely, from small-scale stage design for fashion brands in Europe to megaprojects such as the CCTV headquarters building in Beijing, which had a total budget of 850 million euros. In brand recognition and project delivery, small but highly competitive firms such as OMA can powerfully compete with large architecture firms. OMA and other brand-name boutique firms have no in-house experts specializing in the different fields drawn on by large-scale complex projects; instead, they have the ability to network and mobilize talents and resources for each of their projects.

The following quote from the book *Small, Medium, Large, Extra-large* is a reflection on OMA's global practices by the author and architect Rem Koolhaas:

> Globalization starts 35 miles away from a Dutch office. Sometime in 1987, in our office, international projects and collaborators began to form a majority. Suddenly OMA *was* global, not in the form of multiple offices turning out a single "product," but of one involved more and more deeply in other cultures. We became experts on difference: different possibilities, contexts, sensitivities, currencies, sensualities, rigors, integrities, powers. From then on, we navigated between the potentials for credit and discredit that globalization implied. Some days CNN seems like an oracle, a private bulletin board, each story hitting nerve endings directly related to work.[25]

The global team working on OMA's CCTV project in Beijing offers another glimpse of the power of small (see table A.4). In order to execute the extremely complex structure of the CCTV building, OMA partnered with ARUP—a large commercial architecture and engineering firm with dozens of offices worldwide. ARUP mobilized three of its offices—London, Hong Kong, and Beijing—to work on structural engineering for the project. OMA also partnered with top-of-the-line specialist firms with expertise in lighting, sound, facade engineering, landscaping, theater design, vertical transportation, and food service planning. These partner firms from Japan, the United States, the UK, France, and the Netherlands worked as consultants and provided the technical expertise that OMA does not maintain in-house. The architectural team included hundreds of architects, from the well established to the up-and-coming, from all regions of the world, many of whom collaborated with OMA on a project basis. Many architects working on the CCTV project were of Asian origin, an example of OMA's ability to flexibly tailor its workforce for each of its global operations. The Chinese architect Ma Qingyun, currently the dean of the School of Architecture at the University of Southern California, was listed as the "strategic advisor" for the project. Ma's involvement was indeed strategic for OMA to secure the contract, as he was the key negotiator who eventually persuaded CCTV to choose OMA in the midst of distrust and criticism of foreign architects in 2005 in Beijing. Finally, OMA had to partner with a local design institute—East China Architecture and Design Institute, in Shanghai—to be able to efficiently navigate the unfamiliar Chinese building codes, planning, and construction regulations; meanwhile, the Chinese partner also enabled OMA to tap into the cheaper local design labor force. Boutique firms such as OMA, with their highly recognizable brand names and flexibility to assemble design talent globally according to the specific needs of each project, have been another visible force in the landscape of architectural production, demonstrating the power of small.

A Typology of Cities

> High pressure work in a low pressure city—OMA could never exist without Rotterdam, a city that has no scene, makes no demands, and offers no distractions—a laboratory of indifference.[26]

The quote above from the book *Content* cynically describes the ambivalent relationship between OMA and Rotterdam, the city where it is based. Putting cynicism aside, it also highlights the fact that many highly influential architecture firms are based in smaller cities, as discussed in the last section. The analyses of the office locations of large and small design firms reveal that cities play different roles in the network of transnational architectural production. Some cities, such as Basel, Rotterdam, and Tokyo, are basing points for innovative boutique design firms, whereas other cities, such as Shanghai and Dubai, concentrate the largest numbers of international design offices. Based on these observations, I propose here a typology of powerful cities in the network of architectural production by distinguishing two major types of cities: consumption cities and production cities.

Tokyo, Paris, Rotterdam, Basel, and a number of other European cities are *production cities* with saturated real estate sectors but many small boutique design firms. Highly innovative design concepts and ideas are first produced here and then exported to consumption cities worldwide. Many new design ideas are first conceptualized in production cities, and these places are the imagineering centers that are highly influential for the transformation of built environments in various world cities. Cities such as Beijing, Shanghai, and Dubai are powerful *consumption cities* with the largest numbers of international design offices. These are the places where the resources (i.e., the construction market) are, and they consume design services produced elsewhere. These cities have yet to develop the institutional infrastructure—a network of architecture schools, publications, critics, and so forth—required for architectural design production and innovation. These places are wild frontiers where a variety of design schemes—both avant-garde and banal—are realized in concrete building forms. Star architects rush here to build the dream projects that probably would not be built anywhere else. Young architects rush here as well to be in the action. Although not much innovative work has come yet from these places, the consumption cities exert tremendous power by offering possibilities and posing challenges for contemporary globalized architectural production. They provide strategic terrains on which different cultures, ideas, and design concepts meet and clash. Some cities combine features of both production and consumption cities—London, New York, Los Angeles, and a few others. These places are often locations blessed with the combination of a well-developed infrastructure for architectural innovation, high visibility, and a moderately active construction market, therefore attracting all sorts of architecture firms.

This chapter so far has examined the current configuration of architectural globalization by focusing on firms and cities in the network of architectural production and consumption. Globalization has enabled the separation of the production and consumption of architectural design, and a small number of world cities have become export and import centers of architectural traffic. The increasing separation between where the initial design is conceived and where it is consumed, I argue, is reshaping the landscape of architectural practices, as exemplified by architects' modification of design approaches to minimize uncertainty in the process of construction, over which they often have little control; by the emergence of a new stratum of "brokers" capable of bridging cultural gaps; and by the cross-fertilization of new design ideas and concepts in the process of collaboration. The next section will contextualize some of these observations by locating traces and trends of transnational architectural production in China in different historical periods.

Locating Transnational Architectural Production in China

The post-1990s period witnessed an acceleration of architectural globalization, as seen in the growth of international commissions and the expansion of branch offices of architecture firms. However, the phenomenon of transnational architectural production is by no means a recent one, and the globalization of architectural practices can be traced far back in history. In this section, I will take a historical approach to situate transnational architectural production in the Chinese context. I do not intend to give a detailed account of the development of architectural practices in China, as there are currently a few excellent works addressing the subject.[27] Rather, by highlighting the historical evidence of transnational architectural production in Chinese cities, I intend to shed light on the different *logics* underlying architectural articulation in each period and thus provide a historical context for the discussion on contemporary architectural projects in the following chapters.

The logic governing transnational architectural production in China has changed from a colonial, to a national, and then to a transnational one in different historical periods from the 1850s to the present. The transplantation of architectural design between the 1850s and the 1940s was largely a colonial project, characterized by one-way architectural exportation from the West to China. The destination of such transplantation was largely confined to the multinational concessions in treaty port cities such as Shanghai. The beginning of the socialist period witnessed a strong influence of Soviet monumental-style architecture. But as economic conditions and the relationship with the Soviet Union worsened, orthodox modernism and standardized design production replaced the socialist realist style. The architectural transplantation in this second period, beginning in the 1950s, was part of the larger national project and was aimed at constructing modern yet readable and familiar architectural symbols to represent the new socialist country. Architectural production in postsocialist China marks a radical break from the past. The return of international architects to China after the 1980s is not a neocolonial phenomenon, nor is it a national project as in the socialist period. Rather, the sheer volume and scale of urban construction, as well as the ever-blurring boundary between Chinese and international architects, signal a transnational logic of architectural production, characterized by the integration of the global market and design labor.

The role of the state, and the relationship between the national and the global, produce varying logics of transnational architectural articulation. In the semicolonial period, the foreign concessions were de facto extraterritorial jurisdictions beyond the control of the weak Chinese state. Western architectural and urban planning practices were actively adopted in the foreign concessions. The republican government in the 1920s and

1930s attempted to revive traditional Chinese architecture by searching for a national style, but its effort was circumvented by economic and political uncertainty. Under the socialist state, architecture became a propaganda tool and a representation of the new government. Ideological debates, especially during the years of the Cultural Revolution, largely blocked the freedom of architectural expression and insulated Chinese architects from the outside world. By contrast, the postsocialist Chinese state is an enabler of transnational architectural production, and especially since the 1990s, the state—on different scales—has become a key player in commissioning and sponsoring architectural megaprojects in Chinese cities. However, in contrast to the socialist era, current government involvement in the construction of architectural projects is oriented toward a global agenda rather than a national one. The advanced transnational architectural production since the 1990s does not indicate a loss of control on the part of the state; rather, it manifests how the global and the national are mutually embedded within one another in the shaping of built environments.

The Colonial Project, 1850s–1940s

Until the late nineteenth and early twentieth centuries, most buildings in China were constructed in the distinctive traditional Chinese style with a timber post-and-beam structure supporting a curved roof. Many buildings were one story high, with the exception of pagodas and towers. Building types were limited to palaces, government offices, residential houses, temples, academies, ancestral halls, shops, and gardens. Major building types shared similar spatial layouts—individual buildings were normally arranged around a courtyard, and a few courtyards lined up along one or multiple axes to form a complex.

Western architecture started to appear in foreign concessions in China in the 1850s, introducing new building types and architectural practices.[28] Following the Opium War, the Nanjing Treaty (1842) with Great Britain opened five port cities to foreign trade, including Guangzhou, Fuzhou, Ningbo, Xiamen, and Shanghai. In 1850, the British set up the first foreign concession in Shanghai. Foreign concessions in the treaty port cities became the major sites for the implantation of Western architecture and planning. New building types were introduced to China in this period, such as neo-Gothic and neoclassical churches, customs houses, railway stations, banks, and commercial offices. Foreign concessions increased in number and expanded in territory after the Boxer Rebellion in 1900, and these places became major construction sites for Western-style buildings designed by foreign architects and engineers. Closely following the development of architecture in Europe, foreign architects adopted a variety of revivalist styles then fashionable in the West, such as the neoclassical style, art deco, and later the International Style. Some also built colonial-style bungalows, as seen in the British colonies of India and Southeast Asia.[29]

Between the 1910s and 1930s, China became a goldmine for foreign architects hunting for jobs in East Asia. There were seven foreign architecture firms in Shanghai in 1893, and the number doubled to fourteen by 1910. By 1936, twenty-seven out of the thirty-nine registered architecture offices were led by foreign architects. Local architectural historians Lou Chenghao and Xue Shunsheng recounted, "[Foreign architects] flew between Shanghai, Hong Kong, Japan, and Southeast Asia like migrating birds. They went where the jobs were."[30] As foreigners dominated the market, Chinese builders gradually lost their formal status and became increasingly marginalized, and many of them became apprentices to foreign architects.[31] The domination of foreign architects was largely due to the new regulations in the foreign concessions, as many of the foreign settlements required architects to have professional certifications from RIBA (Royal Institute of British Architects) and the AIA, which disqualified most Chinese builders. The lack of foreign-language skills and connection with the colonial administrators in charge of public works further marginalized Chinese builders and widened the gap between them and the foreign architects.[32]

The Western-style buildings in the foreign concessions were mostly commissioned by colonial patrons and reflected their ambitions. Banks and commercial buildings reached greater and greater heights in Shanghai. International banks brought with them foreign architects to build branch offices in China. Many early bank buildings were designed in the neoclassical style, mimicking their headquarters in the West. The first bank on the Bund in Shanghai was the St. Petersburg Russo-Asiatic Bank, completed in 1901 by architect H. Becker. This was the first building in China constructed with reinforced concrete and equipped with an elevator.[33] The British firm Palmer & Turner, based in Hong Kong, designed the neoclassical HSBC (Hong Kong and Shanghai Banking Corporation) branch in Shanghai in 1921. The American architect Henry Murphy worked with IBC (International Banking Corporation) on six branches in China, and the architecture of these banks clearly symbolized the ascending financial power of the United States.[34] The foreign concessions such as those in

Shanghai thus became strategic terrain for the transplantation of Western architecture to China. As extrajurisdictional territories beyond the control of the Chinese state, these sites enabled the systematic borrowing of Western architecture, urban planning, and administration. With few exceptions, the local context was completely ignored by foreign architects in the one-way transplantation of architecture from the West to China.

The first generation of overseas-trained Chinese architects also played a major role in transplanting Western architecture to China. Supported by the Boxer Indemnity Fund, most of these architects were educated in the Beaux Arts tradition and practiced in private firms overseas prior to their return to China. By 1931, twenty-eight out of the fifty-one architects in the Society of Chinese Architects were educated in the United States, with a number of others educated in Japan and Europe.[35] The returnee architects were clearly more familiar with Western architectural practices than with Chinese architectural traditions. The first generation of these architects designed many neoclassical, art deco, and International Style buildings in the treaty port cities. Their Western orientation was heightened by the nature of their commissions, which were mostly modern buildings previously unknown in China, such as churches, banks, and railway stations.[36] Like their Western counterparts, many of the overseas-educated Chinese architects also ignored the local context and did not attempt to incorporate Chinese architectural elements into their work.

The one-way traffic of architecture from the West to foreign concessions in China, however, did not lead to pure fabrication of Western architecture. As architectural historian Jeffrey Cody argues, architectural exportation is always a hybrid process, with "a spectrum of results from direct imitation to barely discernible architectural genes."[37] Many hybrid forms of architecture with a mixture of Western influence and Chinese traditions appeared in the treaty port cities. In Shanghai, the mix of Western and Chinese architecture gave rise to hybrid shikumen houses combining the Western terrace house tradition with Chinese courtyards (see chapter 4). In the republican period between the 1910s and the 1940s, there also emerged the adaptive Chinese renaissance style, blending traditional Chinese and European architecture. The key practitioners included Henry Murphy, Henry Hussey, and a number of Chinese architects, such as Lv Yanzhi. Calling for more sensitivity to the local context, Murphy argued that essential features of traditional Chinese architecture needed to be preserved intact whenever possible and that foreign architects in China could design architecture in Chinese style and, most important, for the Chinese.[38] Buildings designed in this adaptive Chinese style, such as the

Peking Union Medical College (1916–18) in Beijing, designed by Henry Hussey, were clearly Western classical buildings in scale and function but were decorated with Chinese motifs such as gigantic tiled roofs. The republican government heavily promoted this adaptive Chinese style, seeing it as the "national style" reflecting the glory of Chinese tradition but also the new spirit of the modern era. Murphy served as the chief architectural advisor to the republican government in 1928. Many buildings in Nanjing, the capital of the republican government, were designed in this national style. The Mausoleum for Sun Yat-Sen, designed by Lv Yanzhi and based on the Lincoln Memorial, displayed symmetrical monumentality while incorporating distinctive Chinese elements. Architectural historian Lai Delin describes the mausoleum as the "crucible for defining modern Chinese architecture."[39] The national style, however, was criticized by advocates of the modern movement for being wasteful and not representing the spirit of modern republican China.

Thus, the architectural transplantation in this period is largely a colonial articulation, characterized by the one-way exportation of architectural design from the West to foreign concessions in China. The period between the 1850s and the 1920s saw the transplanting of Western architecture to treaty port cities in China in a wholesale fashion, which was followed later by adaptive approaches that were more sensitive to the local context. As China became a goldmine for foreign architects, private architecture offices and professional associations flourished in large cities. Foreign and overseas-educated Chinese architects had a clear advantage over local Chinese builders, who were increasingly marginalized. The transplantation of Western architecture produced a variety of building forms that had not existed before in China, ranging from straightforward mimicking of revivalist European architecture to various hybrids such as shikumen houses in Shanghai and adaptive architecture in Beijing and Nanjing.

The National Project, 1950s–1970s

After the Communist Party took power in 1949, the influence of the Soviet monumental style became clear in the major institutional projects built in the first decade of socialism in the 1950s. A number of Chinese professors at Tsinghua University studied at the Moscow School of Architecture and brought back with them architectural practices and knowledge from the Soviet Union. Between 1949 and 1957, tens of thousands of Soviet experts were sent all over the country to help build the new socialist China. The Soviet architects working in China promoted design practices blending neoclassical monumentality with Chinese characteristics. Socialist realist architecture appeared in major Chinese cities, and some of the major symbolic buildings were designed by Soviet architects, such as the Soviet Exhibition Hall built in Beijing in 1953, designed by Sergei Andreyev. These buildings are symmetrical both on their facades and in their internal layout. Over the central entrance is usually a high symbolic tower. This building form had a strong influence on modern Chinese architecture through the end of the twentieth century, partly because of the similarity to traditional Chinese architecture, which emphasizes centralizing symmetry.

The Big Roof style—adding traditional Chinese roofs to modern buildings, a practice dating back to the republican period—returned in the 1950s as a result of the search for a new "national style" on the part of the socialist government. However, the socialist national style of the 1950s differed from the national style promoted by the republican government in the 1930s, at least in its theoretical underpinnings. As Peter Rowe and Seng Kuan point out, the national style of the 1930s was mostly driven by the desire of the republican government to celebrate the country's glorious past and rich architectural tradition, whereas the socialist national style of the 1950s was the result of a search for a readable and familiar architectural style to appeal to the masses.[40] Compared with the Chinese renaissance style of the 1930s, socialist realist architecture was much more restrained, using a less massive tiled roof and relying more on minor traditional decorative elements, as seen in some of the Ten Great Buildings constructed in Beijing around 1959 to celebrate the tenth anniversary of the People's Republic of China. The ten buildings were all designed by Chinese architects affiliated with the Beijing Architectural Design Institute. These projects were intended to symbolize progress and the achievements of the new socialist era. Three among the ten adopted the Big Roof style.

The architectural trend of monumentality, formalism, and revival of traditional forms receded and was replaced by orthodox modernism and standardized design construction toward the end of the 1950s. Nikita Khrushchev's speech in 1955 called for an industrialized approach to architecture and construction and put new emphasis on improving efficiency and reducing costs.

> We have an obligation to speed up, improve the quality of, and reduce the cost of, construction. In order to do so, there is only one path—the path of the most extensive industrialization of construction. . . . If an architect wants to be in step

with life, he must be an expert in cost-saving. . . . There are architects who fail to take this into account. . . . This is architectural perversion.[41]

Across the Soviet bloc, socialist realist architecture quickly gave way to standardized construction methods. After the relationship between China and the Soviet Union soured, Soviet experts departed, and China shifted to the orthodox modernist approach to building out of economic necessity. The new approach emphasized low costs, efficiency, standardized design solutions, and mass production. The core of the standardized design solution, for example, in housing construction, was a dwelling unit (*danyuan*) made up of standard building components. Various combinations of these units formed buildings, and multiple buildings formed residential quarters. In the meantime, architectural practices were also reformed, and private architecture firms were abolished and replaced by state-owned design institutes affiliated with different levels of government and with government ministries. Many of these design institutes were comprehensive professional offices often employing thousands of people, and they devised standardized design solutions for residential and governmental buildings across the country. For example, the Ministry of Urban Construction divided the country into six geographic regions (northeast, north, northwest, southwest, central, and southeast), and each region was provided with separate yet standardized design construction methods.[42] Thus, architectural production in China in the 1960s and 1970s continued to follow orthodox modernism, as architects were urged to pay more attention to costs and efficiency. The takeover of socialist realism by modernism in this period was helped by the ideological climate, especially in the years of the Cultural Revolution (1966–76), when formalism and monumentality were not only condemned but also often labeled as revivals of feudalism and antirevolutionary. Self-censorship of architectural expression prevailed among architects, and Chinese architects were increasingly isolated from the outside world during the socialist decades.

In contrast to the architectural transplantation from the West in the semicolonial period, the foreign architectural influence in the socialist period was largely from the Soviet Union, and the destination of transnational architectural flows also shifted from the concessions in Shanghai to Beijing, the new capital of socialist China. The elimination of private property ownership gave the communist party-state enormous power to reshape landscape for legitimating state power and social control, and a large part of the symbolic construction effort undertaken by the new government took place at the center of Beijing. Grandiose government buildings, public squares, and industrial plants were built in the city to symbolize the arrival of a new era. As Mariusz Czepczynski has documented with regard to landscape changes in Central Europe, communism often brought about a new hierarchy of places and buildings.[43] Soviet monumental architecture was positioned in prominent sites in the city; statues of Stalin, Lenin, and Mao were erected in public squares; major roads were renamed after Marx, Lenin, and Stalin; and minor streets were named after other revolutionary heroes. On the other end of the spectrum, places and buildings associated with the prerevolutionary "bad" times, such as those in the foreign concessions in Shanghai, were left to decay slowly during the socialist years. The disinvestment in Shanghai was exacerbated by a population increase, so that many of the formerly desirable residential quarters became densely packed slums by the early 1990s.

The socialist period witnessed significant changes in architectural practices in China, as seen in the departure of foreign architects, the nationalization of private architecture firms, and the emergence of state-owned design institutes that continue to survive today. Chinese architects were more isolated from international developments in these decades than in the semicolonial period. Nevertheless, international linkages of architectural production can still be observed in this period, such as the influence from the Soviet Union and other socialist countries. The architectural articulation in this period was largely a national project by the national government to represent the new socialist order. The shift in the site of major architectural production from Shanghai to Beijing also reflected the transition from the colonial to the national articulation. Standardized design solutions, dictated by the central government and churned out by state-owned design institutes, added a new layer of socialist landscape over the existing traditional Chinese and colonial built environment. The hybrid landscape of socialist Chinese cities was to be transformed again in the 1980s with the Open Door policy and the return of international architects.

Reconnecting to the World: The 1980s

In 1979, at the Third Plenum of the Eleventh Central Committee of the Chinese Communist Party (CCP), Deng Xiaoping outlined his plans for realizing Four Socialist Modernizations and urged greater openness toward foreign investment and technology, thus introducing pragmatic market reform, also called the Open Door policy. The Open Door policy was inaugurated in 1980 with the establishment of four special economic zones (SEZs)—Shenzhen, Zhuhai, Shantou, and Xiamen—in the Pearl River delta in the south. These southern coastal cities were chosen as experimental sites for courting foreign investment, largely because of their geographic location. They are far away from Beijing, the center of national politics, and therefore the capitalist experiments undertaken there were considered "safe" or at least less threatening for the political regime based in the north. The SEZs are also in geographic proximity to the affluent ethnic Chinese communities in Hong Kong, Taiwan, and Macao, which were the targeted sources of foreign investment in the mainland. Shenzhen is the most successful SEZ among the four, with preferential policies attractive to investors and inflows of nonunionized cheap labor from all over the country. Shenzhen was also the first to experiment with land reforms by allowing land leasing to foreign investors and charging land use fees, so that the city government could have sufficient revenue to build infrastructure to attract further investment. Driven by high profit margins, real estate development in Shenzhen and other major cities exploded. Because of the cheap land and construction costs and overpricing by developers, the profit margins of property development often amounted to more than 30 percent.[44] Following the example of the SEZs in the south, in 1984 another fourteen coastal cities opened up to international trade and investment with favorable policies tailored for attracting overseas capital. The Open Door policy of the 1980s officially ended the isolation of the Chinese economy and began to reconnect the country to international finance, trade, and investment. It also opened a new chapter of transnational architectural production in China, with a sudden influx of Western architectural theories and a gradual return of international architects.

The economic opening up was accompanied by a "high cultural fever"—a term coined by Wang Jing, the chronicler of 1980s cultural politics—and a sudden influx of Western theories, from those of Jacques Lacan, Sigmund Freud, and Jacques Derrida to structuralism, poststructuralism, and postmodernism. The introduction of these previously unavailable theories to China was a long-awaited cultural feast for Chinese intellectuals, after decades of the domination of Marxist-Leninist ideology in cultural politics. After the Cultural Revolution (1966–76), during which many intellectuals were sent to the countryside for "reeducation," in the 1980s intellectuals reclaimed their position in society by generating a clearly elitist discourse that placed them in a superior position to that of the peasants and the working class. The resistance to the previous revolutionary ideology and the desire for liberation from it led to the unquestioning embrace of Western theories among China's intellectuals. As Wang put it, "We must understand the 'rush to theory' among young mainland intellectuals in light of their resistance to the indigenous autocratic Father as much as their subjugation to the foreign fathers."[45] Realizing the gap between China and the West after three decades of isolation, Chinese intellectuals in the 1980s were mainly concerned with catching up, copying Western theories rather than contesting and engaging them in the new postrevolutionary Chinese context. The superficial adoption of Western theories among intellectuals was part of, but also reinforced, the larger societal trend of considering anything foreign and Western to be better, more fashionable, and innovative.

Parallel to the arrival of Western theories in art, literature, film, and cultural criticism, Western architectural theories flooded China in the same period, with postmodernism, deconstructionism, and other "isms" introduced through international architects, books, and journal publications.[46] In 1980 senior architect Tong Jun published *New Architecture and Styles,* providing a survey of post–World War II architectural developments in the West. Professional journals such as the *Architect* and *World Architecture* began publication in 1979 and 1980, frequently introducing foreign theory and practices. Postmodernism landed in China in this period too, with a series of lectures delivered by Fredric Jameson at Peking University in 1985. Charles Jencks's works were translated and widely read in the mid-1980s. In 1986, *Architectural Journal* published the essays "Postmodern Pluralism" and "Postmodernism and Contemporary Chinese Architecture," signaling that the debate on Chinese postmodernism in the field of architecture was well under way. The introduction of postmodernism provided theoretical justification for the revival of classical Chinese architecture and "national form"[47] and also, as Wang Jing put it, "fulfilled the quest of those indigenous theorists who were engaged in a mental game that placed China in a continual catching-up race with the West."[48]

In spite of the postmodern hype, the material conditions in the 1980s were not yet ripe to match those in the West, and few had a deep understanding of the imported theory and its social origins. Instead of bringing a true engagement with and contestation of postmodernism and other Western theories, the influence of Western theories in architectural practices in the 1980s resulted in direct imitations of imported iconic images and the uncritical pursuit of novelty designs. The long isolation of architectural discourse and the dazzling influx of Western design ideas made the 1980s an intoxicating period for Chinese architects. But theoretically they were unprepared to digest the suddenly available new ideas, and in practice, the slow-paced urban reform in the 1980s had not yet brought as many opportunities for Chinese architects to build as they would have in the 1990s.

In addition to the sudden influx of Western architectural theories, transnational architectural production in the 1980s could also be located in the return of international architects. In the first decade of the Open Door policy, many cities and developers had little contact with international architects or could not afford them, and international architects were mostly invited by government ministries, or brought in by foreign investors, to work on joint-venture projects explicitly targeting foreign investment and tourism. Private independent firms were still not allowed in this period, and international architects needed to partner with local state-owned design institutes. The significant architectural projects involving international architects in the 1980s were mostly luxury hotel projects in major cities. In 1979, Chinese American architect I. M. Pei was invited to design the Fragrant Hill Hotel (completed in 1982), in collaboration with local design institutes in Beijing. His contemporary design, incorporating many traditional Chinese elements, was well received in the local architectural community as a modern interpretation of traditional architecture. Following the enterprise of the Fragrant Hill Hotel were several other luxury hotel projects commissioned to international architects, many of whom were of Chinese descent, were based in Hong Kong, or had established connections to the mainland via Hong Kong. P & T Group, a Hong Kong–based British design firm with a long history of practice in mainland China, was invited to design the Jin'ling Hotel in Nanjing in 1980, which was the first foreign-funded hotel project in China. Another Chinese American architect, Clement Chen, based in Hong Kong and San Francisco, designed the Jian'guo Hotel in Beijing in 1982, incorporating traditional features such as a Chinese garden and a central courtyard. John Portman designed the Shanghai Center in 1989, using red columns to add a local touch. Although some of these flagship hotel projects incorporated traditional Chinese design elements, most of them were unmistakably modern structures, as explicitly requested by the clients in their attempt to create a familiar cityscape to lure foreign investors.

In contrast to the pre-1949 era, transnational architectural production in transitional 1980s China was much smaller in scale and limited to joint-venture projects in SEZs and a few major cities. To a large degree, transnational architectural flows in this period were channeled through Hong Kong, and Hong Kong architecture had significant influence on mainland architects. The transnational architectural production was also closely monitored by the government. The central and local governments were the main agents that deregulated foreign design practices and invited international architects as special guests to work in China. The goal was to create "pockets" of enterprise zones, such as luxury hotels, to gradually open up the country to foreign investment and tourism. The transnational architectural production in the 1980s, however, also differs significantly from that of the socialist period—the capitalist West replaced the socialist Soviet Union as the source of admiration and inspiration for introducing new architecture. Compared with previous periods, the stance of the state in the 1980s was inconsistent, and often contradictory, in relation to the influx of transnational flows. On the one hand, it was the central state that initiated the Open Door policy, encouraging "commodity economy" and "opening up" to the West; but on the other hand, the party-state was also concerned with "contamination" from Western cultural influence brought by the Open Door policy and foreign investments, so that in 1983 Deng Xiaoping announced the campaign to fight the "spiritual pollution of the bourgeois" in cultural fields. While intellectuals were imagining a utopian future of liberation in political and cultural fields, along with economic reform, the party-state envisioned an economic opening up without modifications to the political status quo. The 1980s were a period of negotiation and contestation between the state and the intellectuals, which eventually ended with the crackdown on the pro-democracy Tiananmen student movement in 1989.

The 1980s were thus a transitional period for the architectural profession in China, as it emerged from its three-decade-long isolation and began to reconnect to the world. Western architectural theories flooded in, and international architects gradually returned. The role of the state was ambivalent and conflictual in endorsing foreign cultural influences, as the state itself was making an uneasy ideological shift from "socialism based on Marxism-Leninism and Mao's thought" to "socialism with Chinese characteristics."

The Transnational Project, 1990s–Present

Transnational architectural practices in China since the 1990s have undergone both a quantitative and a qualitative shift from the previous periods, facilitated by the unprecedented expansion of the construction market, on the one hand, and the privatization and deregulation of design practices, on the other. Architectural production in post-1990s China operates according to a transnational logic, enabled by the globalization of architectural education, the integration of the global design labor market, and the ascending role of the Chinese state in commissioning globally oriented architectural megaprojects. These forces have turned urban China into fertile ground for wild architectural experimentation (see table 2.8).

The forces of both the market and the state worked together in the reshaping of the architectural design landscape in the post-1990s period. The sudden expansion of urban construction, enabled by urban renewal programs and land and housing reforms, attracted new players—international design firms and private Chinese design firms—to the design market. But the entry of these new players would not have been possible without the deregulation and privatization initiated by the state. In the mid-1980s, foreign design firms were allowed under the condition that they partner with state-owned design institutes. In 1994, the Ministry of City and County Construction and Environmental Protection allowed private practices to be established by Chinese architects. In 1995, the Ministry of Construction granted special status to twenty private architecture firms in Shenzhen, Guangzhou, and Shanghai as an experiment.[49] In the meantime, privatizing reforms of state-owned design institutes were well under way, as the government no longer allocated projects to these institutes, which therefore had to survive on their own in the competitive marketplace. Under these deregulatory changes, international firms and local private firms quickly entered the market and ended the previous monopoly of state-owned design institutes. The current architectural design field is therefore divided among three types of architecture firms—state-owned design institutes, international firms, and private Chinese firms—each having its comparative advantages.[50]

State-owned design institutes are a legacy of the socialist urban planning system. A design institute is often affiliated with a particular level of government, such as a province, city, or county, or with a government ministry, such as agriculture, railway, or commerce. In the socialist period, construction contracts were allocated to design institutes from within their affiliated governments and ministries; therefore, there was rarely any competition among institutes for project commissions. Since the 1980s, design institutes have undergone significant reforms. On the one hand, new design institutes are established according to changes in administrative boundaries and hierarchies. On the other hand, large design institutes have split into many smaller units and set up branches in different cities

TABLE 2.8 **Select list of megaprojects designed by international architecture firms in Beijing and Shanghai, 1998–2008**

Type of megaproject	Project name	City	Architect/architectural firm	Nationality of design firm
Airports	Shanghai Pudong International Airport	Shanghai	Paul Andreu	France
Master plans	Beijing Capital International Airport, Terminal 3	Beijing	Foster & Partners	UK
	SoHo City master plan/Beijing Logistic Port (unbuilt)	Beijing	Zaha Hadid with Patrik Schumacher	UK
	Huamao Center Masterplan	Beijing	Kohn Pederson Fox Associates	US
	Central Axis master plan of Olympics	Beijing	Albert Speer & Partners	Germany
	Expo 2010 master plan	Shanghai	Albert Speer & Partners	Germany
	Shanghai Huangpu River Waterfront & Key Area master plan	Shanghai	SOM	US
	Suzhou Creek master plan	Shanghai	EDAW	US
Corporate/financial/ mixed developments	Jiushi Corporation Headquarters	Shanghai	Foster & Partners	England
	World Financial Center	Shanghai	Kohn Pederson Fox Associates	US
	Plaza 66	Shanghai	Kohn Pederson Fox Associates	US
	Jianwai SOHO	Beijing	Riken Yamamoto & Fieldshop	Japan
	Shangdu SOHO	Beijing	Peter Davidson	Australia
	Xintiandi	Shanghai	Wood & Zapata	US
	Jinmao Tower	Shanghai	SOM	US
	Wealth Center	Beijing	GMP	Germany
	Zhongguancun West, BSTP Lot 21	Beijing	Kohn Pedersen Fox Associates	US
State organizations	Chinese Central Television Headquarters	Beijing	Office for Metropolitan Architecture	Holland
	Bank of China Head Office	Beijing	Pei Partnership Architects	US
	China Natural Offshore Oil Corporation Headquarters	Beijing	Kohn Pederson Fox Associates	US
	China Petro Headquarters	Beijing	Henn Architekten	Germany

Category	Project	City	Architect	Country
Convention/exhibition centers	International Automotive Expo	Beijing	Henn Architekten	Germany
	Beijing International Sports and Exhibition Center	Beijing	RTKL	US
Cultural institutions	National Theater	Beijing	Paul Andreu	France
	Oriental Art Center	Shanghai	Paul Andreu	France
	Chinese Museum of Film	Beijing	RTKL	US
	National Museum	Beijing	GMP	Germany
	Museum Archives and Exhibition Hall for Urban Development, Pudong	Shanghai	GMP	Germany
	National Library	Beijing	Office for Metropolitan Architecture	Holland
	Shanghai Grand Theater	Shanghai	Jean-Marie Charpentier and Studios Architecture	France
	Beijing Book City	Beijing	Office for Metropolitan Architecture	Holland
	Capital Museum	Beijing	RTKL	US
	National Art Museum of China	Beijing	RTKL	US
	Museum of Science and Technology, Pudong	Beijing	RTKL	US
Sports stadiums	Olympic Green	Beijing	Sasaki Associates	US
	2008 Olympics Wukesong Cultural and Sports Center	Beijing	Burckhardt + Partner	Switzerland
	National Stadium	Beijing	Herzog & de Meuron	Switzerland
	National Swimming Center	Beijing	PTW and ARUP	Australia
Newtowns	Anting International Automobile City and Newtown	Shanghai	Albert Speer & Partners	Germany
	Songjiang Newtown	Shanghai	Atkins	US
	New Jiangwan City master plan	Shanghai	Johnson Fain & Partners	US
	Pujiang Town City Planning and Urban Design	Shanghai	Gregotti Associati International	Italy
	Shanghai New Harbor City master plan	Shanghai	GMP	Germany

where the market is strong. Many of these spin-offs are de facto independent private practices, but they still operate under the names of state-owned institutes. Project commissions are no longer allocated by governments or ministries but have to be fought for in the marketplace. Thus, many state-owned design institutes have reinvented themselves as "quasi-private architecture firms"[51] and compete with one another for contracts. By the early 2000s, there were about 250 class-A design institutes, many of which employ more than one thousand architects and have branches in major cities all over the country.[52] On account of their manpower and government connections, the reinvented design institutes take the lion's share of the construction market and are responsible for the mainstream urban landscape. Although a number of state design institutes managed to spin off independent studios led by brand-name architects, most institutes are anonymous, collective players, operating on the principles of speed, efficiency, mass design, and standard production.

International architecture firms arrived in China in large numbers in the 1990s, after the deregulation of the domestic design market. Currently there are three major subtypes of international design firms active in China. First are the star-driven prestigious firms led by celebrity architects. The second type are large corporate architecture firms, such as SOM, ARUP, and other lesser-known commercial firms. The third type, and the most recent entry, are the small, not-yet-known, but up-and-coming firms from all over the world that are attracted to the possibility of building something in China, such as the Ordos 100 project. The first two types illustrate the previous discussions in this chapter on the power of "large" and "small." Based on their advantages in resources, technology, and advanced management, corporate architecture firms have obtained commissions for many complex large-scale megaprojects, such as the fifty-five-story Jinmao Tower (SOM) and Chongming Ecological Island in Shanghai (ARUP). The star-driven firms, with their high visibility and public recognition, can appeal to clients who aspire to be associated with brand names and are willing to take risks for new and sensational design, as seen in SOHO China's collaboration with various international architects (chapter 3) and many of the Olympic structures in Beijing (chapter 5). The third type of international firms are new to the scene, and they often work on commissions for individual buildings in group projects, such as the well-publicized Commune by the Great Wall, designed by twelve Asian architects; Jinhua Architecture Park, in which seventeen international and Chinese architects participated; and also the Ordos 100 project in Inner

Mongolia, in which each of one hundred architects is assigned to design a villa. Some of them have come to China in search of opportunities to build and experiment, while others had no previous interest in or knowledge about China and have landed Chinese commissions by chance.

Overall, international architects and firms working in China are far from a homogeneous group, with various scales, agendas, and practice principles. Compared with Chinese firms, international firms have difficulty penetrating the Chinese market and navigating the local politics and unfamiliar cultural practices. Most of them choose to partner with local firms or directly localize their workforce by hiring Chinese architects in their offices. The most common type of collaboration is between corporate or star-driven international firms and state-owned design institutes—with the former bringing the symbolic capital of fame, prestige, reputation, and new design concepts, and the latter providing the manpower, government connections, and local knowledge.

Private Chinese firms began to appear in the mid-1990s. They are less prestigious than international firms and have fewer connections to the government than do state design institutes.[53] However, they have the advantage of being familiar with both local conditions and international trends, as many of the founders of these firms are returnee Chinese architects who studied and worked abroad in the 1980s and 1990s. The most successful—in terms of public, professional, and market recognition—include MADA s.p.a.m., founded in Shanghai in the late 1990s by Ma Qingyun, a graduate of the University of Pennsylvania; MAD Design, registered in New York in 2004 and currently based in Beijing, founded by Yale graduate Ma Yansong; and Urbanus, a progressive young firm, founded in 1999 in Shenzhen and Beijing by partners Liu Xiaodu, Meng Yan, and Wang Hui, who all have architecture degrees from the United States.

Ma Yansong is the first Chinese architect to win a major international commission—for the Absolute Tower in Canada, which is widely referred to as the "Marilyn Monroe building" for its sensational curves. The headshot of the thirty-three-year-old Ma Yansong together with the model of his Marilyn Monroe building has appeared in hundreds of fashion and lifestyle magazines in China. Critic and editor of *Urban China Magazine* Jiang Jun commented that the making of Chinese "starchitects" such as Ma Yansong was based on two crucial elements. The first is the "Chinese card." The crucial period of urban construction has made it advantageous to be a Chinese architect in an international architectural context, as the world is "gazing at China curiously, wondering what kinds of stars would rise from the drastically changing China."[54] The second element is the "international card," and in the case of Ma Yansong, it includes the combination of a degree from Yale, an intern experience at Zaha Hadid's office, a firm registered in New York, and an international list of partners. In the epilogue of the book *MAD Dinner,* Jiang Jun wrote,

> The Chinese card interests the world, while the international card excites China: this logic of a "besieged fortress," where people trapped within want to go out and vice versa, exemplifies the instauration of China's modernity. It's also the logic that enables dual-background architects . . . to negotiate in both a domestic and international context—a collective positioning of the next generation of free-thinking Chinese architects.[55]

If MAD Design is an example of star-driven private Chinese firms, following the paths of their international counterparts, then Urbanus is an example of the new generation of Chinese design firms, less geared toward achieving stardom but more committed to creating designs sensitive to history and the constantly changing local urban conditions. Since its first project, a district library in Shenzhen in 2001, Urbanus has been involved in the architectural design and planning of a wide range of more than two hundred projects across the country. As the leading example of a progressive Chinese design firm, Urbanus has produced a number of cutting-edge works that have received high professional recognition and appeared in numerous international exhibitions and publications. As Canadian curator and artist Adrian Blackwell observed, the best work from Urbanus is infill architecture that responds to local conditions and everyday life, embracing each situation in all its complexity.[56] Its recently completed (2009) social housing project in Guangzhou is one such case. The commission was to design an apartment complex of 220 units for low-income migrants in Guangzhou. As migrants pour into large cities and few social housing projects are built by governments, most major cities in China face a housing crisis for the poor. In cities such as Shenzhen and Guangzhou, many migrants have ended up in squalid "urban villages"[57] with extremely high density and poor infrastructure. Urbanus has been conducting research on such migrant enclaves in urban villages, and in its *tulou* project, it reworked a housing prototype originating from Hakka communities in Fujian province three hundred years ago, designed to protect villagers from pirates, vagrants, and other intruders, into an intimate living space for migrant families and communities. Its sensitivity to history and social context has turned Urbanus into a progressive exception and a role model for other Chinese firms to emulate.

Architectural production entered a transnational era in the 1990s, with the breakdown of previous trade barriers and the integration of the international design and labor market. China has become the largest and fastest-growing construction market and has attracted international architects from all over the world. These international architects working in China are far from a homogeneous group. A few major types can be identified. The first are the jet-setting starchitects who receive the most media attention and have a large crowd of local admirers and followers. For these starchitects, China provides not only a market but also a heuristic site to explore the possibilities of architecture, thanks to the magnitude of urban construction, unchecked state power and sponsorship, and abundance of cheap labor. The second type includes "corporate parachutes"—corporate architects, engineers, and project managers sent from their home offices. Many of these expatriate architects have limited local knowledge and tend to impose Western design concepts and management styles squarely on their Chinese projects. Their operation in China is largely a strategy to diversify corporate portfolios, and their success hinges upon "hiring locally" in their project offices in order to bridge the knowledge gap. The third type is a group of more research-oriented architects, from Europe, Japan, and the United States, temporarily based in China, designing, researching, and writing about Chinese cities.[58] They are much more informed about local conditions than both the starchitects and the corporate parachutes. Their experience of living in China has enabled them to observe the action from up close and has given depth to their writings that is rarely seen in the "hit-and-run" Western journalism on Chinese cities. The last type are the dual-track Chinese architects, who have hands-on knowledge of both local conditions and international trends. Some of them have emulated the paths of international starchitects and devoted much effort and attention to self-promotion through the media, while others, such as Urbanus, are producing cutting-edge and progressive design with high sensitivity to social and historical contexts.

In the 1990s, the previous monopoly of state design institutes was ended, first by the entry of international design firms, and later by the rise of private Chinese firms. It is only a matter of time before state design institutes further disintegrate into smaller and independent practices and the two newcomers—international firms and private Chinese firms—gain a greater share in the architectural design market. The strong presence of international firms and private Chinese firms since the 1990s very much resembles the market configuration of the pre-1949 era, when both foreign and Chinese professional architecture practices flourished in the foreign concessions. But a crucial distinction must be drawn between the semicolonial period and the post-1990s era, and that is the role of the state in regulating transnational architectural flows. In contrast to the semicolonial period, when architectural flows were directed from the West to extrajurisdictional foreign concessions in China, over which the weak Chinese state had little control, transnational architectural production since the 1990s has been facilitated by state deregulation for private design practices and government sponsorship for architectural megaprojects. Therefore, the state is a major enabler for transnational architectural production taking place in Chinese cities in the post-1990s era.

Ordos 100

> The scope of the project is to develop 100 villas in Ordos, Inner Mongolia, China, for the client, Jiang Yuan Water Engineering Ltd. FAKE Design, Ai Wei Wei['s] studio in Beijing, has developed the master plan for the 100 parcels of land and will curate the project, while Herzog and de Meuron have selected 100 architects to participate. The 100 architects hail from 27 countries around the globe.[59]

The above quotation is from the project statement of the Ordos 100 project, currently under construction (2008–10). In 2008, one hundred architects, from countries as far as Israel, Chile, Mexico, and South Africa, convened in the city of Ordos and presented their design proposals to Cai Jiang, the client and developer of the project (see table A.5). Most of the architects are young and up-and-coming, chosen by Jacques Herzog and Pierre de Meuron to participate in this typically Chinese exercise of city building—from scratch. Ordos is located in the region of Inner Mongolia, which is rich in coal, gas, and other natural resources. The city has been capitalizing its natural resources and is among the fastest-growing cities in the country. The local government is building a new district of the city for a projected population of two hundred thousand by 2020. Artist Ai Wei Wei's studio FAKE Design drafted the master plan and divided the parcel into one hundred lots for the construction of one hundred upscale villas. The lots were assigned to architects by lottery. Most architects invited for the project have never built in China before, and their involvement in the project is only at the initial design stage—detailed design drawings and construction will be turned over to local partners.[60]

It is hard to speculate about the impact of this experiment of concentrating one hundred designs in one quarter of an unbuilt city, but the project nevertheless showcases the continuing course of transnational architectural production under way in China. Following the examples of Beijing and Shanghai, second-tier cities have begun to use architecture as a strategy to draw world attention. While construction is under way, Ordos has already received considerable media attention—*Domus* magazine reported on the project, and design models for the hundred villas have begun to be circulated on major architecture websites. In this sense, the unbuilt Ordos 100 has already realized its goal.

This chapter has examined the geography of global architectural production by focusing on the globalization strategies of large and small architecture firms, as well as on the different roles and positions of cities in the global network of architectural design. The transformation of the built environment of Chinese cities has to be understood in light of the positions of Chinese cities in the global city network. The analyses presented in the chapter have revealed that Beijing, Shanghai, and other large Chinese cities are crucial consumption sites in the global design network, offering a fertile ground for architectural experimentation. International architects, from various backgrounds, are actively involved in the architectural experiment under way in China. Although there are trends showing that local private Chinese firms are catching up, the case of Ordos 100 well illustrates that the appetite on the part of local clients for international architects is unsatisfied and still growing. By 2020, China will have more than one hundred cities with a population over one million. The magnitude and scale of urbanization will turn Chinese cities—not only the biggest and most glamorous ones, but also the small and previously unknown ones—into the new territories of transnational architectural experimentation. The next three chapters will examine the current transnational architectural practices in the two largest Chinese metropolises—Beijing and Shanghai.

Architecture, Media, and Real Estate Speculation

In the middle of the four-square-kilometer area designated as Beijing's new CBD was Beijing Er Guo Tou liquor factory. The place was infamous among local residents for its smelly twice-weekly brewing sessions. In 1997, a real estate company, SOHO China, acquired the land, and in less than five years, it replaced the former liquor factory with SOHO NewTown—a high-end residential complex of modern high-rise apartment towers painted in bold orange, red, and blue. SOHO NewTown was the first residential building project in Beijing that used bright colors. In 2001, Beijing No. 1 Machinery Factory, also sitting within the CBD, was demolished by implosion. The land was leased to the same real estate firm, SOHO China. By 2005, the former factory workshops had already been replaced by Jianwai SOHO—a cluster of two office skyscrapers, eighteen apartment towers, and more than three hundred retail shops, all designed with ultramodern, minimalist chic.[1] Jianwai SOHO is one of the few building projects in Beijing to have eliminated bulky balconies. The SOHO properties were priced at the highest level at the time in Beijing, but they were sold out long before the projects were completed. Following the success of SOHO NewTown and Jianwai SOHO, the company has continued to use design—mostly from prestigious international architects—to brand its projects. As of 2009, SOHO China has expanded its real estate operation to the entire CBD with seven SOHO projects, and it has developed more commercial space in Beijing's CBD than any other real estate firm.[2]

SOHO China is the epic symbol of the creative mixing of art, architecture, media, and real estate speculation under Chinese market capitalism.

It is not the largest private developer in the country, but it is the most publicized because of its design-intensive and concept-driven development model. Every SOHO project is packaged as a concept—of new styles of urban work and living—to the growing Chinese middle class. Along with selling apartments and office space, SOHO China is also selling dreams to the new middle class—dreams of making a fortune by investing in real estate, and dreams of living in Beijing just as New Yorkers, Londoners, and Parisians live in their global cities.

This chapter will first take a historical detour and examine how the center of economic activities in Beijing has shifted from the older inner city to the new CBD that was once outside the city limits. I will then examine the use of international architecture and design firms by both the public and the private sectors in the making of the new CBD. Last, through the case of SOHO China, I will zoom in on the overlapping urban circles of real estate developers and the cultural elite—architects, artists, writers, and other creative types—to examine how the symbolic capital of architectural design is ultimately linked to the accumulation of economic, political, and cultural capital for the urban elite. The spectacles of place making have produced a fragmented city of urban glamour zones surrounded by pockets of the dispossessed.

From Peking to Beijing: A Genealogy of Downtowns

I use "Peking" to refer to the city before the market reform in 1978 and "Beijing" to refer to the new city rapidly transformed by institutional reforms and restructuring after that year.[3] Downtown is understood here as the business and commercial center, that is, the *economic* center, of the city. Throughout much of its history, the political and economic centers of Beijing have often been two separate spheres. In the imperial and socialist periods, downtown Peking was the political center of the empire and of the communist government, respectively; it was largely defined and shaped by its national and regional roles. It was suppressed and overshadowed as a commercial space. In the brief republican period, downtown Peking emerged as a cosmopolitan international space, largely produced by translocal flows of people, goods, and economic activities in a semicolonial setting. In the most recent global phase, older historic downtowns have become subcenters for retail and tourism, and the entrepreneurial city government has built a new CBD on the former urban fringes. Drawing on the existing scholarship about the urban and social history of Peking, this section will trace how downtown Peking has continuously changed its location, function, and meaning from the imperial period until today, and how the downtown(s) has/have been made or unmade by local and translocal processes throughout this history. Then I will turn to the contemporary period and examine the efforts by the city government to use international design firms to promote the new CBD.

Imperial Peking, 1400s–1911

Peking/Beijing is an ancient city that has served as the capital of five imperial dynasties and one modern regime.[4] Imperial Peking—during the Ming and Qing dynasties from 1403 to 1911—was the node of the government and administration networks of the Chinese Empire.[5] The tremendous economic, political, and cultural resources commanded by the state "connected Peking indissolubly to the empire."[6] Imperial families and the government were the largest employers in the city, and their activities overflowed into many aspects of local urban life. Economic centers were submerged under the shadow of the political center, the imperial domain. The dominance of political spheres over economic spheres left clear imprints on the cityscape.

Ming and Qing Peking consisted of several walled cities nested in concentric rings (fig. 3.1).[7] The Forbidden City, as the residence of the imperial family, was located in the geographic center. It was the focal point of imperial Peking and a world closed off from the city's residents. The Imperial City surrounding the Forbidden City enclosed private gardens, lakes, and workspace exclusively reserved for the ruling family and high-ranking bureaucrats. The sparsely populated palaces and the eunuch-managed Imperial City were off-limits to the public. This inaccessible space occupied a large proportion of the built-up area of the city, and it was both the geographic center of Peking and the political heart of the empire. Compartmentalization by walls and gates was fundamental in organizing the society of imperial Peking. The concentric orientations of imposing city walls asserted the centrality of the emperor and played a symbolic role in constructing Peking as the capital of the empire.

The spatial layout of Peking was divided into the square-shaped Inner City in the north and the rectangular Outer City in the south. The major commercial center of imperial Peking developed around the central city gate—Qianmen, which still connects the Inner and Outer City today.

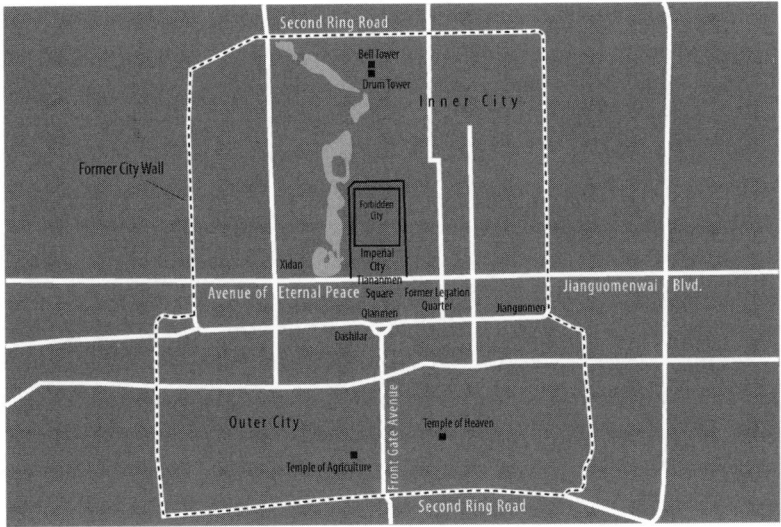

FIGURE 3.1. The historical center of Beijing

The Outer City was smaller than the Inner City and lacked the majestic imperial center. Owing to the presence of the imperial palaces, there were more residences—mostly of noble families and high-ranking bureaucrats—in the Inner City, and more commerce in the Outer City. During the Qing period, as the new ruling Manchu elites ordered all Chinese residents and commercial activities to be relocated to the Outer City, the economic center of gravity further shifted to the Outer City. Imperial City walls imposed significant barriers to traffic, and city gates became major transportation arteries.

A downtown section appeared near the streets and markets in the densely populated area just outside Qianmen in the Outer City. Here developed a great congestion of merchants, shopkeepers, peasants, workshops, and laborers. Residents were concentrated in the highly commercialized, densely settled lanes and alleys near Qianmen. As the commercial area expanded, reedy swamps were gradually drained; shops appeared outside the walls between the Inner City and the Outer City, and residential neighborhoods multiplied. Although other subcenters also emerged during the Ming and Qing periods,[8] Qianmen occupied the top rank with its large number of permanent shops catering to the demands of the city's officials and aristocrats for luxury goods. As the primary downtown of imperial

Peking, the commercial and entertainment quarter at Qianmen attracted sojourners from throughout the empire and beyond.

The political and economic system of the imperial period thus produced an imbalance between the Inner and Outer City.[9] In spite of the burgeoning economic activities in the downtown Qianmen area, residents of imperial Peking felt that the Outer City could not match the elegance of the palaces and imperial domains in the Inner City. According to historian Susan Naquin, the local urban life in the Outer City was only sketchily represented in visual media before the nineteenth century, and the recommended tourist sights in popular guidebooks in this period were mostly limited to places in the Inner City and the countryside.[10] Downtown, as the economic center of Peking, was conceived by its residents as an inferior secular space, in sharp contrast with the sacred imperial domain. The physical and symbolic centrality of the imperial domain skewed the locations of markets and defined the meaning of downtown in imperial Peking.

Republican Peking, 1911–1937

The fall of the Qing dynasty in 1911 marked Peking's transition from tradition and imperialism to modernity, and Wangfujing emerged as the new downtown commercial center in republican Peking. The republican period witnessed major changes in the market system and the locations of downtowns in Peking, with the Inner City gaining an upper hand over the Outer City.[11] The Qing-era restrictions on Inner City commerce had vanished, and the concentration of wealthy families there provided the clientele for high-end markets. The variety and number of businesses increased, and old and new styles of commercial establishments proliferated. Hosting new styles of specialty shops, department stores, and indoor markets, Wangfujing surpassed Qianmen and became the emblem of new consumerism and cosmopolitan urban life in Peking. The rise of Wangfujing as the new economic center in republican Peking was due to its geographic proximity to the foreign community. It was the transnational connections in semicolonial republican Peking that redefined the economic geography and reordered power relations between places in the city.

The history of Wangfujing is the history of Peking's encounter with the West.[12] After its defeat in the Opium War in 1860, the Chinese government signed the Treaty of Tianjin, which sanctioned the establishment of a permanent international settlement in Peking—the Legation Quarter. The arrival of a large number of foreign bureaucrats, diplomats, and politicians in the early 1900s contributed further to the growth of Wangfujing as a cosmopolitan marketplace. Many of the commercial establishments at Wangfujing were owned by foreigners, and almost all of them sold imported goods from Europe, Japan, and the United States. Wangfujing's growth was propelled by the economic clout and tastes of foreigners from the Legation Quarter.[13] The foreign community was the key clientele at Wangfujing's specialty shops and antique dealers. Local Chinese bourgeois and aristocrats rubbed shoulders with foreigners while strolling along its paved and well-lit shopping promenades.

Wangfujing, Xidan, and Qianmen formed a triangle of commercial centers within and around which lived the wealthiest residents of Peking.[14] Among the three centers, Wangfujing was characterized as the most Western and modern, while the older Qianmen market appealed to the masses with cheaper and traditional products. By the 1930s, Wangfujing had gathered all the elements of a modern downtown, with theaters, department stores, cafes, and other cultural institutions in place. Replacing the imperial political domain, the new downtown district of Wangfujing became the center of Peking's spatial organization and the focal point of cosmopolitan urbanism.

Socialist Peking, 1949–1978

Chinese communist leaders developed strong animosities toward the conspicuous consumption and urban lifestyles of the previous republican period. The new rulers saw cities as places of vice, corruption, and class exploitation. Although the CCP was active in the cities in its early days, after 1927 it was driven into the countryside by the Nationalist Party and had to devise means for mobilizing a rural revolution while watching the Nationalist Party rule the cities.[15] After the CCP came to power in 1949, the government initiated a series of reforms to purge urban evils and to transform the pre-1949 consumption cities into socialist production centers. These measures included, for example, eliminating foreign control and influence, deporting foreign residents, building heavy industrial facilities in city centers, reducing service sectors, and eliminating private ownership of property. For the country's leaders, the ideal socialist city was a spartan and productive place with minimal lifestyle distinction and conspicuous consumption.

The anti-urban bias of the communist leadership had a devastating impact on the urban economy. Between the 1950s and the 1970s, Peking and other mainland Chinese cities suffered severe disinvestment, shortages, and poor quality of goods and services. Many stores were closed down, and those open were often staffed with unfriendly clerks. According to Martin Whyte and William Parish, Peking had 10,200 restaurants in 1949, when the population was less than two million. But by the 1970s, when the total population was almost five million, the number of restaurants shrank to only 656. The number of shops declined from 70,000 in the early 1950s to 10,000 in 1980.[16]

Earlier downtown commercial centers invariably suffered from the anti-urban disinvestment policies. During the socialist period, Wangfujing's cosmopolitan and international character quickly diminished, as foreigners were deported and private shops were replaced with state-owned department stores. Foreign signs and road names were changed to Chinese names with strong socialist appeals; for example, the main street of Wangfujing was renamed People's Street. Most goods were allocated through the local government in the centralized planning system, and state-owned retail establishments lacked incentives to compete for customers. The department stores in Wangfujing failed to update their facilities and continued selling substandard products, and Wangfujing quickly lost its former cosmopolitan glamour and appeal.

After a short-lived commercial renaissance in the republican era, downtown Peking in the socialist years became subordinated again to the political domain. The communist leaders set up their administrative apparatus inside the compounds of the former Imperial City and transformed Tiananmen Square into the most sacred site in the country. With the iconic portrait of Mao and monumental museum complexes narrating Chinese revolutionary history, Tiananmen Square became the symbol of the new socialist China and a highly politically charged space.[17] The government complex and Tiananmen Square formed the focal point of the city, organizing the urban society and spatial structure of socialist Peking.

Global Beijing, 1978–Present: Making the New CBDs

The market reform in 1978 fundamentally reorganized urban spaces in the city, and modern financial districts have replaced historic downtowns as the center of the urban economy. As a result of intensified interdistrict competition, three clusters of business districts appeared over the course of the 1990s—Zhongguancun in Haidian district, with a specialization in the high-tech and electronics industries, Financial Street (Jinrong Jie) in Xicheng district, and the CBD in Chaoyang district (fig. 3.2). Among the

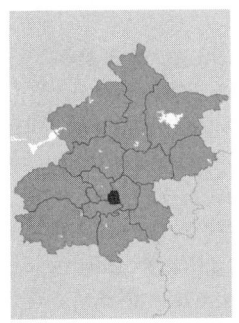

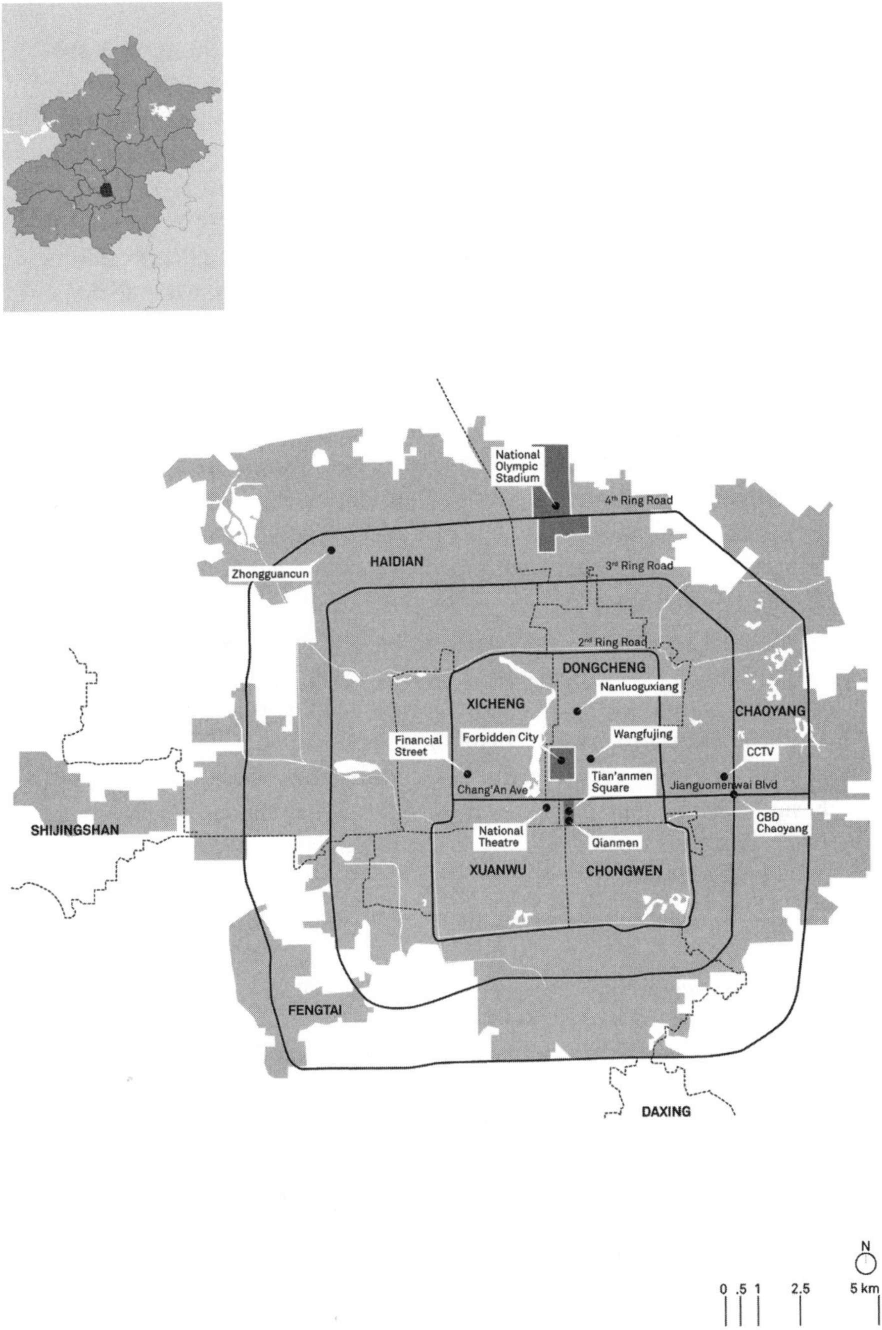

National
Olympic
Stadium

4ᵗʰ Ring Road

Zhongguancun

HAIDIAN

3ʳᵈ Ring Road

2ⁿᵈ Ring Road

DONGCHENG

Nanluoguxiang

XICHENG

Wangfujing

CHAOYANG

Financial
Street

Forbidden City

CCTV

Chang'An Ave

Tian'anmen
Square

Jianguomenwai Blvd

SHIJINGSHAN

National
Theatre

Qianmen

CBD
Chaoyang

XUANWU

CHONGWEN

FENGTAI

DAXING

N

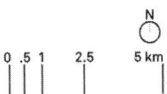

0 .5 1   2.5   5 km

FIGURE 3.2. Map of Beijing

three, the CBD in Chaoyang district has the largest concentration of specialized business services firms. The development of the CBD is a product of targeted state policies. The city government strategically used urban master plans from international design firms in the planning stage of the CBD.

The plan to build a CBD was first proposed in the *Beijing General City Plan*, which was approved by the State Council in 1993. It stated that "a modern central business district with multiple functions of finance, insurance, trade, information, commerce, culture, and entertainment should be built in Beijing."[18] In 1998, the Beijing city government issued the *Specific Controlling Plan* indicating that the CBD would be located in Chaoyang district in the eastern part of Beijing.[19] The city government established the CBD Administration Committee to supervise all development activities. In 1999, the central government appointed Wang Qishan, the former executive of the China Construction Bank, as the mayor of Beijing. Since then, it has become one of the primary goals of the city administration to build a financial district that can lure multinational firms and financial institutions to Beijing.

The area allocated for the CBD is approximately four square kilometers at the crossing of East Third Ring Road and Jian'guomenwai Boulevard. The site used to be an industrial area with a number of large manufacturing facilities. Approximately fifty-four thousand families worked and lived in the area.[20] However, the city government envisioned a new modern business district emerging from there. The existing manufacturing facilities had to be relocated elsewhere, old residential buildings demolished, and residents evicted. The first step in turning the area into a modern business district was to draft a master plan accommodating global business functions.

In the preparation of the CBD master plan, Beijing followed Shanghai's practice of inviting international architecture firms for publicity.[21] In 2000, the Chaoyang district government organized the first international design competition for master plan proposals and selected eight international firms.[22] The local and national media competed to report the participation of international architecture firms in the design competition. To reflect the international character of the design process, the organizers also put together a jury committee of international experts. The committee finally selected the design by Johnson Fain & Partners (US) for the first prize. In 2003, the city government organized the second international design competition to select a detailed plan for a smaller core area of the CBD, and it chose the design proposal from Pei Cobb Freed & Partners (US).

Although two American firms won the design competitions, neither of their designs was used as the final master plan. Instead, Beijing Planning and Design Institute, an affiliate of the city government, combined features from different proposals and made the final master plan. For the city government, it did not matter much that the final master plan was an eclectic selection from different proposals—what mattered more was that the final master plan resulted from *international* design competitions, and, therefore, it was a *global* product. As with the development of Pudong financial district in Shanghai, the city government in Beijing used international design firms in the first publicity campaign to promote the new CBD.

In contrast to older commercial centers such as Qianmen and Wangfujing, there is little cultural heritage or history associated with the four-square-kilometer site chosen by the government for the new CBD. To fill the cultural vacuum, private developers and the city government commissioned prestigious international architects to design various architectural megaprojects. In the few short years leading up to the 2008 Olympics, the CBD saw construction of dozens of signature buildings—office skyscrapers, luxury hotels, shopping plazas, high-rise apartments, and cultural institutions—from various renowned architecture firms. The flagship architectural projects not only provided the state-of-the-art physical infrastructure for a modern CBD but also created the symbolic cultural capital desperately needed by local boosters for place making.

The city government officials used a rich repertoire of images of other global cities as reference points in their discursive construction of the new CBD. Most of these references were drawn from CBDs in the West, especially Manhattan in New York City. On the official website of the CBD Management Committee of Beijing, a flashing picture of Manhattan's skyline is prominently displayed.[23] Under the gleaming image reads a slogan: New York/Manhattan—Beijing/Chaoyang. Downtowns and CBDs—in Tokyo, London, Paris, Frankfurt, Toronto, and other global cities—have thus become part of the official imagination of urban modernity for city builders in Beijing. The imagined modernity is centered on office skyscrapers, new infrastructure, and the priority of attracting investment. In the documents accompanying the master plan, the city government clearly emphasized the significance of creating a modern cityscape symbolizing a financial district (fig. 3.3). A vertical "finanscape" with concentrated skyscrapers was seen as the right urban form to symbolize the rise of Beijing as a global city. The new CBD could not be just another downtown. It had to be built to thrill. The master plan of the CBD reads,

FIGURE 3.3. Central business district, Beijing, 2009. Photograph courtesy of SOHO China.

The core area of the CBD is designed to concentrate a large number of sky-scrapers. It is to be occupied by buildings such as the CCTV, the World Trade Tower, the Silktie Center, and Jianwai SOHO. Major buildings are allowed to exceed three hundred meters in height and form the symbolic central block of the CBD. . . . The design is to create a perfect urban image with outstanding symbolic buildings and to form a focal point in the mass of high-rise towers.[24]

The Beijing municipal government issued a series of policies designed to attract multinational and Fortune Global 500 companies to establish their regional headquarters in the CBD. These policies aimed to reduce the operation costs for business services firms by providing tax cuts, subsidies, and other benefits. By 2004, a large number of business services firms had moved into the new CBD.

From the imperial period to the most recent global phase, the economic center or downtown of Beijing has been remade and reinterpreted, from an inferior space submerged under the political domain to a transnational space of global flows. The CBD is a state project intended to attract global capital and transform Beijing into a global city. Architecture, urban design, and planning are the new tools used by government bureaucrats for promoting the CBD. For Beijing, which lacked the infrastructure for its financial sector in the 1980s and 1990s, the new CBD functions as the nodal point reconnecting the city to the global financial circuit. The imperial palaces and communist government compounds, once the signifiers of power and centrality, have been replaced by signature architecture that houses the work of globalization in the new CBD.

Architectural Spectacles: From SOHO NewTown to the Commune to Jianwai SOHO

SOHO China distinguished itself from other real estate firms by creating a self-portrait as a patron of contemporary architecture. The company was founded in 1995 by an entrepreneurial couple. The chief executive, Pan Shiyi, established himself as a private developer with his property development work in southern China in the early 1990s, when the state had liberalized the property market and real estate speculation had just begun. His wife, Zhang Xin, studied economics at the University of Cambridge in the late 1980s and worked on Wall Street before coming back to China in the early 1990s. The husband-and-wife team used innovative architecture and urban design extensively in the building of their real estate empire in Beijing.

SOHO NewTown

Pan Shiyi and Zhang Xin's first major project in Beijing—SOHO New-Town, completed in the late 1990s—is a high-end residential project of twenty-two hundred apartment units located within the CBD (fig. 3.4). Back then Chinese developers paid scant attention to the design of their buildings. Most new apartment buildings were unfurnished cement shells, and homeowners would need to spend months on renovation, interior decoration, and remodeling before they could move in. Breaking away from this practice, SOHO NewTown provided fully furnished apartments and set a number of records—it was the first residential development project to advertise its apartments in newspapers, the first to use bright colors for the building facades, the first to display artists' works in its public space, and also the first to introduce the "SOHO" concept to Beijing's new middle class.

SOHO stands for "Small Office, Home Office." SOHO apartments, with homes doubling as offices, are inspired by the loft-style apartments

FIGURE 3.4. SOHO NewTown, Beijing. Photograph courtesy of SOHO China.

in the West. The individual apartment units at SOHO NewTown, many of which are as large as 250 square meters, combine dwelling and work areas and have few fixed partitions so that tenants can divide the space as they see fit. The concept also clearly evokes the SoHo gallery district in New York, a reference frequently made by Zhang Xin when recounting her days working on Wall Street. The developers claimed their project to be a "revolution in housing" and "the way of the future," as it broke free from the traditional practice of dividing a space into living areas and bedrooms. According to the developers, SOHO apartments are intended to meet the demands of the information age by offering the urban middle class new styles of work and living. As Pan Shiyi wrote,

> With the development of the information industry and a networked society, everything has become much more flexible and fluid. Today it is impractical to design a house or building with strictly delineated functions. . . . We are bringing the most progressive and the most advanced notions and concepts to our cities. . . . We design for the stylish middle class.[25]

The mixed functionality of space—the same apartment can be used for home, office, and other purposes—is not only meant to address lifestyle concerns but is also a very well calculated strategy on the part of the developers to maximize profits. The ambiguity between residential and commercial use allowed higher investment returns for those who purchased properties at SOHO NewTown, since they could rent out spaces not only as apartments but also as office and commercial space. A shift from residential to commercial uses took place at SOHO NewTown and all other SOHO projects—over time, residents gradually moved out, and most commercial and residential space has been rented out to small firms in the media, publishing, art, and advertising sectors.

SOHO NewTown caused a sensation in Beijing. Together with the promotion of the SOHO concept, Pan Shiyi and Zhang Xin also commissioned many established Chinese artists, including Ai Wei Wei, Yin Xiuzhen, and Ding Yi, to install artworks in the public space at SOHO NewTown. When the presales began in 1999, buyers were queued up for the apartments priced at 9,000 RMB per square meter, which was in the highest price range of apartments in Beijing back then. Many of them belonged to a new class of Beijingers—technology-savvy thirty- to forty-year-olds who worked in the arts and media sector. SOHO China published a number of statistics highlighting the success of SOHO NewTown:

> Between 1997 and 2001, 282 sales people attended to 112,050 clients during the construction of SOHO NewTown. They received 1,680,750 telephone calls and generated 0.41 billion RMB in sales. During that period, there were 21,620 media reports on SOHO NewTown.[26]

Architecture played a relatively minor role in the development and branding of SOHO NewTown. Pan Shiyi and Zhang Xin worked with architects from Tsinghua Design Institute, one of the most prestigious local design firms. However, design institutes in China are large and anonymous organizations often without a brand name. The developers thus could not identify one celebrity architect to promote their projects. Pan Shiyi and Zhang Xin expressed frustration with Chinese architects:

> Chinese architects tend to think of architectural design only as paper drawings and engineering, and they don't see it also as art. What I want is something different from others, something that will surprise people, and something people will talk about.[27]

> When I first worked with Cui Kai (from Tsinghua Design Institute), design firms in Beijing were called No. 1 Design Firm, No. 2 Design Firm and so on.

Architects were employed as technicians, not as creative people. They were not taught to think creatively. Their job was to carry out instructions.[28]

The Commune

To achieve more media exposure and greater branding effects in their next projects, the developers shunned anonymous Chinese design institutes and reached out to international architects. In 2000, the company finished its second project—the Commune by the Great Wall. It is a cluster of twelve ultramodern luxury villas in the rolling mountains near the Great Wall, each house designed by a prominent Asian architect, including the Japanese architects Shigeru Ban and Kuma Kengo and Chinese architect Chang Young Ho—currently based at the Massachusetts Institute of Technology. The Commune, as part luxury hotel and part vacation homes, attracts image-savvy multinationals for company events and wealthy Beijing residents for resort weekends. In 2002, Zhang Xin was awarded a special prize for her individual patronage of architectural works at the Venice Biennale for this project. In 2004, the Commune won Zhang Xin another prestigious recognition—the Mont Blanc de la Culture Arts Patronage Award.

The success of the Commune was the result of a well-orchestrated media operation and publicity campaign. Using her networks, Zhang Xin reached out to internationally renowned museum curators, architects, and critics. For the Venice Biennale, Pan Shiyi and Zhang Xin brought with them dozens of reporters and photographers from mainland China, Hong Kong, Japan, and Taiwan, providing minute-to-minute detailed feeds for the news media back home. As the professor of architecture at the London School of Economics, Ricky Burdett, wrote, the Commune is "a sophisticated real-estate operation" that "places contemporary Asian architecture at the center of a global stage."[29]

Zhang Xin is confident and extremely explicit about her approach of combining real estate speculation and architectural experiment, as she commented, "the more effective way to advance architecture is commercialization . . . without commercialization, architecture and art could not interact with the public."[30] But the "public" who can have access to this hidden cluster of luxury resorts is limited—the Commune is an unmistakably elite project marketed to the economically privileged few. After the project gained international recognition, Zhang Xin and Pan Shiyi decided not to sell the villas but instead to turn them into a "private collection of contemporary Asian architecture." In the next few years, they expanded the project to build about forty more villas—mostly replicas of the original ones, but built at a cheaper cost—and outsourced the management to a five-star hotel chain. The luxury villas at the Commune are fully booked all year long for extravagant private parties and events.

Since the spectacular success and publicity exposure of the Commune, SOHO China has accelerated its design-intensive model of real estate expansion and has worked with a number of prestigious international architects on its various SOHO projects in the CBD, including Japanese architects Riken Yamamoto (on Jianwai SOHO) and Kuma Kengo (Sanlitun SOHO), Australian architect Peter Davidson (SOHO Shangdu), Korean architect Seng H. Seung (Chaowai SOHO), and British architect Zaha Hadid (master plan of SOHO City, unbuilt; Chaoyangmen SOHO).

Jianwai SOHO

From the earliest design stage of Jianwai SOHO, the developers intended to make it a new landmark in Beijing's CBD with bold architectural statements.[31] In October 2000, SOHO China invited Arata Isozaki, Riken Yamamoto, and Rocco Yim to submit design proposals. The developers were looking for a design that would be at once modern, non-Chinese looking, and marketable to wealthy Chinese investors and foreigners alike. The design submitted by Isozaki was complete with Chinese metaphors in abstract forms, integrating features found in traditional animal figures such as the phoenix, turtle, and crane. It is ironic that a design full of Chinese references was actually proposed by a Japanese architect. However, the developer was looking for a completely modern design and was not impressed by Isozaki's China-inspired proposal. Pan Shiyi commented, "Chinese elements don't have to be expressed in specific architectural languages."[32] Rocco Yim's design was rejected as well, the reason being that it was too impractical—the design reduced the usable area of space for residence and shops and therefore would imply a smaller profit margin for the developers. Pan Shiyi commented, "This is a very interesting design, but it's too experimental, and nobody would buy a house like this in Beijing." There are limits to the patronage for avant-garde architecture—experimentalism has to be practiced within the bounds of marketability. Finally, Riken Yamamoto's ultramodern design was selected out of the three. Yamamoto's design stresses minimalism, with modern looks and strong visual appeals, all characteristics sought after by the developers. In an interview, the chief architect of Yamamoto's design team, Sako, commented,

Our design was chosen because the developer wanted something with impact, something different from surrounding buildings, and something that can be a new landmark.[33]

The developers and architects used a variety of rhetorical tools in their articulation of the architectural sophistication of Jianwai SOHO, stressing, for example, the minimalist design feature of the buildings, the openness and accessibility of the streets within the complex, and the linkage to local architectural traditions. Minimalism is a striking feature of Jianwai SOHO's architectural style. All buildings at Jianwai SOHO are white, square, and completely lacking any architectural adornments (see fig. 3.5). The sales brochure states that "Jianwai SOHO follows the principle of simple and concise." "Less is more," a famous saying by Mies van der Rohe, is cited many times in the brochure. The developers' preference for minimalism is not a coincidence. During the massive construction boom in China, Chinese developers and architects copied architectural styles from different countries and historical periods. It is not unusual to see a neo-classical building standing next to an International Style building, while not far off stand Chinese-style pagodas. Most buildings are heavily decorated in order to grab attention. In this jungle of different architectural styles, a minimalist building can strike a great contrast with surrounding buildings and therefore have a strong visual appeal. Moreover, a minimalist approach can totally break free from Chinese architectural style and thus can be perceived as modern, foreign, and futuristic. The developers believed that such minimalist design could distinguish the project and appeal to the fashion-conscious new urban middle class.

The developers and architects also emphasized the small scale, walkability, and open access of Jianwai SOHO and called it "democratic architecture." Yamamoto used sixteen small streets to connect different residential and office buildings. He put many piazzas, gardens, and benches on the streets. There are no fences or walls. However, the open and "democratic" architecture has a purpose, and it is a commercial purpose. By keeping the shopping streets connected to Chang'An Avenue, the developers could draw crowds to the shops at Jianwai SOHO. The acclaimed "public" space is an illusion, since even without gates and fences, the price ranges of the shops can easily keep out those who cannot afford them.

It is a common practice among international architects working in China to claim that their design is inspired by Chinese cultural elements and therefore has local roots. This can be seen in all SOHO projects com-

FIGURE 3.5. Jianwai SOHO, Beijing. Photograph courtesy of SOHO China.

missioned to international architects, who invariably make reference to Chinese culture or architecture to show they have taken the local context into consideration. Traditional courtyard houses seem to be the favorite reference for international architects. Architect Yamamoto claims that his design of little winding streets connecting different buildings was inspired by Chinese hutongs.[34] The ultramodern and minimalist towers at Jianwai SOHO bear little resemblance to Chinese courtyard houses.

The happy union of celebrity developers and star architects could be vividly observed at a celebration event for Jianwai SOHO's completion in 2004, to which a number of international and Chinese architects were invited, including Zaha Hadid, Patrick Schumacher, Ito Toyo, and the returnee Chinese architects Ma Qingyun and Zhu Pei, as well as a few others who had worked for SOHO China on its different projects. The architects

invariably expressed excitement about Beijing and China as well as about
working with the celebrity developers.[35]

> The developers asked us not only to design a residential space, but also to pro-
> pose a new concept of urban living. Jianwai SOHO better incorporates work
> and living than the projects I worked on in Japan. In Japan, many good ideas
> can't be realized. In China, basically everything is possible. For me this is very
> attractive. Beijing has a huge capacity to absorb all kinds of new things. People
> in Beijing have a strong desire for new things. They are looking for a different
> style of living from before, something new, and that's why they're eager to ac-
> cept new things. . . . Beijing is big, projects are big, and construction sites are
> big. The scale is very attractive. I'm willing to try all kinds of projects here.
> (Riken Yamamoto)

> China is an exciting place right now. Twenty years ago, when traveling in Eu-
> rope and the US, I was proud to say I worked on projects in Tokyo. Now in the
> US and Europe, people ask, "Do you have projects in China?" China is the
> most exciting place. (Ito Toyo)

> SOHO China is the dream of every architect. It's a precious experience to work
> with them. (Peter Davidson)

Using star architects for place making is not unique to China, but the
"Bilbao effect," or the buzz generated by signature architecture, is more
spectacular in China than elsewhere. This must be understood in relation
to specific local characteristics, such as fast development cycles and over-
dependence on presale revenues. The speed of construction is extremely
fast in Chinese cities, especially in the prime locations such as the CBD in
Beijing in the pre-Olympics years. The period from architectural design
to construction to sales is often less than a few months. In the case of Jianwai SOHO, the developers wanted to start construction as soon as possible and gave the architects only three months for the design of the whole
project.[36] Because of the lack of other channels, such as a stock market and
bank mortgages, for raising capital for construction, presales and down
payments from property buyers—often 20 to 30 percent of the total purchase—are crucial for developers to maintain cash flow. If developers can
generate enough buzz, they can attract potential buyers and succeed in
presales. In the case of SOHO China, the company can often finish selling
all units even before anything is built. Presales are risky for property buyers, since they need to make decisions before the buildings are built, and

sometimes even before construction starts. SOHO China has packaged each of its projects into a lifestyle with architectural design to boost investors' confidence. In a market of unbalanced information and resources—for developers and investors—the use of media and architecture can help build investors' confidence and encourage their decisions to invest.

Architectural projects from celebrity developers and star architects embody symbolic capital in the real estate market in China. The symbolic capital of distinguished architectural design can lend credit and trust to developers, who then skillfully turn it into cultural, political, and economic capital. In the case of Jianwai SOHO, the developers have accumulated cultural capital by frequently appearing in talk shows on TV and being interviewed by international media.[37] They have also, meantime, built strong connections with government and city planning bureaus so that their projects can always be given priority and quick approval. As the developers expected, the sale of office and residential properties at Jianwai SOHO far exceeded that of other projects in the CBD.

Public Spectacles and Place Making

On a sunny afternoon in April 2005, when I was doing my fieldwork in Beijing, in the public plaza of Jianwai SOHO, a young man climbed into a "birdcage"—made of tree branches and supported by a ten-meter-high steel tripod—to the accompaniment of media reporters' camera flashes (fig. 3.6). Ye Fu, a performance artist, would stay in his birdcage for a month without coming down to the ground. Food and water were provided with a rope and basket by the staff at Jianwai SOHO. Ye Fu wrote poems, text-messaged, and occasionally chatted with visitors who would climb up to his birdcage. The whole event was broadcast on SOHO China's website. According to the curator, Zhu Qi, this performance art project was an experiment in urban living—to experience living in the middle of Beijing, in a literal sense. The site for the art project was close to East Third Ring Road, a hectic transportation artery always crowded with traffic on both tiers of its elevated highways. April is the driest month in the city and also known as the time for sandstorms. The time and place for the art performance created harsh conditions for this experiment in urban living. SOHO China organized the event as part of its effort to increase popularity and foot traffic and to attract media attention to the newly opened Jianwai SOHO complex.

FIGURE 3.6. Performance art project at Jianwai SOHO, 2005. Photograph courtesy of SOHO China.

This birdcage performance art project was one of the many public spectacles staged by SOHO China. During my fieldwork, I witnessed a wide variety of cultural events, ranging from book fairs, fashion shows, and lectures and symposiums on architecture and urban culture to poetry readings and lavish private parties. In combination with architectural spectacles, these well-orchestrated cultural events continued the place making and helped to create buzz about the tabula rasa of the new CBD.

On April 26, 2005, Xu Yang, then the media director at SOHO China, called me and asked if I would be interested in interviewing the artist and writing a short piece for Sina.com, a major Chinese-language website. I arrived at Jianwai SOHO around 4 p.m. I saw a few rows of bookstands—apparently a book fair was going on. The selection of books was random, and the fair attracted few visitors. The public square felt a bit empty, and not far away, construction workers were still working on the last phase of unfinished apartment buildings. Although most units were already sold by spring 2005, there were not many residents living at Jianwai SOHO. At one corner of the square, I found the "birdcage." A few people were sitting at two tables, chatting and drinking beer. Artist Ye Fu, dressed in a bright red traditional Chinese silk suit, was also in the crowd. The artist and his friends looked bored. Everybody was waiting for the executives from SOHO China and media reporters. I chatted with one of the artists in the group, who cynically commented on SOHO China's culture-based branding strategies:

> Now Pan Shiyi has become a celeb, and there's no need to use ads anymore to sell his buildings. He's trying out other things for marketing. Last year they organized a summer festival at Jianwai SOHO, but it was not that successful. The people who came were mostly youngsters who didn't have other places to hang out. So this year, they changed strategies again. This brother [pointing to artist Ye Fu] will be up in the air for a month. It'll attract a lot of attention, and it doesn't cost anything.[38]

Finally, Pan Shiyi, dressed in a light-green shirt and wearing a pair of thick-framed designer glasses, walked out of one of the sleek office towers. He brought with him a group of reporters from television and newspapers, all equipped with notebooks, recorders, and cameras. Pan Shiyi was soon surrounded by more journalists who were already waiting on the site. The media was clearly more interested in the star developer than in the little-known artist. After taking a few rounds of handshakes and routine questions—mostly on the skyrocketing housing prices in Beijing—Pan Shiyi walked to the cage and climbed a few steps on the rope ladder leading up to it. The moment was well recorded by journalists' cameras. The well-planned event attracted high-prestige media networks including CCTV and BBC News and put Jianwai SOHO again under the media spotlight. Curator Zhu Qi seemed to be satisfied with the media exposure of the event. Zhu Qi had done many experimental art projects over the past few years in the outskirts of Beijing, where several artists' villages are located, but none of them caught the same kind of attention from the media. He was surprised to see so many reporters and some "bigwigs" in Beijing's cultural circuit showing up. The young curator was impressed; he commented, "This never happened before. This is the power of Pan Shiyi."

The performance art quickly attracted another crowd, but of a different sort: migrant workers from the nearby construction sites. The migrant workers had limited cultural and entertainment opportunities, so whenever Jianwai SOHO organized events, they were among the first to come see them (see fig. 3.7). The crowd of construction workers kept at some distance, but they were curiously and very attentively observing the "birdcage." It was no doubt a strange scene for the migrant workers—a

FIGURE 3.7. Migrant workers waiting to be taken to a cinema, Beijing, 2005. Photograph by the author.

well-dressed man, surrounded by a sea of cameras, climbing into a make-shift cage in the air. Throughout the event, the two groups did not mingle—the artists, journalists, and developers were near the cage, chatting, shaking hands, and networking with one another, while not far away, migrant workers in their work uniforms were standing by, watching and wondering what was going on. The urban glamour world of the rich and famous and the world of migrant workers were two parallel universes that never crossed at any of the cultural events at Jianwai SOHO. The distance between migrant workers and sophisticated urbanites was a striking feature of all these public spectacles. Security guards would not allow them to sit in the audience seats at various fashion shows, film screenings, and other events, as the seats were reserved for the privileged urbanites. The media director Xu Yang told me, "These two types of people just don't mix."

When I was about to leave, Pan Shiyi called me to join him and a few friends for afternoon tea. By then—spring 2005—it had been more than a year since I started research fieldwork, and the main executives of SOHO China were already quite comfortable with my regular presence at their events. We were joined by a few other major figures active in the cultural circuit of Beijing: Liu Suola, a singer and blues musician, and Zha Jianying, a Chinese-English bilingual writer and occasional contributor to the *New Yorker*. Both women had lived abroad for many years and returned to Beijing, which has become common in the Chinese diaspora of artists and writers. Also at the table were a young poet and a writer from *Sanlian Life*—a well-known weekly magazine in China. The chat was casual but filled with cultural "code words." The topic quickly shifted from everyone's favorite recent movies, to Chinese and Greek philosophers, to Durkheim and Tocqueville, to problems of Chinese translations of Western classics, and, in the end, to the bashing of the post-'80s generation for its cultural ignorance.

This afternoon tea session was a perfect "ethnographic moment" to observe the overlapping real estate and culture circuits in Beijing. In terms of education and overseas exposure, Pan Shiyi is a bit out of place in this circle of cultural elites. Having grown up in remote Gansu province on the Yellow River plateau, he attended an average college and speaks no foreign languages. But he is a fast learner, and by spending time in the circle of Beijing's cultural elites, he has quickly accumulated personal cultural capital at the same time as he has been developing his real estate enterprise. When asked at the table about his favorite movie, Pan Shiyi answered *Hero*—a blockbuster mixture of historical drama and martial arts, directed by Zhang Yimou. Quickly the others at the table explained to Pan why the movie is in poor taste, from both the technical perspective of filmmaking and camera work and the artistic perspective of the conceptualization of the historical story. Pan patiently listened to everybody's criticisms, and in the end, albeit reluctantly, he dropped *Hero* as his favorite movie. Fortunately, the developer was rescued by a phone call from a high-ranking official in the Ministry of Land, who was sending him a friendly reminder to be careful with his comments to the media about housing prices.

The next day I went again to the site of the birdcage to see how office workers and residents nearby would react to this performance art project. Artist Ye Fu was managing well, although he looked a bit tired after a rough night—the wind was strong and he had had to cover his cage with a large sheet of plastic. It was lunchtime, and many office workers were outside taking a break and strolling in the public square. The birdcage clearly attracted public attention, but most people did not seem to know how to interact with the artist in the cage. One middle-aged woman, working in a boutique shop at Jianwai SOHO, told me that the artist was the same age as her son and that she wondered if the family of the artist would be worried about his radical act of living in the cage for a month. An elderly man came close to the cage and asked me what this was. Upon learning that it was a performance art project, the old man repeated the word "art" a few times as if trying to convince himself that this was art. Then he said to himself, "What's the difference between this and those little shabby houses in the countryside fields where we peasants used to watch watermelons? I've spent years in shabby cages like this." The crowd laughed and dispersed.

Apparently there was a large gap between the circuit of developers, media, and artists and ordinary people, such as the shop attendants and migrant workers, in their attitude toward this performance art act. But the gap did not seem to be of any concern to SOHO China, since the public at large was not the target group whose attention SOHO China wanted to attract. Just as its building projects targeted the top of the income pyramid, the various public spectacles staged at Jianwai SOHO clearly aimed to reach major television networks and newspapers. Artist Ye Fu continued his month-long experiment of urban living in the middle of Jianwai SOHO's public square. It was a lonely act—most pedestrians watched him from afar and did not know how to make sense of the artist in the cage.

SOHO Xiaobao: From Sales Brochures to a Literary Magazine

In addition to attracting mainstream media by staging various spectacles, SOHO China has also turned itself into a media platform through publishing and the Internet. *SOHO Xiaobao* (*Xiaobao,* "newsletters"), started as a real estate sales brochure in 2000, has become a high-end literary magazine with regular contributions from central figures in the art, media, and literary scenes. Through the example of *SOHO Xiaobao,* this section will examine the curious mix of media, high culture, and crude speculation in the concept-driven real estate sector in Beijing.

Many real estate firms in China regularly produce internal newsletters for property buyers, because presales are a common practice and property owners want to be updated on the progress of construction. These newsletters normally report progress, give sales statistics, list recent activities of company executives, and include glossy images of computer models of the unbuilt buildings. These colorful brochures are called *loushu* (*lou,* "building," *shu,* "book"), and they are widely distributed at major housing fairs as well.

SOHO China is no exception, and it started the publication of its newsletter, *SOHO Xiaobao,* in 2000, as a monthly internal report to investors who had bought properties at SOHO NewTown. But the company soon realized that this was a waste of resources, since the newsletter had limited impact as an advertising tool. Xu Yang and Li Nan, two managers in charge of the newsletter, decided to turn *SOHO Xiaobao* into a literary magazine and to invite prominent writers, academics, and other types in Beijing's cultural circuit to contribute short essays on a variety of issues beyond real estate. *SOHO Xiaobao* became a remarkable success in the crowded magazine publishing market, partly owing to the financial support from SOHO China. The publication is free, and therefore the publisher does not need to worry about sales and circulation, and this gives the editors greater freedom in their choice of monthly topics. In a mere three years, by 2003, *SOHO Xiaobao* had already become a well-known, but still "internal," publication of SOHO China. The reputation of *SOHO Xiaobao* was spread by word of mouth among editors, writers, artists, and journalists in Beijing. Although anybody can request a free subscription, the readership has not expanded to the general public, as the magazine was intended by SOHO China to be an elite publication for the elite. Every month, twenty thousand copies are sent free of charge to readers based in Beijing, other major cities in the mainland, Hong Kong, and Taiwan. Another two thousand copies are circulated to sales offices of various SOHO projects as well as to major housing fairs and real estate conferences. Considering the remarkable success of the magazine and the buzz it has generated, it is surprising that the publication does not have any full-time editors or staff. As "editors," Xu Yang and Li Nan have been running the magazine in addition to their full-time job, which is selling more apartment and office buildings.

In an interview, editor Xu Yang told me about his core strategy for running the publication—inviting prominent figures in the academic and literary circuit to write and, more important, making sure to let the contributors know who else is writing for the magazine. According to Xu Yang, many people will put extra effort into their essays once they know that novelist X or writer X is also contributing to the same issue. Thus, the success of *SOHO Xiaobao* stems not only from its financial backing and editorial freedom but also from its skill at generating and manipulating peer pressure among the cultural elites in Beijing. Over time, SOHO China has been able to invite a wide range of academics, critics, writers, and journalists to contribute articles.

With the confidence gained from its success with *SOHO Xiaobao,*
SOHO China has also ventured into book publishing. In addition to
dozens of glossy photo albums devoted to each of its projects, between
2003 and 2008 the company put out four collections of essays previously
published in *SOHO Xiaobao.*[39] In 2005, the publisher Changjiang Wenyi
put out a book, titled *Urban Circles,* containing a collection of about a
hundred essays previously published in *SOHO Xiaobao* in 2003 and 2004.
As suggested by the book's title, the contributors are drawn from a small
circle of Beijing's urban elites active in the media and cultural fields. The
top three categories of contributors are professional writers, university
professors, and editors from major newspapers and magazines (such as
Xinzhoukan and *Economic Observer*), followed by leading film directors
such as Jia Zhang Ke, architects such as Ma Qingyun, and internationally
renowned Chinese curators such as Feng Boyi and Fan Di'an. These central figures active in the cultural and literary scene in Beijing were invited
to write about a wide range of themes—from the city, urban culture, and
architecture to major events and catastrophes (e.g., the Olympics and the
Sichuan earthquake in 2008) and social problems, as well as occasionally
nostalgic subjects (entire issues devoted to the '70s and '80s). These publications are hybrid mixes of fiction, cultural critiques, and promotions of
SOHO projects, and the list of contributors demonstrates the increasingly
overlapping urban circles of economic and cultural elites.

Started as a real estate brochure, *SOHO Xiaobao* has thus quickly been
turned into a high-end urban literary magazine for Beijing's cultural elite.
The various publications from SOHO China do not intend to build a mass
readership; instead, the targeted readership is the small group of people,
mostly in publishing, media, and academic circuits, who have the most
influence on public discourse. These publishing enterprises have become
important channels for SOHO China to further develop its rapport and
networks with prominent figures in the cultural circuit and the media.

Developers and Policy Making

The various SOHO publications also function as a media outlet for the
developers to express opinions on a variety of policy issues and have
their voices heard by the government. The last few pages in each issue of
SOHO Xiaobao are always devoted to the writings of Pan Shiyi, discussing new government regulations for the land and real estate sectors. Pan

Shiyi's personal blog—ranked as one of the most visited blogs in main-land China—has also become a powerful media platform from which to publicize the company, advertise its new projects, and sometimes influ-ence government policy making.

Developers frequently give positive forecasts about the real estate market through the media and encourage people to buy properties for investment. One of the often-used tactics among developers is predicting that housing prices will continue to rise—so that, as their logic goes, it would be wiser to buy now before the prices become completely out of reach. Developers often cite ad hoc statistics about migration flows to cities as evidence that the demand for urban housing will just keep grow-ing. In early 2008, when clear signs of economic recession started to be seen in China, major developers, such as CEO Wang Shi of the company Vanke, expressed concerns about a possible turning point in real estate sales in China. Wang Shi also urged potential homebuyers to be cautious, to "wait three or four years," or "not to buy before age forty." Wang Shi's remarks and negative predictions for the real estate market caused great controversies among developers across the country. Pan Shiyi heavily criticized Wang Shi, and in an essay published in *SOHO Xiaobao,* he de-clared that China's real estate market was healthy and had not reached a turning point, in spite of the global economic recession. Many developers and newspapers enthusiastically endorsed Pan Shiyi's "no turning point" argument.[40]

In addition to housing prices, access to land has been a major concern for real estate developers in China. Although the land reform is currently in its third decade, the urban land market is still a murky area full of cor-ruption and uncertainties. The central government has passed a number of policies, such as Document No. 11 in 2006, in order to regulate land transactions by introducing more transparent methods of allocating land such as public auctions and bidding, but the policies have not been well fol-lowed. Owing to the often unclear land-use rights, most land transactions still take place through backstage negotiations among local governments, developers, and other types of landholders, instead of through public bid-ding and auctions.

Acquiring land in central locations has been at the top of the agenda for private developers. Although rich in cash flow, SOHO China lacks connections to governments in comparison to state-owned real estate firms and often finds itself unable to get prime land through public auc-tions. SOHO China often has to negotiate with land-rich developers in order to get prime locations. For example, the company paid Huayuan Group—another major developer in Beijing with significant government connections—over 0.1 billion RMB to purchase a piece of land in the CBD for the development of SOHO Shangdu. On his blog, Pan Shiyi has repeatedly criticized current practices in land transactions and urged the government to further reform the land market so that developers with sufficient funds can get prime land through open auctions. He wrote, "I spend one third of my time looking for land. The biggest problem facing the real estate market is lack of institutions that can guarantee full-fledged market transaction of land."[41]

Fair and open access to bank loans is another major concern among real estate developers, as the channels for raising funds within China are still relatively limited. Real estate financing is an area where the interests of developers and regulators (i.e., the government and central banks) clash the most. Real estate financing has introduced greater risks to the national banking system. It is common among developers to acquire land from either the government or other developers with a small initial down payment and then to use the land as collateral to acquire loans from banks and proceed with construction. They use advertisements to attract buyers, and presales start far before the projected completion dates. With the revenue from presales, the developers gradually pay back banks, construction companies, and state-owned land reserve centers from which they obtain land. To get more access to capital, developers repeatedly urge the government to deregulate the banking sector and increase bank lending to developers and homebuyers.[42]

On June 13, 2003, the Bank of China issued Document No. 121, titled "Notice regarding Further Regulating Real Estate Financing." The policy aimed to tighten government control over bank lending to all major parties in the property market, including developers, property buyers, construction companies, and land reserve centers. Specifically, Document 121 restricted bank lending for high-end luxury property developments. Although "high-end" was not clearly defined, most of the SOHO projects are clearly high-end by dint of their sales prices, which are often four to five times above the city average. The policy also restricted presales practices by allowing banks to issue mortgages to property buyers only when the construction is close to completion. This would have been a major blow to many developers, since it would have substantially delayed presales and created a severe shortage in the cash flow needed to continue construction. Document 121 raised the down payments for purchasing properties from 20 percent to 30 percent and raised interest rates for people buying a second home and those buying commercial properties. Most of SOHO China's investors belong to this group of buyers. The full implementation of Document 121 would have changed the rules of the game, and its release created an immediate panic among real estate developers all over China.

Developers quickly mobilized to oppose the new regulatory policy. Zhang Baoquan, the CEO of Antaeus Group, told the media that "the new policy grouped together developers with strong performance and those with poor performance through administrative means, and killed fair competition between firms."[43] Apple Community, a large residential project that Zhang was working on, was far from finished; under Document 121, his project would have had to wait another two to three years to be able to collect presale revenues. Ren Zhiqiang, another mover and shaker in the real estate sector and the CEO of Huayuan Group, made similar comments: "There are all kinds of birds in the forest and you can't kill them all because of a few bad ones."[44] In an article circulated to the media titled "The Winter Has Come," Ren strongly opposed the new policy by arguing that it would freeze the real estate market and would do just what the SARS epidemic did to the real estate market in the early months of 2003; the "winter" of the real estate market would come if Document 121 were carried out. In another article, titled "Hatred toward the Rich," he wrote that Document 121 was a policy full of hatred, directed not only at the rich but also at people trying to get out of poverty. As he wrote, "The radical measure adopted by the Bank of China to limit consumption and blame the rich would bring negative effects to China's economic growth and shake people's confidence in getting rich."[45]

On the day that Document 121 was released, Pan Shiyi immediately circulated an article to major websites and journalists and also published it in *SOHO Xiaobao,* listing twenty possible outcomes of Document 121—most of them were negative. For example, he argued that the implementation of the document would lead to more widespread corruption, as cash-poor developers would bribe bank and government officials. Pan Shiyi commented on the negative impact of government intervention in the property market:

If Document No. 121 were implemented, then many developers would close shop. . . . We've seen the negative legacies of the planned economy in the past. Document 121 would have a negative impact on our country's economic

growth . . . in the market economy we can't use one-size-fits-all types of policy
to solve problems. It would be naïve to say the real estate sector in China has
no problems, but it would be equally biased to say the real estate sector is full
of problems. Every city, every region is different. The Bank of China realized the problems and issued Document 121, but the proposals lack careful
consideration.[46]

In addition to circulating commentary articles to the major media, developers also organized frequent discussion forums in the three months
after Document 121 was released. Major newspapers, magazines, websites,
and TV channels took turns sponsoring these activities. On August 16,
2003, major developers organized a full-day conference titled "Chinese
Real Estate Credit Policies Forum" in Beijing, also inviting academics and
government officials. But the voices of developers criticizing the new government policy overwhelmed those of the government officials. *Beijing
Youth Daily, Bankers Magazine,* and *Economic Observer,* as well as sohu
.com, all reported the forum. A week later, the newspaper *21st Century
Economic Report* organized a real estate conference at Boao Canal Vil-
lage—a project developed by SOHO China on Hainan island in the south.
The same group of developers, including Pan Shiyi, Ren Zhiqiang, Zhang
Baoquan, Feng Lun, and others, were all present, giving speeches criticiz-
ing Document 121. Feng Lun, the CEO of Vantone Real Estate based in
Beijing, commented that "for the first time the voice of business people
overwhelmed that of the government."[47]

On September 1, 2003, seventy-eight days after Document 121 was released, the State Council issued Document 18, titled "Notice regarding
Promoting Continuous and Healthy Growth of the Real Estate Sector."
The new policy reconfirmed the strategic importance of the real estate
sector—as one of the four key industries—for the national economy and
reversed many proposals listed in Document 121 regarding regulating
bank lending. Certain regulatory measures listed in Document 121, such
as those restricting bank loans to individuals, developers, and construction companies, disappeared altogether. Instead, the new Document 18
encouraged further development of the real estate financing system, as
well as bank lending to developers in good standing. Ultimately Document 18 reversed the previous assessment of Document 121 that the real
estate sector was overheated and introduced great financial risks to the
national banking system.

Real estate developers unanimously celebrated Document 18, calling it
"a victory of market economy over planned economy."[48] Pan Shiyi wrote

another widely cited commentary in *SOHO Xiaobao,* titled "Chinese Are No Longer Snails"—a metaphor describing people tied to their apartments in socialist times—praising the importance of the new policy for the continuing growth in the real estate development sector.

> The planned economy did not bring wealth and progress. Only the market economy has made people richer. . . . My impression is that government always intervenes in fields where it shouldn't, and for those areas it should regulate, it often doesn't do a good job. The government allocation of housing in the socialist period turned Chinese into snails—people and houses were inseparable. . . . Document 18 separated people from their apartment, and Chinese don't have to be snails again. . . . Document 18 guarantees smoother transactions in the housing market, and the government can gain more taxes and land revenues.[49]

The story of the two contradicting government policies, Document 121 from the Bank of China and Document 18 from the State Council, illustrates how the circle of real estate developers mobilized the media and influenced government policy making. Zhang Jingping, a journalist at *Nanfengchuang* magazine, commented that "No matter if the original policy is flawed, or if the developers' critiques are justified, the fact that the policy was reversed shows the power of the private business groups to influence government decision making."[50] The change of direction of Document 121 also illustrates the strategic importance of the media for real estate developers in advancing their interests.

The Art of Sales, the Game of Survival

The previous sections in this chapter have explored how SOHO China has successfully branded its projects using art and architecture and influenced government policy making through the media. In this section, I will examine its sales tactics and practices: how the sales professionals have framed and sold various SOHO shops, apartments, and offices to a variety of investors. As I will illustrate below, the SOHO properties, packaged as the embodiment of a new concept of urban living and work, appealed to investors as an attractive financial product. In this process, the symbolic capital of architectural design is ultimately linked to the accumulation of economic capital.

Jianwai SOHO targeted the group of people at the top of the income hierarchy. The total sales of Jianwai SOHO reached more than US$0.1

billion in 2004, which was the highest among all projects in the CBD. The project also targeted a wider range of domestic Chinese investors beyond Beijing. Local Beijing-based buyers made up only a small percentage of the investors. According to a report released by SOHO China, in Jianwai SOHO's 2004 sales, 54 percent of the purchases were made by wealthy Chinese from other provinces, 18 percent by foreigners, and only 28 percent by local Beijing investors. Among the buyers, 180 people spent more than $10 million each.[51]

SOHO China invented a unique system of managing its sales department, widely referred to as "the survival game." Most of the sales staff are young people in their mid-twenties and early thirties. They receive a base wage of only about 1,000 RMB a month, and they make their main income from commissions, which are set at a flat rate of 0.5 percent of the sales amount after taxes. Since the properties at Jianwai SOHO are among the priciest in the city, the transactions can easily amount to tens of millions of RMB. Therefore, the young sales staff can turn themselves into millionaires just from commissions in a very short period of time. All sales managers and staff are divided into small teams, and the average length of labor contracts is only three months. Every three months, the company routinely fires the team with the lowest sales record. By contrast, the team with the highest sales record is given a prize—a bag of 40,000 RMB in cash. Thus the labor contracts are renewed every season, and the competition restarts every three months. Pan Shiyi often reminds the sales staff that they are not regular but only temporary employees and that anybody can be fired anytime. But he also tries to convince them that the experience of working for SOHO will prove to be beneficial for their future careers, even if they are fired.[52] In spite of the job insecurity, the work pressure, and the constant threat of being fired, SOHO China's sales department regularly retains over one hundred employees. The high commission fees attract young people from all walks of life to join the company's sales team.

For the sales staff, to survive the game and be able to stay, the key is to "dig out" potential clients. Owing to the high prices, the clientele for Jianwai SOHO is quite limited. For example, the price of an apartment at Jianwai SOHO is above $2,000 per square meter. To buy a two-bedroom apartment of about 140 square meters costs roughly $280,000, while the annual salary of a well-paid, white-collar worker in Beijing is only around $10,000. Many of the customers buying at Jianwai SOHO are investors who previously bought at SOHO NewTown, or those investors' relatives and friends. Ms. Liu, a twenty-seven-year-old member of the sales staff, commented,

> People who can afford SOHO apartments are limited in number, so we have to continue to keep our existing clientele base and at the same time explore new sources. I would make hundreds of phone calls and send text messages every week, just trying to keep in touch with clients. Sometimes I would get a list of investors from other developers, and sometimes I need to pay for such information. It's worth the money.[53]

The young salesmen and women combine a variety of tactics in selling SOHO products to the new rich. The quotations below describe their various ways of persuading clients to invest, by appealing to the SOHO brand, new concepts of urban work and living, and ultimately the potential for investment return. Along with selling apartments, they are also selling dreams—dreams of making a bigger fortune by investing in the hot real estate market in the capital.

> I always tell my clients that we are not only selling apartments, but also building our brand. . . . I had a client who was planning to spend 2.6 million for an apartment. I helped him with the investment analysis. I suggested he use the 2.6 million as a down payment, and use bank loans to buy a whole floor of office space. In that way he can use half of the floor for personal use, and half for rental, and he can also use the rental income to pay back the mortgage. . . . After the April holiday when our office reopened, he brought a huge suitcase of 2.6 million in cash and signed a contract of 13.4 million for the whole floor of office space I recommended. . . . From the beginning to closing the contract, he only came to see our place once. That's the power of a brand. (Ms. Sun, twenty-eight years old, highest weekly commission: 170,000 RMB)[54]

> A few days ago I closed a deal with a client from Dongbei [i.e., the Northeast region]. We only talked for about an hour the first time. Later on the phone he expressed concerns about the market in Beijing. There are so many government regulations for the real estate market, and he's worried about how much money he can make from investing in real estate in Beijing. I sent him lots of information on government policies. . . . In the end, he signed a contract for an apartment unit. I wanted to recommend that he buy a whole floor of office space, but I sensed maybe he's not interested or didn't have that much money. He called again the morning after he bought the apartment and he sounded a bit excited.

He told me, "Mr. Yao, I didn't sleep the whole night, thinking about your buildings, and I've decided to buy another whole floor of office space." (Mr. Yao, twenty-nine years old, highest weekly commission: 30,000 RMB)[55]

One day I received a phone call from a client who's interested in commercial property. From her experience, only storefronts facing streets are worth investment. But Jianwai SOHO is a new kind of property, and facing streets or not really doesn't matter that much. So I told her our buildings belong to the third generation of commercial property in Beijing, which is the walking and shopping complex. As Beijing becomes more international, places like Jianwai SOHO will become like a showcase connecting the city to the world. She's convinced, and made a one-time payment for a commercial space. I'm glad that she changed her traditional way of thinking and accepted new concepts. (Ms. Li, twenty-four years old, highest weekly commission: 20,000 RMB)[56]

During my fieldwork with sales staff and investors, the topic of architecture and branding was routinely mixed with talk of investment return. Most sales staff would talk first about how fashionable Jianwai SOHO is, the style, the taste, the design, and soon the conversation would shift to investment return—that you cannot lose money if you buy the SOHO brand. Ms. Yang, an attractive twenty-nine-year-old saleswoman, seemed to be genuinely satisfied with her job of combining design and sales. She commented,

I think I'm lucky to work for SOHO China, because their buildings are a symbol of our time. Selling such products is a lucky job. Once a client told me, "Jianwai SOHO, in a certain sense, has interesting architecture. If you look around in Beijing, you don't have many places like this—dynamic and energizing." But architecture and buildings are after all products of people working on different things—from planning to design, from construction to sales. I'm lucky that I'm part of this.[57]

The wealthy Chinese property owners at Jianwai SOHO can be roughly divided into two groups: business owners in sectors such as mining, manufacturing, and trade, and high-income urban professionals such as lawyers, accountants, and business executives. Coal mine owners from the nearby Shanxi province make up one distinctive group of property owners at Jianwai SOHO. According to local newspapers and the company reports, in the last quarter of 2005, SOHO China achieved sales of $0.12 billion, more than half of which was spent by coal mine owners from Shanxi province. Owing to soaring energy prices and China's increasing demand for energy, many coal mine owners have quickly amassed a fortune and heavily invested in real estate in big cities. A saleswoman described her first sales experience with a client from Shanxi. The case illustrates how huge surplus capital accumulated in a primary production sector such as mining is channeled into the real estate sector.

> When I met the client for the first time, I wondered if he could afford to buy anything at our place. He didn't even take a flight to Beijing. He arrived by train! And I had to pick him up at the dirty train station. He has a mining company in Shanxi province. He's interested in buying a commercial space on lower floors for investment. We had many long talks negotiating the price. In the end, he didn't say anything and left. A few days later, I got a phone call from him saying he would come to Beijing again. This time, he brought his older brother with him. After a final check, they bought a large storefront worth more than $10 million. (Ms. Dan, twenty-five years old, highest weekly commission: 20,000 RMB)[58]

Along with coal mine owners, another distinctive group of property owners are high-income urban professionals working for international firms. When the Jianwai SOHO Property Owners Committee was set up in 2005, most elected representatives were young and highly educated urban professionals.[59] A corporate lawyer might share little with a coal mine owner in cultural and consumption tastes, but both groups belong to the economically privileged few who can invest their surplus capital in the booming real estate market in Beijing. Enter the trendsetters, international architects hired by entrepreneurial developers: by creating a never-before-seen urban space in Beijing, local developers and international architects have provided a rare, and design-intensive, commodity for investors. The architectural design of various SOHO projects does not need to appeal to the diverse tastes of investors, since most of them soon rent out their purchased space to small firms in the media, education, advertising, and retail sectors. Functioning as symbolic capital, distinctive architectural design can build trust in development projects in the uncertain real estate market, and by appealing to the end-users—small firms renting office space in various SOHO buildings—it can also translate into higher financial return for investors. The transformation of the symbolic capital of design into economic capital underlies the operation of the SOHO enterprise combining real estate, cultural industries, and media.

The Divided City

Beijing is a concept-driven city, and its real estate sector is a concept-driven field. With varied degrees of sophistication, real estate professionals often evoke images of other global cities in branding their projects. The most common practice in this kind of "imagineering" is giving projects foreign names. Among more than four hundred property listings in one issue of *iHome* magazine in 2005, a large number of the new properties on the market had exotic foreign names, such as Vancouver Forest, German Impression, Portland Garden, Paris Station, California Town, Sunny Stanford, Venice Garden, Hollywood, Rome Garden, Style Berlin, Fifth Avenue, Park Avenue, Milano Sunshine, Australian Town, and Long Island. In addition to foreign names, "international" (*guoji*) and "new" (*xin*) are two words frequently used in property names.

These naming practices reveal the strategies used by developers and the marketing professionals they hire to articulate their projects as translocal spaces, spaces located in Beijing but largely isolated from the rest of the city. The various Venice Gardens and Park Avenues are imagined to be separate from their immediate urban context of Beijing and to have more in common with other global cities. By referencing other cities, the developers are projecting a new cosmopolitan lifestyle that they believe is attractive to wealthy upper-middle-class Chinese. They suggest to potential investors that people can experience the lifestyle of cosmopolites in other global cities by living and working in these estates with foreign names.

SOHO China has perfected this invocation of other global cities, not through naming, but by publishing a large number of essays and articles explicitly comparing Beijing to other global cities. Here is a quote from an essay written by Zhang Xin:

> There are restaurants, shops, offices and people living here at Jianwai SOHO. It is like the center of New York, Paris, and London. . . . Beijing needs this cosmopolitan lifestyle. . . . Beijingers took off their gray people's suits, gave up their bicycles, and with confidence, they have started to live a lifestyle like that of New Yorkers, Parisians, and Londoners in their newly built city.[60]

By contrast, the majority of local residents have clearly been excluded from the imagining of a global Beijing. Most of them have witnessed the transformation of their city and their own marginalization as Beijing quickly globalizes. In 2005, I ran into a retired factory worker from Beijing

No. 1 Machinery Factory—the factory demolished to make space for Jianwai SOHO, who told another, not-so-glamorous story of the city.

> I started working in the factory when I was seventeen years old. Now I'm sixty. I was laid off ten years ago with other workers. I get 200 RMB [about $30] every month for living, and I don't have to tell you if that's enough. . . . After I was laid off, I did any jobs I could find. I even collected garbage on the street. . . . This whole area used to be Beijing No. 1 Machinery Factory, but now everything has changed. Now there are expensive shops and restaurants. Sometimes I take a walk here but I don't buy anything here.

Shifting Centers, Shifting Powers

New geographies signify new power relations. By tracing the changing locations, functions, and meanings of downtown Peking/Beijing, I examined in the first section of this chapter the larger socioeconomic forces that have defined the downtown space in the city in different periods. The shifting power balance of the economic, political, and cultural spheres largely explains the making and unmaking of the downtowns. As the commercial and business section of the city, downtown Peking in the imperial period was Qianmen, located in the inferior Outer City, separated from the Inner City by the city walls. The power of the empire organized the spatial patterns of the city, with the imperial political domain occupying both the geographic and the symbolic center. Transnational connections in the republican period reordered such power relations, as Wangfujing replaced Qianmen and emerged as the most cosmopolitan marketplace, mainly catering to the foreign community. The short-lived commercial renaissance vanished quickly after communist leaders took power in 1949. The political power of the communist regime reorganized the spatial relations in the city, and as manufacturing replaced commercial activities downtown, Peking was transformed from a consumption city to a socialist production city.

In the recent global phase, the entrepreneurial city government planned a new CBD at the former urban fringes, aiming to attract global business firms. By providing state-of-the-art infrastructure and favorable policies, the new CBD has become a space of centrality with a large agglomeration of multinational business firms. Thus, the economic center of gravity shifted again as the new CBD became a strategic node connecting Beijing to transnational flows. Centrality in the global urban setting, therefore, has to be disconnected from geographic entities such as center, near-center, and peripheries. Rather, it should be understood as a function of power.

Using SOHO China as a case, this chapter has examined the symbolic power of architectural design in the making of the new CBD. The entrepreneurial developers at SOHO China staged one architectural spectacle after another by collaborating with prominent international architects. With various publications in print media and on the Internet, SOHO China constructed an image as a sophisticated patron of avant-garde architecture instead of a profit-driven speculator. Mobilizing the media, SOHO China has also built a closely tied network with the cultural elites in Beijing, and together with other developers, it has had significant influence on government policy making. Transnational architectural production has become a major strategy of capital accumulation, as the symbolic capital of architectural design is transformed into economic, cultural, and political capital in the process of making the new CBD.

Urban sociologist Sharon Zukin writes, "Shifts in a dominant class' accumulation strategy generally invoke new cultural norms in order to justify and facilitate the exercise of unaccustomed forms of social control."[61] This applies well to SOHO China's practice of packaging each of its SOHO projects into a new concept of urban work and living. By selling the SOHO apartments as undivided residential or office space, the developers have introduced new models of urban living. By portraying their projects as translocal spaces, the developers are also selling a dream that by working and living in SOHO projects, Beijingers can experience the lifestyle of their counterparts in other global cities. As exemplified by various SOHO projects, the new urban landscape in the CBD should be understood as the product of intersecting transnational flows of design professionals, images, and investment capital, as well as the mediation of these global and local processes in the built environment. The majority of city residents, however, are largely excluded in the official imagination and discursive construction of Beijing as a global city.

CHAPTER FOUR

History, Cosmopolitanism, and Preservation

The ubiquitous Chinese character 拆, painted in white on buildings slated for demolition, has become a popular symbol synonymous with the machinery of urban renewal and displacement (fig. 4.1). Since 1990, when local governments started to renew neighborhoods with "old and dangerous houses," a large number of historic buildings have vanished under the wrecking ball. The scale of destruction and displacement has prompted widespread criticism, and in response, the government has passed preservation laws, increased conservation funds, and tightened control over developers to ensure fair compensation for the displaced. But in spite of these progressive measures, the pace of demolition and residential displacement has yet to slow down. On the contrary, in Beijing and Shanghai, the 2008 Olympics and the 2010 World Expo have further fueled the machinery of urban renewal. It is against this background of urban destruction that the discourse of urban preservation has emerged. This chapter examines the politics of urban preservation and the role of international architecture firms in the process.

The preservation discourse comprises different concerns, interests, and proposed solutions. Local urban planners and architects tend to focus on the technical aspects of preservation, and some have proposed alternative models of preservation that are more sensitive to urban textures and residents.[1] Preservationists and activists working in various nonprofit organizations tend to focus on the legal dimensions of preservation, by raising public awareness of preservation laws and monitoring discrepancies between laws and implementation.[2] For instance, the Beijing Cultural Heritage Protection Center, an urban preservation nonprofit, has

FIGURE 4.1. "Chai," the demolition sign, Shanghai. Photograph by the author.

mobilized hundreds of volunteers to monitor illegal construction within government-designated protection zones and sends an annual report to the city government making policy suggestions. Journalists have recorded many stories of neighborhood renewal, displacement, and the destruction of historic architecture. The most famous is Wang Jun's best-selling book published in 2003, *Cheng Ji* (Beijing Record), in which he documented the destruction of the city walls of Beijing between the 1950s and 1970s.[3] Artists, photographers, and filmmakers have produced their own accounts of *chai* (demolition), documenting the unprecedented urban change, the violation of urban citizenship rights, and the loss of history.[4] Last but not least, academics have studied urban preservation in the larger socioeconomic, political, and cultural contexts, attributing the destruction of the historical built environment to the burgeoning property market, the growth machine of government and business, the unclear property rights and lack of incentives for preservation among residents, the Chinese culture of destruction, and the power split among government agencies in charge of preservation that results in a lack of unified action.[5]

   In spite of the rise of the discourse on preservation, a few critical issues remain missing from the debates. First, there is little discussion about how the different values of historic architecture—economic, cultural, and symbolic—are weighed by different interest groups. Growth-oriented local governments and developers emphasize the economic value of historic buildings over cultural and other symbolic values. Local residents are more concerned with relocation and compensation than with the cultural heritage of architecture. The intellectual group of preservationists tends to advocate the preservation of physical buildings and to ignore the poor living conditions of residents. These conflicting interests need to be taken into account to understand the politics of preservation.

Second, in the current preservation discourse, there is little critical reflection on the relationship between preservation and modernization, as most critics see preserving the old as the opposite of modernizing. Contrary to the common expectation that urban preservation and modernization are incompatible, I argue that in the Chinese case the two are very much compatible—urban preservation plays the same role of remaking a modern urban landscape as the construction of iconic new buildings.

Third, few have noted the critical role of international architects in reversing urban development policies from demolition to preservation. Since Xintiandi's commercial success in Shanghai, local governments and developers across the country have reached out for international architects to undertake various high-visibility projects of preservation. Local governments, developers, international architects, and the media are all part of the preservation coalition that churns out new heritages and prestigious addresses by reworking the historical built environment.

Pragmatic motivations for urban preservation and narrow interpretations of the past reinforce each other and have led to superficial preservation practices. This chapter will first examine the logics, targets, and practices of urban preservation. I then use Shanghai as a case to examine changes in urban policy from demolition to pragmatic preservation. I zoom in on the intricacies of the development process at Xintiandi, a flagship preservation-based development, and examine the collaboration, negotiation, and conflicts among governments, investors, architects, and local residents. As much of the preservation discourse is focused on buildings but neglects the residents living within, I devote a separate section to a discussion of the displacement and relocation of residents. I examine how residents' rights to housing have been largely compromised in the process of urban renewal and preservation, and how they negotiate with governments and fight for their right to the city. A comparison of Beijing and Shanghai at the end of the chapter reveals the different trajectories of urban preservation.

Deciphering Preservation in Urban China

The disappearance of historic architecture in Chinese cities has gone through several distinct phases since the mid-twentieth century. The main threat to historic buildings has changed from anti-urban ideology under socialism, to urban renewal and demolition in the 1990s, and to gentrification after 2000.

During the socialist period, some historic buildings and monuments were purposefully destroyed for ideological reasons, especially during the Cultural Revolution, as they were seen as remnants of the feudalist or colonial past. But owing to the lack of resources for development, most of the pre-1949 built environment was preserved by "benign neglect," as described by photographer Greg Girard, and was left largely untouched until the dawn of the market reform.[6]

In the 1990s, many of the old buildings and neighborhoods, preserved by accident under socialism, were torn down in the process of urban renewal to make inner-city land available for the construction of high-rises. Since around 2000, as a few preservation-based redevelopment projects scored high investment returns, developers and city governments have suddenly realized the economic potential of historic buildings, as a resource to promote tourism, raise property values, and provide a catalyst for neighborhood upgrading. In recent years, as old buildings are landmarked and neighborhoods are designated as historic districts, these places are quickly being gentrified as upper-class newcomers and tourists replace the original residents. In the post-1990s period of large-scale urban renewal and rapid gentrification, Chinese urban preservation has been driven by pragmatic motivations of urban development, has been based on a heavily edited interpretation of the past, and has resulted in superficial practices. It is in this context that the involvement of international architects becomes significant, as they can further add symbolic capital to the various preservation projects in the process of cosmopolitanizing Chinese urban landscapes.

Urban preservation in China is mostly driven by economic and political interests rather than by concerns for protecting cultural heritage. The recent policy shift from demolition to preservation can be seen as a state response to widespread criticism of demolition, displacement, and the loss of cultural heritage. The government has passed numerous preservation laws in order to pacify the critics of urban renewal and demolition. Historic preservation has been carried out for the recovery of the economic value, rather than the cultural and historic value, of old buildings. Old buildings have regained attention and been saved from demolition mainly for their economic potential as catalysts to renew neighborhoods and raise property prices. Therefore, preservation has become a sophisticated instrument to facilitate growth and development.

Preservation requires an act of symbolic interpretation of the past.[7] The pragmatic nature of urban preservation explains why certain styles of buildings from specific periods are eagerly sought out to be saved, while others are neglected. Grandiose imperial structures (e.g., the Forbidden City in Beijing) and examples of Western architecture (e.g., the neoclassical buildings on the Bund in Shanghai) have always been given priority over vernacular forms such as hutong and *lilong* neighborhoods. Republican-era architecture and cityscapes are actively restored, while communist-period architecture is largely neglected, as seen in the selective reconstruction of Old Shanghai (*Lao Shanghai*) and Old Beijing (*Lao Beijing*), focusing exclusively on structures from the 1920s and the 1930s. The focus on the republican era is an obvious choice, since that was the time when the country began to modernize and Westernize; therefore, reviving the architectural heritage of the republican period can showcase Chinese cities' cosmopolitan past. The following socialist period, from the 1950s to the 1970s, by comparison, is perceived as isolationist, parochial, and noncosmopolitan, a period that deviated from the progressive path of modernization and disconnected from the West. Most types of communist-era buildings, such as factory workshops and workers' villages, have rarely appeared on the government's preservation list.

The developmentalist ideology and the focus on the 1920s and 1930s have led to superficial practices. The most common practices include *reconstruction*—tearing down the authentic and replacing it with the inauthentic for a face-lift, as in the case of the rebuilt Yongding Gate in Beijing; *symbolic preservation*—preserving a small part symbolically and destroying the rest to reap real estate gains, as in the case of Xintiandi in Shanghai; *urban acupuncture*—concentrating resources for restoration on a few architectural monuments, such as the Forbidden City and temples in Beijing; and last, *remodeling,* as in the case of the lavishly renovated mansions in the gentrified neighborhoods of Beijing and Shanghai. These practices of preservation are largely cosmetic and geared toward political legitimation and revenue generation. Among the four types of practices, international architects are more involved in symbolic preservation and remodeling, as will be examined in the case study on Xintiandi.

From *Chai* (Demolition) to *Bao* (Preservation)

Shanghai experienced massive demolition in the 1990s (see table 4.1). In 1992, Deng Xiaoping's tour of southern China marked the real beginning of the pragmatic market reform. In the same year, at the Sixth Communist Party Congress of Shanghai, the Shanghai municipal government announced the famous 365 Plan, declaring that by the year 2000, the city would finish demolishing 365 hectares of "dangerous houses" (*weifang*) and increase the living area per capita from 6 to 10 square meters. The plan was based on a survey conducted in the previous year, which confirmed 15 million square meters of old-style *lilong* housing in the city and identified 365 hectares as being in dangerous condition.[8] The term "dangerous," however, was never clearly defined. Neighborhoods that promised good investment returns, such as those in central locations and with low residential density, were deemed to have "dangerous housing" and slated for demolition, even if the housing stock was in good condition. In

TABLE 4.1 **Demolition and relocation of residents in Shanghai, 1995–2008**

Year	No. of households relocated	Area demolished (in million square meters)
1995	73,695	2.54
1996	86,481	2.59
1997	77,388	3.63
1998	75,157	3.44
1999	73,709	2.48
2000	68,293	2.88
2001	71,909	3.87
2002	98,714	4.85
2003	79,077	4.75
2004	41,552	2.33
2005	74,483	8.52
2006	76,874	8.48
2007	49,092	6.90
2008	51,288	7.54
Total	997,721	64.80

Source: Shanghai Statistics Yearbook (2009).

comparison, many neighborhoods in desperate need of housing improvement, but with less promising investment prospects, were carefully bypassed by developers and local governments.

Land and housing reform were the two institutional changes crucial for the implementation of the massive urban renewal programs. The housing reform abolished the system of free allocation of housing by work units to their employees, a practice dating back to the 1950s. Since the 1980s, housing has become a commodity that can be purchased on the market.[9] Similarly, the land reform abolished (only partly) the practice of land allocation by governments to state-owned enterprises and turned land-use rights into a commodity to be exchanged on the emerging land market.[10] Municipal and district governments were authorized to transfer urban land-use rights to private developers in return for a substantial land-leasing fee. In Shanghai, the first piece of land was leased to foreign investors for a fee in 1992. By 1995, 9,214 hectares of urban land were leased, and the leasing fees obtained by the municipal government amounted to $84.6 million.[11] Housing and land reforms did away with the institutional constraints that had prevented urbanization and development in the forty years of the socialist era and greatly decentralized power to municipal and district governments so that entrepreneurial measures could be taken to attract investments and promote growth.

To achieve the goal set in the 365 Plan, the Shanghai city government issued a series of policies to speed up demolition and redevelopment. Document No. 18 issued by the Department of Construction in 1996 gave district governments approval rights over redevelopment proposals from private developers and thus further decentralized power from the municipal to the district level. Moreover, the city government reduced all kinds of taxes and fees that should have been levied on private developers. In some cases, even the land-leasing fee, the major revenue source for local governments, was reduced. For example, among the five grades of urban land, nonprime land from the third to the fifth grade was leased to private developers at a 40 to 60 percent discount.[12] Developers were also allowed to increase building heights and density regardless of zoning regulations. Thus, a large proportion of the profit from urban renewal was channeled to private developers.

Because of the limited market demand for housing and offices in the mid-1990s, it was a daunting task to demolish 365 hectares of "dangerous houses." By 1997, there were still 125 hectares left to be demolished. In 1998, the Department of Construction issued Document No. 33, which further reduced the land-leasing fee and, in addition, provided subsidies to private developers partaking in the 365 Plan. Developers were awarded from $40 to $110 for every square meter demolished according to project location and housing condition.[13] Finally, in 2000, the city government announced that the 365 Plan had been successfully accomplished. According to official statistics, during the 1990s, 27 million square meters of old housing were demolished, 640,000 households were relocated—mainly from inner-city neighborhoods to suburbs—and 0.1 billion square meters of new housing were constructed. Many historic buildings and neighborhoods were bulldozed in the implementation of the 365 Plan.

Real estate development in Shanghai accelerated after 2000, and the city government announced one demolition campaign after another to make inner-city land available for commercial redevelopment. The "New Round of Urban Renewal," carried out between 2001 and 2004, targeted neighborhoods with more than 70 percent old-style *lilong* housing. The city identified 307 such areas, and many neighborhoods in decent condition were also slated for demolition at the insistence of district governments. An estimated three hundred thousand households were relocated in this round of renewal. Although by the beginning of the 2000s, the demand for housing was strong and property prices were high enough for developers to make good profits without government subsidies, the city and district governments continued to offer favorable policies to developers. Document No. 68, issued in 2001, abolished land-use fees and reduced other fees for developers. The urban renewal and demolition continued with the Eleventh Five-Year Plan (2006–10), in which the city government set the goal of renewing four million square meters of old housing and relocating another two hundred thousand households.

It is apparent that demolition of "dangerous houses" has become the most important instrument used by city governments to intervene in the land and housing markets. By demolishing old low-rise houses in the inner city, where land prices are the highest, the government can requisition land, transfer land-use rights to developers, and boost municipal revenues from land-leasing fees. Each wave of demolition creates tens of thousands of displaced residents, who then look for housing elsewhere in the city. Thus, massive demolition directly creates huge demand for more housing, especially in the suburbs, where property prices are lower, but also in the secondhand housing market. The city government has control over the pace of urban renewal and demolition, making it more aggressive and faster in some years than in others, to boost the real estate market during recessions and prevent the market from getting overheated in boom times. In 2007, when property prices peaked in Shanghai, the government slowed down the pace of demolition to control the demand for housing, while in 2009, in the midst of the global economic recession, the government sped up urban renewal again and set the goal to "improve the living conditions of 200,000 households" and renew eight million square meters of old houses in five inner-city districts—Hongkou, Zhabei, Yangpu, Huangpu, and Putuo (see fig. 4.2).[14] The scale of demolition and relocation in Shanghai is unprecedented. From 1990, when the 365 Plan was announced, to 2008, the city demolished 70 million square meters of houses and relocated 1.2 million households from inner-city districts.[15]

Since the 1990s, the Shanghai city government has shown steady movement toward historical preservation, by passing a series of preservation laws and landmarking a large number of historical buildings. The city has rapidly expanded the list of historical buildings designated for preservation from a mere 50 initially to more than 700 locations. The first list of historical buildings for preservation was generated in 1989, including only 50 locations. In 1994, a second group of 175 locations was added. Five years later in 1999, another 162 locations were designated for preservation. In 2004, a group of 235 locations with more than 600 buildings were listed by the Shanghai Cultural Heritage Bureau for preservation. The buildings listed for preservation are predominantly examples of Western-style architecture from the colonial period. Buildings from the following socialist era are mostly regarded as worthless for preservation and eligible for demolition as they age. Only recently, in response to criticism about the lack of preservation for architecture from the socialist era, were a few buildings built after 1949 added to the preservation list.

In addition to the preservation of individual buildings, there is another initiative to preserve large areas with multiple heritage sites. In 2003, the city government designated twelve historical and cultural heritage areas (*lishi wenhua fengmao baohuqu*) for preservation, with a total area of 27 square kilometers.[16] This is roughly one-third of the inner-city area of Shanghai. Among the twelve areas, nine were chosen because of the presence of a large number of historical buildings from the colonial period, such as the Bund, which was the former International Settlement, and Hengshan Road—the former French Concession (see table 4.2). In March 2005, the city government proposed to add another thirty historical and cultural heritage areas in Pudong New District and outer districts, a total of 12 square kilometers. There are no specific guidelines for preservation

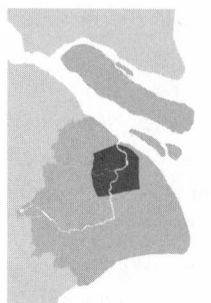

Twelve Historical & Cultural Heritage Areas

1 The Bund
2 People's Square
3 Old City
4 Hengshan Road & Fuxing Road
5 Hongqiao Road
6 Shanyin Road
7 Jiangwan
8 Longhua Road
9 Tilanqiao Road
10 West Nanjing Road
11 Yuyuan Road
12 Xinhua Road

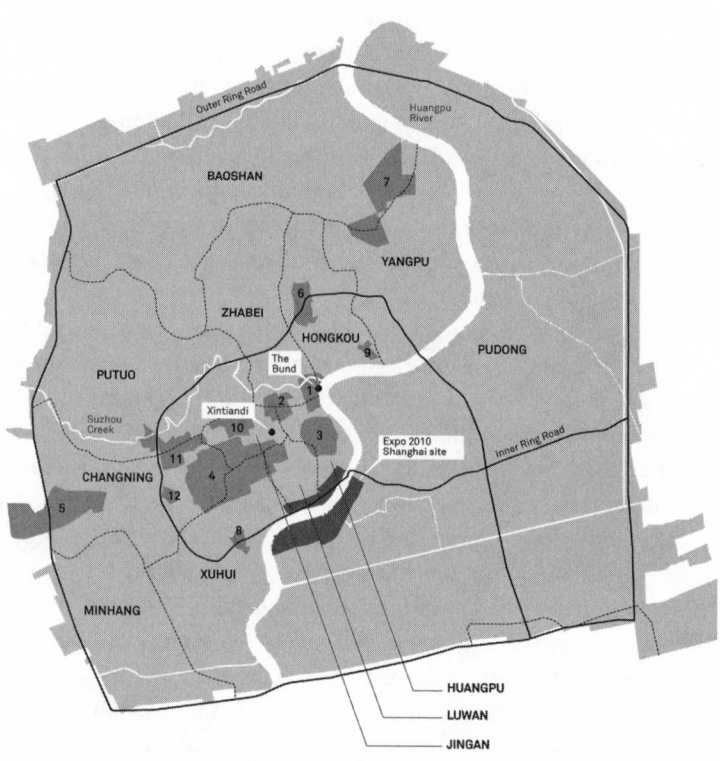

FIGURE 4.2. Map of Shanghai

TABLE 4.2 **The twelve historical and cultural heritage areas of 2003, Shanghai**

Rank	Heritage Area	Target for preservation
1	The Bund	Neoclassical and art deco buildings in the former International Settlement
2	People's Square	Revolutionary sites and excellent modern architecture
3	Old City	Traditional Chinese city
4	Hengshan Road and Fuxing Road	Garden villas in the former French Concession
5	Hongqiao Road	Suburban villas from the colonial period
6	Shanyin Road	Modern Shanghai dwellings
7	Jiangwan	Modern urban planning
8	Longhua Road	Revolutionary sites, religious temples
9	Tilanqiao Road	Jewish quarter in the 1930s and 1940s
10	West Nanjing Road	Former International Settlement
11	Yuyuan Road	Chinese and Western-style architecture from the colonial period
12	Xinhua Road	Garden villa

Source: http://www.shanghai.gov.cn.

practices in these historic districts. Anticipating the potential economic return, local district governments rushed to identify and encircle more sites as preservation zones.

What marked the transition from demolition to preservation in Shanghai was the flagship redevelopment project at Xintiandi, where two blocks of shikumen houses, Shanghainese tenements built by Western landlords for Chinese tenants in the colonial period, were turned into a posh entertainment quarter by international developers and architects, with support from local governments. Although it is questionable what is actually preserved at Xintiandi, the commercial success has sent a clear message to mayors and developers across the country that history can sell, and very well. Since Xintiandi opened, Shanghai has begun to preserve much more architecture than it ever did before. As most financial institutions moved to modern office towers across the river in Pudong, the neoclassical buildings on the Bund were renovated as spaces for galleries, boutiques, and upscale restaurants and clubs. In 2004, an American-Chinese businessman, Handel Lee, turned one of the buildings along the Bund, Three on the Bund, into a space for the Shanghai Gallery of Art, an Armani boutique, an Evian Spa, and a Jean-Georges Vongerichten restaurant with an interior designed by Michael Graves. Various preservation and redevelopment plans followed for other buildings on the Bund. Old warehouses along Suzhou Creek and factory workshops in Yangpu district were turned into artists' studios, galleries, and offices for media firms. In 2004, Wu Jiang, a former architecture professor at Tongji University and currently the head of the Shanghai Municipal Planning Commission, announced that the city government would welcome the participation of private investors and developers in the preservation of Shanghai's historic buildings and that major contributors would be awarded government subsidies.[17] Han Zheng, the mayor of Shanghai, delivered a new slogan in August 2004: "Building new is development, preserving old is also development."[18] The new slogan summarizes well the nature of historical preservation efforts in Shanghai—preservation is another instrument, a more sophisticated one than demolition, to promote urban growth.

Xintiandi: New Heaven and Earth

There were several previous preservation-based redevelopment projects in Shanghai, but none of them have been as commercially successful as Xintiandi, nor have they attracted the same media attention nationally and internationally. Since its opening in 2001, Xintiandi has become the top entertainment and tourist destination in Shanghai.[19] The project's success has helped to raise property values in the area significantly and turned the surrounding area into the most expensive real estate in the city. The project has had a significant impact on urban policy making in Shanghai and beyond. It has generated a new awareness among government officials and developers concerning the economic potential of historic buildings. By examining the redevelopment process of Xintiandi, this section explores how the material history of shikumen is reinterpreted to suit the new development goal of making Shanghai into a global city and the role of international architects in the process.

A Brief History of Shikumen

Before redevelopment, the area of Xintiandi consisted of dilapidated shikumen houses. Shikumen houses are residential row houses built by Western landlords for Chinese tenants in the former foreign concessions of Shanghai. Foreign concessions were established in Shanghai in the 1840s after China lost the Opium War. Shanghai was forced to open as a treaty port, and the city was divided into three parts—the old Chinese city, the French Concession, and the International Settlement of British and

FIGURE 4.3. Shikumen houses used by multiple families. Photograph by the author.

American Territories. Each of the three parts had its own police, courts, and government jurisdictions. In the 1860s, to escape from the upheavals of the Taiping Rebellion (1851–64), a large number of refugees flooded into Shanghai from nearby provinces. For many of these refugees, the destination was the foreign concessions. Targeting this influx of Chinese migrants, Western landlords started building shikumen houses in the foreign concessions. This was the first wave of shikumen construction. Later, in the 1920s, when the French Concession expanded westward and incorporated more territory, shikumen construction peaked again. Most of the shikumen houses that remain today were built in the 1920s and 1930s—the golden age of colonial Shanghai.[20]

Originally designed by European architects, shikumen blends European architectural elements such as slate-gray bricks and French windows with Chinese features such as courtyards and stone gates (see fig. 4.3). In the Shanghai dialect, shikumen means "gates-wrapped-in-stone." A shikumen gate is two wooden planks wrapped by a stone frame, with a big bronze ring fixed on each plank, and elaborate stone sculptures on top. Behind the shikumen gate is a courtyard, and further inside is a living room, locally known as a parlor. Then there is the back courtyard, kitchen, and back door. Left and right wings flank the courtyard and the parlor. The layout of the second story is similar to the one below, except that there is a garret above the kitchen covered by a flat roof. To maximize the efficiency of land, shikumen houses were built on two sides of narrow lanes no more than four meters wide. The houses were connected, with their shikumen gates facing the main lane. At the end of a lane, there was a bigger gate, which separated the neighborhood from the outside. Houses facing the streets were used as shops, and those inside for residence. The closed structure of shikumen neighborhoods, with their multiple layers of gates and walls, was popular among the migrants longing for security and safety in chaotic colonial Shanghai.

Shikumen was the major residential form in Shanghai until the 1980s. Except for the very rich and very poor, most residents in Shanghai lived in shikumen houses. Wealthier families occupied larger units in shikumen neighborhoods in prime locations, and less well-to-do families crowded into smaller units in less desirable locations. A large block of shikumen houses could have hundreds of households, while a smaller one usually comprised eight to ten households. In 1949, when the communist regime took over Shanghai, there were about nine thousand neighborhoods with shikumen houses, accounting for 64 percent of the total built area of the city.[21]

In the socialist era, many buildings were used in ways never intended, and most shikumen houses deteriorated quickly for lack of repair and overcrowding. Because of the limited resources of local governments, very few new housing projects were constructed in this period; in the meantime, the city experienced a sharp spike in population growth. As a result, shikumen houses, originally designed for single-family use, were divided to accommodate multiple households. The private clubhouse of the developer of Xintiandi—Shui On Group—a renovated 1930s-era shikumen house, is such a case. The house was owned by a wealthy merchant family in the 1930s. After the communist regime took over Shanghai in the 1940s, the family fled overseas, and the house was confiscated by the Shanghai city government. Later, it was allocated to a few working-class families as a residence. During the period of severe housing shortages in the socialist era, more and more families moved into the house. Right before the renovation, this single-family mansion was partitioned and occupied by thirty-six households. Families shared common kitchens and bathrooms, and private lives spilled over into public spaces. The developer relocated the residents, restored the former glory of the mansion, and turned it into its private clubhouse and gallery.

By the early 1990s, a large proportion of shikumen houses built in the early twentieth century had become densely packed slums with poor sanitary conditions. At Xintiandi, however, the slum image of the shikumen houses was carefully erased by international developers and the design professionals they hired. The history of shikumen is rewritten: the decayed row houses are now a symbol of Shanghai's glamorous colonial past.

The Public-Private Coalition at Work

In 1996, Shanghai's Luwan district government signed an agreement with Shui On Group from Hong Kong to develop the Taipingqiao area where Xintiandi is located. In the 1990s, the area covered fifty-two hectares of land and consisted of twenty-three residential neighborhoods with some seventy thousand residents and eight hundred work units. There were more than two hundred lanes of shikumen houses in the area, built between the 1900s and 1930s, with a total built area of one million square meters.[22]

In the Shanghai dialect, good neighborhoods are called *shangzhijiao* (upper corner) and bad ones are called *xiazhijiao* (lower corner). Taipingqiao is a typical "lower corner." Although located near the former French Concession, Taipingqiao was actually a zone in transition. It was bounded by the exclusive villas and mansions of the French Concession on the west, the Old Chinese City on the east, the upscale shopping boulevard, Huaihai Road, on the north, and the Zhaojiabang shantytown (*penghuqu*) on the south. Modern Shanghai is often portrayed as a shining metropolis, but little is known about the less glamorous corners developed on the periphery of foreign concessions, such as the Taipingqiao area. By 1949 the residents in Taipingqiao were mostly lower-middle-class families.

Shui On Group could not have secured the development rights to these fifty-two hectares of inner-city land without good relations with high-ranking city officials. Because of his extensive government connections, Vincent Lo, the president of Shui On, is called "the red capitalist" and "the king of *guanxi*" in the local business community. *Guanxi* means "connections." Based in Hong Kong, Vincent Lo entered mainland China's real estate market in 1985, when the country had just opened up to foreign investment. Over the years, he has gradually built good connections with city and district government officials in Shanghai. In 1985, Lo partnered with the Shanghai branch of the Communist Youth League and built the modest City Hotel. When the City Hotel went into debt in the late 1980s, Lo used his own resources to finance the hotel. It was through this collaboration that he started building his political capital in Shanghai. Many 1980s mid-level bureaucrats were promoted to high-ranking positions in the 1990s. Han Zheng, the leader of the Communist Youth League in the 1980s, has now become the mayor of Shanghai. Although foreign developers are in a relatively disadvantaged position compared with domestic developers because of their lack of connections with government, Shui On has reversed the usual situation through a long and patient courtship of local politicians. As Lo commented, "Now many of these people have moved up to very senior positions, and we have been through some hard times together, so our friendship has a solid base."[23] Lo is an honorary citizen of Shanghai and also a member of one of the top advisory bodies consulted by the central government.

According to the contract signed between Shui On and the district government, the company was to provide capital for the redevelopment, and the Luwan district government would provide subsidies and take responsibility for the relocation of residents. The fifty-two hectares of land in Taipingqiao were leased to the company for fifty years. Shui On agreed to invest $0.3 billion over the next fifteen years, which was 97 percent of the total investment. The remaining 3 percent was provided by the Fuxing Development Corporation, a state enterprise owned by the Luwan district government. According to the agreement, two or three blocks would be leased out every year for redevelopment based on negotiated land prices.[24] Around 2002, Lo made three trips to the United States and Europe to drum up investment. He managed to borrow $45 million from four banks—Citigroup Venture Capital International, Standard Chartered Bank, Value Partners, and Jebsen and Co. The balance was paid by Shui On itself.[25]

Developers have great autonomy in deciding the pace, direction, and magnitude of their projects. In 1997, owing to the Asian economic crisis, Shui On decided to delay the construction of office buildings and luxury apartments and begin the rehabilitation of shikumen houses and the construction of Taipingqiao Park. With help from the Luwan district government, it took only forty-three days to relocate thirty-eight hundred households and 156 work units in order to make way for the park.[26] Between October 2000 and June 2001, a brand-new urban park of thirty thousand square meters and an artificial lake of ten thousand square

FIGURE 4.4. Taipingqiao Park built on former neighborhoods. Photograph by the author.

meters were built on the site of four former residential neighborhoods (see fig. 4.4). The project was proposed as a present for the eightieth anniversary of the CCP by Lo. The construction of Taipingqiao Park cost 0.1 billion RMB, which was put together by Shui On, the city, and district governments. The three parties collaborated closely throughout the redevelopment process.

Old Shikumen Repackaged

At one corner of Xintiandi is the old party hall. In July of 1921, Mao Zedong and his thirteen comrades held the first meeting of the CCP in the shikumen building here. As the birthplace of the CCP, the old party hall is listed as a national landmark and cannot be demolished. When Shui On was given the development rights, one stipulation was that the old party hall had to be preserved. Shui On commissioned an American architecture firm—Wood & Zapata—for the renovation work. The principal architect, Ben Wood, worked on renovating Boston's 150-year-old Faneuil Hall Marketplace. The developer's original idea was to keep the CCP building,

FIGURE 4.5. Renovated shikumen building as Starbucks. Photograph by the author.

tear down the surrounding shikumen houses, and build luxury low-rise villas. However, Wood persuaded Lo to preserve the whole two blocks of shikumen together with the CCP building and turn the area into a festival marketplace. Having worked on various renovation projects in the United States, Wood knew about the economic potential of historical architecture. Although the theme-park-like historic downtown is a repeated exercise in the West, in China in the 1990s there was little preservation, and the concept of preserving a few buildings and turning them into an entertainment district was groundbreaking.

The two neighborhood blocks at Xintiandi were densely packed with about thirty lanes of shikumen houses. To create a more open composition, the architects at Wood & Zapata first removed many of the crumbling houses. About one hundred shikumen houses were kept in their original positions. In the north block, most of the original buildings were kept, while in the south block, a modern shopping complex replaced many shikumen houses (see fig. 4.5). The facades of the old houses were repaired, and the original color and texture were restored. The interior space was gut-renovated by Shanghai's best interior design firms. The slate-gray bricks and stones from old residences were used for new construction and as pavement for pedestrian streets. The heavy wooden gates were replaced with glass storefronts displaying brand-name luxury goods.

The "creative preservation" at Xintiandi is enabled by the classification of the area's shikumen houses as fourth-grade historic architecture. According to a regulation passed in 2002, historic buildings are divided into four grades, each of which has different requirements for rehabilitation.[27] Whereas first-grade historical architecture allows no alterations to facades, structures, and interiors, buildings categorized as fourth grade can be radically changed, except that their facades should be kept as original. Fourth-grade historical buildings are the most sought-after properties in Shanghai because of the large leeway left for remodeling and expansion. When asked how authentic the renovated shikumen is, architect Ben Wood commented,

> Xintiandi came along at a special historical moment. Even if I didn't do it, somebody else would have done it. I'm not a preservationist. I've never done a project like Xintiandi before, preserving old buildings. . . . Sometimes you can't save a building, and you have to make it up somehow. . . . I would say 80 percent of it is authentic and 20 percent is made up. . . . Xintiandi is contemporary Chinese architecture.[28]

Although the architect claimed authenticity for the renovated shikumen and called it "contemporary Chinese architecture," the refurbished shikumen is barely recognizable for local Shanghainese. When I asked the locals how they felt about Xintiandi during my fieldwork, many longtime residents laughed and told me, "That's not shikumen." The new shikumen at Xintiandi has been gutted, polished, and sterilized and, therefore, "preserved." The inauthentic was quickly driving out the authentic altogether. Most shikumen houses sitting within the fifty-two hectares of land were demolished to make space for the developer to build high-rise modern towers. Mao and his thirteen comrades who convened here in 1921 probably could never have envisioned that, eight decades later, the old party hall would be surrounded by brand-name shops for hyperconsumption.

Shanghai Nostalgia

The architects also turned one well-kept shikumen house into a museum, which features a permanent exhibition showing the everyday life of former shikumen residents in colonial Shanghai. Old family photos, furniture, and other objects are carefully selected and arranged to reproduce an image of old Shanghai as a modern city. According to the museum's brochure, the typical family living in shikumen houses in the 1930s was a well-to-do middle-class family who sent their children to English-speaking schools, went to theaters on weekends, watched Hollywood movies, and listened to jazz. The theme of the exhibition, "Yesterday Meets Tomorrow, at Xintiandi Today," is printed on the museum pass, with a background photo of old shikumen gates. Not all histories are equally marketable. Only those with connections to the colonial period of Shanghai are actively preserved in an attempt to show that Shanghai was once an international metropolis. In contrast, the history of shikumen as decrepit slums throughout most of the twentieth century is carefully erased in the reconstruction of old Shanghai.

The nostalgia for 1930s Shanghai, ubiquitous in the themed environment at Xintiandi, does not imply a longing for a glamorous past. As urban historian Lu Hanchao observed,

> Unlike nostalgia that in most cases rejects mainstream culture, the Shanghai nostalgia is part of it. Unlike nostalgia that usually protests about the present, the Shanghai nostalgia celebrates it. Unlike nostalgia that is commonly negative, dispirited, and withdrawn, the Shanghai nostalgia is positive, spirited, and receptive.[29]

The nostalgia for a selectively remembered colonial past serves the social and political agenda of Shanghai's transformation into a global city.[30] The rehabilitation of shikumen, rather than protecting "cultural heritage," is intended to project Shanghai's bright global future by reconnecting to the city's colonial past. The popularity of Xintiandi, with its themed environment referencing 1930s Shanghai, is not evidence of nostalgic localism. The locals love to go to Xintiandi not because the place reminds them of the past that is long gone but because the place makes them feel that they live in a modern and cosmopolitan city.

Contrary to the common juxtaposition of localism and cosmopolitanism, local cultural elements have become a constitutive part of global cosmopolitanism. When cities become more homogeneous as they are integrated into the global economy, local cultural differences become rare commodities sought after by mobile consumerist elites. For the audience of foreign expatriates and wealthy Chinese to whom Xintiandi is marketed, the marks of cosmopolitanism include not only international-brand shops but also exotic local cultural elements such as the refurbished shiku-men. To Chinese visitors, the place looks foreign and modern. To foreign visitors, Xintiandi looks Chinese and traditional. It is the juxtaposition of the old and the new, the Chinese and the foreign that has generated a hybrid diversity that constitutes cosmopolitanism. Shanghai's shikumen houses never looked as polished as those at Xintiandi. The old historical fabric of shikumen is used as a component to create a completely modern space. Just like the Shanghai nostalgia that is receptive to the present, historical preservation in Shanghai is part of the larger project of modernization and urban development.

Accumulating Economic and Political Capital

Xintiandi's success has pushed up property values in the nearby area, which is also developed by Shui On Group. Lake Ville, a high-end luxury apartment complex near Xintiandi, was sold out at the price of $6,000 per square meter even before it was released onto the market, making it the most expensive property in Shanghai in the early 2000s. Wood & Zapata, together with Japanese architecture firm Nikken Sekkei International, executed the architectural design of the complex. According to Shui On's promotional brochures, individual apartments at Lake Ville "recall the style of old Shanghai shikumen courtyard houses." Not far away, Corporate Avenue, a development of two high-rise grade-A office towers, was built on the banks of Taipingqiao Lake. Shui On invited the Hong Kong–based architecture firm Palmer & Turner to give the buildings a touch of art deco style, evoking again 1930s Shanghai. The two office towers were soon fully occupied by branch offices of multinational firms.

Xintiandi helped both the development company and the architects to further build their political and economic capital. Ben Wood moved his operation from Boston to Shanghai. He set up a design office in a corner unit at Xintiandi and leads a multinational team of young architects from Australia, Germany, the United States, and local Tongji University. Ben Wood never had to get projects through design competitions. His reputation as the designer of Xintiandi has easily led to other major commissions in Beijing, Hangzhou, Nanjing, Tianjin, Chongqing, and Zhujiajiao in Shanghai.

Building on the success of Xintiandi, Shui On also acquired the development rights for several other high-profile projects in Shanghai. The largest among these is the Knowledge and Technology Community in Yangpu district. The Yangpu district government established a joint venture with

Shui On to develop an area of eighty-four hectares. The San Francisco office of Skidmore, Owings & Merrill drafted the master plan for the project. The success of Xintiandi has also paved the way for Shui On to enter the real estate markets in other Chinese cities. Mayors have sent invitations to Vincent Lo and Ben Wood asking them to clone Xintiandi in their cities. The first such clone, Xihu (West Lake) Tiandi, has already been completed in the nearby city of Hangzhou. Chongqing Tiandi, with a total budget estimated at $0.12 billion, is currently under construction in Sichuan province.

Creating a New Address

The media and local academic institutions played an auxiliary role in promoting Xintiandi. Xintiandi attracted a wide range of media coverage from both the local and the international press. Most media reports uncritically embraced the transformation of the place and identified Xintiandi as a symbol of Shanghai's global future. *People's Daily,* a national newspaper and the major government propaganda outlet, wrote that Xintiandi demonstrated "the respect for, and the cherishing of, history and culture by the municipal government and enterprises."[31] The *Los Angeles Times* praised how the area of dilapidated colonial row houses had been recast as a "consumer's paradise."[32] The *Economist* ran a story and compared Shanghai to other global cities: "China's commercial capital is starting to take on the chic of Paris, the sophistication of New York, and the futuristic vibes of Tokyo."[33] In the local newspaper, *Xin Min Weekly,* the head of Luwan district commented that Xintiandi should be taken as an inspiration for old architecture renovation projects in the future.[34]

Local academic and cultural institutions are also active players in promoting Xintiandi. The Department of Architecture and Urban Planning at Tongji University has worked closely with Shui On as consultants. In 2002, the faculty and students at Tongji published the first book dedicated to the project, *Shanghai Xintiandi.*[35] The book highly praised the preservation-based redevelopment led by Shui On and suggested that the "Xintiandi model" be employed in other preservation cases in Shanghai and other cities.[36] Local architecture and planning journals competed to publish articles featuring the restoration of shikumen houses at Xintiandi. While praising the success of Xintiandi, the media carefully ignored controversial issues, such as the demolition of shikumen houses in surrounding areas and the displacement of residents. Together with local governments and international developers, the professional and cultural elites—architects, planners, and design consultants as well as the media—are active boosters who have helped turn Xintiandi into a new icon.

Shui On carefully limited its commercial tenants to high-end, image-savvy luxury shops. Among the seventy-nine tenants in the renovated buildings, the majority (forty-one) are upscale restaurants, bars, nightclubs, and coffee shops. Architect Wood opened his own bar, DR at Xintiandi, and it has become a popular hangout for architects and designers. Another twenty-seven tenants are fashion, art, and gift shops. The rest are boutique hotels, beauty spas, and a cinema complex. Xintiandi has triggered a reshuffling in the hierarchy of nightclubs and bars in Shanghai, and it has become the new center of nightlife. In his historical ethnography about the transformation of Shanghai's nightlife, sociologist James Farrer describes how previous organic bar districts, such as the one on Maoming Road, have been replaced by the high-profile new developments at Xintiandi and the even newer ones on the Bund, which represent "unprecedented levels of both transnational investment and local government involvement . . . leading to a gentrification, stratification, and increasing regulation of Shanghai's bar culture." Farrer also rightly points out that encouraging large-scale urban entertainment districts such as Xintiandi has become an integral part of the government's promotion of Shanghai as a global city.[37]

The shikumen setting is frequently used by marketers to differentiate Xintiandi from other shopping and dining venues in the city. For instance, a French restaurant housed in a former shikumen named itself Shikumen Bistro. In its brochure, the restaurant assures the discerning Shanghai cosmopolites of the finest French-Mediterranean cuisine in a refined shikumen setting. Sophisticated diners can "watch Chef Jean Alberti create seasonal fare from the exhibition kitchen, relax in the sumptuous Cigar Lounge, or have a drink on the Veranda Café overlooking the Shanghai Skyline."[38] The marketing department of Shui On also organizes cultural and promotional events to draw a large crowd and create an urban scene at Xintiandi Square. In summer 2005, upon the visit of a senator and business delegation from Hawaii, Shui On organized a Hawaiian festival. Consumers could have "a unique Hawaii experience by shopping at the different stores at Xintiandi," according to the event flyers.

Although the price range of the high-end shops at Xintiandi is out of reach for most Shanghai residents, the growing population of foreign expatriates and wealthy Chinese has brought a steady supply of customers. The place has also become a tourist mecca since its opening. About thirty thousand people stroll through the shops at Xintiandi on a daily basis. According to Shui On's estimates, about 70 percent of the visitors are Chinese, and 30 percent are foreign tourists and expatriates. The place becomes jam-packed on major holidays and in high tourist seasons. In May 2005, a delegation led by Lian Chan, the ex-president of the Kuomintang Party of Taiwan, visited Xintiandi. They were greeted by the developer Lo and a select group of Luwan district officials at the entrance to Xintiandi North Block. The visit came during the Labor Day holiday, one of the busiest tourist weekends. The main road leading into Xintiandi Square was packed with Chinese and foreign visitors, as well as media reporters. Lian Chan had to cancel his original plan to walk through Xintiandi and ended the visit.

Xintiandi symbolizes how Shanghai has been increasingly integrated into the global economy and how new consumption patterns have been generated as locals adapt to global culture. Until recently, restaurants in China did not have outdoor seating. However, the sidewalk cafes at Xintiandi are even more popular than places with indoor tables because of the theatricality of the space—it is a place to see and be seen. The place is especially popular among young and affluent urban professionals. One of my interviewees, a female office worker in her early twenties, told me that she came here two to three times a week, hanging out with friends in bars and clubs, and that she would feel old-fashioned if she did not visit Xintiandi often.

Is the development at Xintiandi a form of gentrification? Gentrification in Western cities often involves the movement of young professionals into the central city in search of affordable housing in close proximity to employment opportunities, for both economic and cultural reasons. The Chinese gentrification happening in inner cities exhibits some different features. First of all, the government plays a much bigger role in fostering neighborhood change, since urban renewal and redevelopment programs are mostly initiated and directed by municipal and district governments. Also, the newcomers are not young, well-educated, and affluent urban professionals. Instead, they are wealthy Chinese—both locals and people from other provinces—and foreign expatriates who can afford the highest rents in inner cities. Moreover, the motivations for resettlement differ. In China, the newcomers do not resettle in inner cities in order to "live close to work," nor are they motivated by the spirit of "frontier and salvation," to quote sociologist Sharon Zukin's description of artists who move into warehouses, rehabilitate the space, and regenerate neighborhoods on the urban frontier.[39] Instead, the resettlement of higher-income social groups in inner cities is largely driven by expectations of financial return from the appreciation of property values. What is common to gentrification in both Chinese and Western cities is the displacement of lower-income groups by higher-income groups.

Beyond Xintiandi

After Xintiandi, large and small preservation-based redevelopment projects mushroomed across the urban districts in Shanghai. Chinese and international architects have participated in the design and planning of these projects. Some of the projects imitated the practices of Shui On, while others experimented with new preservation concepts, trying to preserve more of historical architecture than just facades and to improve living conditions for the residents without much displacement. Several pilot preservation projects have been carried out in places such as Duolun Road, Sinan Road, and Tianzifang on Taikang Road. As the knowledge and understanding of historical preservation among local planners became more sophisticated, they gradually adopted a critical stance toward Xintiandi and reevaluated its impact on both historic shikumen architecture and local residents. Some questioned Shui On's practice of dislocating all original residents in order to preserve a small part of the neighborhood and use the rest for commercial redevelopment. Senior architect and planner Zheng Shiling from Tongji University commented,

> The evaluation of Xintiandi has become more objective. In the beginning most opinions were extremely positive. Now many people agree that Shui On has destroyed a larger part of the place and only preserved a small piece. The preservation is just to raise the value of the surrounding real estate properties.[40]

Social preservation, aiming to preserve not only historic architecture but also the culture and lifestyle of residents living in the old buildings, gradually gathered support among local planners.[41] In 2005, Shanghai Urban Planning and Design Institute announced an ambitious plan to turn a three-kilometer stretch along the southern bank of Suzhou Creek in Huangpu district into an area of rehabilitated shikumen alleys, warehouse galleries, museums, and teahouses by 2010.[42] The project aimed to keep the original living atmosphere of the neighborhood, and most residents would not be forced to leave their homes. The city government provided most of the funds to support the conservation of old houses, while private developers will be invited to rehabilitate nonresidential structures such as warehouses and convert them for commercial uses such as restaurants and galleries.

Social preservation, together with other sophisticated and sensitive design concepts, is widely adopted by local planners as a better approach to the historical fabric of cities. However, it often encounters great difficulties in implementation, especially in places where the exchange value of real estate properties is the highest. As the land prices in inner-city Shanghai keep rising, the incentive to redevelop older neighborhoods and dislocate residents is simply too strong to resist for both city governments and private developers. One example is the well-known Bund Origin Project (Waitanyuan). The location is where Suzhou Creek meets the Huangpu River, and it has a large number of historic buildings from the colonial period, including the former site of the British consulate. Chang Qing, an urban planning professor at Tongji University, proposed a detailed master plan for preservation in his 2003 book *Strategies of Preserving Architectural Heritage*. Later, the government organized international design competitions to seek creative design proposals for developing the area while preserving the landmark buildings and streets. However, the design proposals were set aside when the city government started to negotiate with foreign investors, including Morgan Stanley and Rockefeller International. In just the first phase of the project, 95 percent of the residents were displaced. Now architects and planners are trying to persuade the government at least not to demolish many of the historic buildings, and the request has become increasingly difficult as investors demand higher and denser construction to increase investment returns. The top-listed landmarks will probably stay, but the rest of the neighborhoods and residents have been wiped out. The Bund Origin Project illustrates the difficulty of going beyond Xintiandi and planners' powerlessness to implement social preservation plans in the midst of the real estate boom in Shanghai.

Displacement, Relocation, and Compensation

In a neighborhood in its final stage of demolition, amid the rubble and smashed buildings, it's not unusual to see a single stranded house, often half-demolished, glowing from within at night. Indeed, an occupied home: with a family watching television, people cooking and eating dinner, kids doing homework. These little islands of stubbornness (Wounded justice? Greed? Denial?) float there for a few days before finally, through coercion or persuasion, the electricity is cut, the tenants are moved out and the men with sledgehammers descend.[43]

The quotation above, together with the haunting images from Greg Girard's photo essay book, *Shanghai Phantom,* captures well the typical Shanghai neighborhood in the final stage of demolition. During my fieldwork, I used to take long walks in the neighborhoods near Xintiandi that were slated for demolition. Sometimes I found myself in a no-man's-land, surrounded by debris, piles of garbage, and skeletons of shikumen houses without roofs or walls. Occasionally, I could spot old newspapers, toys, and pieces of furniture that told stories about the families who had lived in these houses. I could also see some old trees standing in the rubble, telling the age of the neighborhood, and the lavish green leaves, full of life, struck a sharp contrast with the surrounding ruins. Other times, I found I was not alone. Some shikumen doors were still intact, and in the second-floor windows of the houses, I could see light and people still living in these half-demolished buildings. I also often found myself being watched by migrant workers doing demolition and recycling. Squatting families, migrant recyclers, and demolition crews are the common types one encounters in a typical Shanghai neighborhood being demolished. This section discusses residential relocation and displacement taking place alongside preservation.

The Legalization of Forced Demolition

Demolition and residential displacement are contentious issues for urban renewal, but few observers have noted that forced demolition in Chinese cities has been made legal through a number of government policies. The legalization of demolition without residents' consent is no less crucial than housing and land reforms in explaining the speed of urban destruction and renewal taking place in China. This section will examine the laws and policies that have shaped practices of demolition, residential relocation, and compensation.

The 1991 Demolition Regulation guaranteed local governments the authority and power to issue demolition permits without seeking residents' consent and to enforce demolition in disputed cases.[44] Households were compensated according to the number of officially registered individuals—that is, only the family members with urban registration. Residents without urban registration, even if they had lived in their houses for decades, could not be compensated. Tenants of public housing were also not eligible for compensation. In cases in which disagreements occurred, the regulation stated that "residents can appeal to the People's Court, but demolition should not be delayed during the appeal if residents are provided some form of compensation or temporary housing" (article 14). If the People's Court ordered developers to proceed with demolition but residents refused to be removed, then forced demolition (*qiangzhi chaiqian*) could be carried out (article 15). Soon after the central government drafted this regulation, the Shanghai city government followed suit and drafted a local version, which specified the role of city and district governments as being to persuade residents to be relocated for the "needs of city construction."[45] By legalizing forced demolition, these regulations paved the way for large-scale urban renewal programs.

Mass demolitions and evictions throughout the 1990s resulted in widespread resistance against urban renewal. In response, the State Council revised the Demolition Regulation in 2001, loosening the requirements for compensation eligibility and tightening control over demolition.[46] Developers are now required to show evidence of sufficient relocation funds in order to obtain a demolition permit. The revised regulation expanded compensation coverage to nonregistered individuals and public housing tenants.

However, the power imbalance remains unchanged, as no consultation with residents is yet required and housing authorities can still carry out forced demolition. The 2001 regulation also encouraged developers to provide evicted residents with monetary compensation, radically departing from the previous regulation's stipulation of on-site rehousing. The amount of monetary compensation is calculated according to the size and assessed price of demolished houses. The assessed price is often far lower than actual market prices, and what is more controversial is that the increasing value of central city land is not taken into account in the calculations. Invoking the public ownership of urban land, local governments and developers often claim that residents have no entitlement to compensation for the requisitioned land, thus ignoring the actual land-use rights of residents. In most cases, former inner-city residents have to relocate to urban peripheries, as the compensation is not sufficient to allow them to purchase flats in the more expensive areas where they used to live.

The Negotiations

The glamour of the space of conspicuous consumption at Xintiandi is multiplied when contrasted with the poor neighborhoods nearby. Across Taicang Road, the northern boundary of Xintiandi, was a cluster of old shikumen houses scheduled to be pulled down (see fig. 4.6). This was part of the next phase of the Taipingqiao project. In the summer of 2005, about

FIGURE 4.6. The neighborhood near Xintiandi being demolished, 2006. Photograph by the author.

three hundred families refused to accept the compensation offered by Shui On to resettle elsewhere. A year later, in the summer of 2006, only thirty families were still remaining. The remaining families were those with fewer resources and special needs. To oust these residents, demolition companies tore down most of the empty buildings and left construction debris uncollected on the ground. On some occasions, water and electricity supplies were cut off. The families had to live amidst this environment of dirt, noise, and waste. And just across the street they could see the fancy shops and wealthy customers at Xintiandi.

The negotiation process for relocation compensation in China is an informal but coercive one. First of all, developers in general do not engage in any dialogue with the local community. For example, according to the agreement reached between the Luwan district government and Shui On, it is the district government's responsibility to relocate residents. Shui On hired specialized demolition companies (*chaiqian gongsi*) to clear the site. The demolition companies were paid a lump sum by Shui On, which covered compensation for residents and demolition costs. Second, the negotiation between the district government and residents was an informal process, carried out on an ad hoc basis. Together with monetary compensation, the Luwan district government used a combination of other incentives to persuade residents to move out, such as giving job offers to certain family members, providing ready apartment units in exchange for the current ones, or offering retirement pensions and medical insurance for elderly family members. Specific terms were negotiated according to each family's needs, and resettlement plans varied case by case.[47] Third, although the negotiation with residents was a flexible and informal process, it was also a coercive one. If a family had members working in the public sector—for example, in government branches, work units, or schools—the Luwan district government would put pressure on these public employees, asking them to persuade their families to move out. The remaining thirty families across the street from Xintiandi were forcibly removed by December 2006. The final deadline was decided by the municipal government for the construction of a new subway line in the area, as a part of Shanghai's ambitious mass transit program.[48]

The unfair compensation is the single most important factor explaining why some families have refused to move. In the beginning of the redevelopment at Xintiandi, relocated families were compensated an average of $15,600. This was considered a good deal in 1997, and many families were content to take the monetary compensation and left. However, real estate prices in Shanghai skyrocketed in the next few years. Although the compensation was raised to $20,000, it was far from enough to purchase an apartment unit in the city. The remaining families at Xintiandi were mostly lower-income residents living in extremely crowded conditions. Since the calculation of compensation is based on living area (i.e., square meters) instead of number of residents, it was impossible for these families to buy an apartment in the city that was large enough to accommodate all family members. The families negotiated with the local government for on-site relocation.[49] Some residents I interviewed expressed their concerns regarding the redevelopment and compensation:

My family has lived here for three generations. Before the Liberation (1949), my grandfather bought the house. I have the contract. I don't want to live in the suburbs. There are no hospitals. It takes hours to get to the city and see a doctor by bus. (Resident A, a man in his fifties)

The compensation by living area is unfair. Most families here are big families squeezing into small apartments. The compensation should be based on counting people, not square meters . . . the government and developers don't talk to us directly. We can only negotiate with demolition companies. They are thugs. Sometimes they beat people up and break our windows. We don't do protests and demonstrations, because police will arrest us. But we will stay till the last minute. (Resident B, a woman in her sixties)

Now I'm unemployed. But I can still make a living here in the city center by collecting bottles and cans for recycling. Each makes 5 cents, and I don't starve. What can I do in the suburbs? We don't want to move elsewhere. We don't want compensation. We want a flat in those high-rises after redevelopment. (Resident C, a young woman in her early thirties)

Vincent Lo lives just across the street. But he never paid a visit to us. He built a park, but not for us. There are always concerts and all kinds of events, but we can't afford a ticket. And they block the roads to the park when there are events. . . . The shikumen houses preserved at Xintiandi are not real ones. They're expensive shops for the rich people. These [pointing to the neighborhood where he lives] are real shikumen. (Resident D, a man in his mid-forties)

The rage and discontent of residents focus on unfair compensation, forced demolition, poor infrastructure in suburbs where cheaper apartments are available, and the increasing income gap between the rich and the poor. For these residents, the polished shikumen at Xintiandi just across the street are a constant reminder of this increasing inequality. The economic profit from the historical preservation of shikumen is captured only by private business and local governments. Neighborhood residents have to bear the cost of the redevelopment.

Housing Rights Activism

Overall, incidents of housing activism in Shanghai have increased over the course of urban renewal as residents have begun to combine various tactics to fight for their rights.[50] The combination of a nonelectoral political system and a booming property market has led to new forms of housing activism in Shanghai. Instead of street actions and direct confrontations, residents tend to use other, more subtle tactics in their resistance. Some residents register extra family members and build extensions to gain better compensation; others mobilize the media to bring attention to their cause; still others engage in "rightful resistance" by framing their struggles in terms of legal rights.[51]

A small group of housing activists has emerged in Shanghai, most of them lawyers advising residents who have lost their homes on how to negotiate with the government for fair compensation. However, as the state does not tolerate organized demonstrations for fear of social instability, many leading activists have been persecuted by the government. Zheng Enchong, a lawyer in Shanghai, had his law license revoked in 2001 and was sentenced to a three-year jail term in 2003. He was charged with "revealing state secrets" after communicating with human rights organizations abroad about housing demolition in China. Zheng Enchong's sentence sent a reminder to other lawyers about the risks of representing demolition cases. Organized street protests are generally less successful, as organizers must first obtain authorization from the government to stage a legal protest. Many organizers are jailed when applying for authorization, and the police are quick to arrest and disperse protesters. Mass petitioning to the central government in Beijing is equally unsuccessful, as petitioners are often stopped by government security on their way to Beijing and then sent back. Increasingly, residents file lawsuits in local People's Courts, despite the fact that the courts are often not independent from the government.

Many residents try to delay construction efforts by standoff, simply staying in their apartments and refusing to leave even when demolition crews arrive, thus becoming so-called *dingzihu* (nail households). *Dingzihu* refuse to be evicted even after courts' final decisions. Some *dingzihu* also register extra family members and build extensions to their houses in order to negotiate for better compensation. The Internet has become a powerful medium for residents to communicate with one another, to seek legal advice, and to get their stories out. Compared with the tight censorship over conventional media, the government has less control over the content circulated on the Internet. Stories, photos, and even live videos of forced demolitions can be easily found online. Numerous websites offering legal services to evicted residents have been created in recent years. Even with the risks of defending demolition cases, an increasing number of lawyers are now more willing to take such cases, partly impelled by a sense of justice, but also partly driven by the lucrative market for demolition lawsuits.

Changing State Responses

Housing activism, although rarely consisting of direct confrontations, has nevertheless led to significant changes in state responses. In 2003, the new administration led by Hu Jintao and Wen Jiabao called for "building a

harmonious society" and issued a series of social policies in an attempt
to address the grievances of the urban poor. Relocation of displaced residents was listed at the top of the policy agenda. The central government
issued an "Urgent Notice" in 2003, instructing local governments to monitor demolition to ensure social stability and quell unrest. Although the
notice did not prohibit forced demolition, it urged local governments to
regulate forced demolition by private companies, which had been viewed
as the most contentious issue stirring housing activism and social unrest.
The notice also, for the first time, emphasized "the interests of the people"
over "the speed of urban construction."[52]

One year later, the central government issued another notice freezing
all large-scale demolition projects except for infrastructure construction.[53]
The 2004 notice banned "barbaric demolition" practices and ordered local governments to sever their ties with demolition companies. The most
important change was the endorsement of standardized legal procedures
to replace arbitrary mediation in resolving demolition disputes. In 2005,
Shanghai ratified a bylaw prompted by the 2004 notice that required demolition companies to secure at least 70 percent of relocation housing
prior to demolition, stop ad hoc negotiations, and apply transparent and
standardized procedures for compensating families.

In 2007, the central government passed the landmark Property Rights
Law, which has had significant implications for housing rights. The new
Property Rights Law contradicts the earlier demolition regulations, as
those regulations had legalized forced demolition of private property. At
the time of writing, there have been petitions from lawyers in Shanghai to
Prime Minister Wen Jiabao, pointing out the contradiction in the two sets
of laws and requesting that the legislative council abolish the preexisting
regulations and immediately put a stop to forced demolition.[54]

In 2009, for the first time, the Shanghai city government passed a policy
requiring developers to seek residents' consent before demolition.[55] According to the policy, before any demolition and neighborhood renewal
take place, developers should first seek residents' agreement to the demolition and then discuss relocation and compensation plans with them.
For demolition to take place, developers should have consent from the
majority of residents. In addition to the conventional monetary compensation and relocation to suburbs, the government encourages nearby
relocation—resettling the displaced not far from where they had lived.
Although many crucial details are left unspecified in the document, such
as the percentage of residents whose consent should be obtained, this
is nevertheless a radical step in China, since it is the first time that the

government has showed willingness to consult with residents regarding urban renewal. These changing state responses from 2003 to the present reflect the extra-electoral opportunities available to residents to fight for housing rights and make new claims to their city.

Beijing Preservation

Historical preservation and redevelopment in Beijing exhibit dynamics similar to those in Shanghai. However, a discussion on Beijing preservation is nevertheless necessary in order to fully explore the complexity of urban preservation in China. Unlike the much-Westernized Shanghai, Beijing is an ancient Chinese capital, and therefore it takes different efforts to reinvent the city's historic architecture and to market it to today's consumer culture.

A Tale of Two Cities

Urban preservation and redevelopment in Beijing since the 1990s have taken a path similar to that in Shanghai. In 1990, the city government began the Old and Dilapidated Housing Renewal Program, declaring a goal of renewing three million square meters of old housing stock by 2005, in plenty of time for the Olympics. As in Shanghai, the city and district governments in Beijing offered various incentives to developers to partake in the urban renewal, and a large proportion of the profit was channeled to the private sector. In the process of urban renewal, historic buildings and neighborhoods vanished, and millions of residents were relocated from the inner city to the urban periphery. As urban destruction in Beijing sparked sharp criticism internationally, and with the Olympics quickly approaching, the city government passed a number of conservation plans in the early 2000s to demonstrate its determination to preserve historic buildings and to stage a "Humanistic Olympics." As in Shanghai, the repertoire of urban preservation in Beijing has become increasingly ambitious, expanding from monuments and individual buildings to entire preservation districts. In 2001, the city designated twenty-five historical preservation areas; however, just as in Shanghai, the designation did not entail any specific measures of preservation, and both developers and governments frequently ignore zoning regulations. In the 1990s, in spite of opposition from all fronts, Xicheng district government built Financial

FIGURE 4.7. Hutongs being demolished, Beijing, 2008. Photograph by the author.

Street on 103 hectares of land within the Second Ring Road, razing hundreds of historical hutongs. Soon other district governments followed suit to compete, such as the notorious Oriental Plaza project on Chang'An Avenue in Dongcheng district and the International Financial Center in Xuanwu district.

In spite of the similar issues facing urban preservation in the two cities, Beijing, after all, is a very different city from Shanghai, and historical preservation in Beijing has its own problems and dilemmas. Beijing has a much longer history than Shanghai and, therefore, many more layers of a historic built environment and architectural heritage. Unlike historic architecture in Shanghai, which is mostly modern and Western, historic architecture in Beijing is mostly Chinese. Hutongs and courtyards, the traditional residential forms in Beijing, have been the focus of its preservation debate. And indeed, Beijing's hutongs are vanishing at an alarming rate (see fig. 4.7). In 1949 there were about 6,074 hutongs in Beijing, but the number shrank to 1,572 in 2005.[56] Among the remaining hutongs, only 671 are within designated protection areas, while about 900 are outside these zones and are under constant threat of demolition. In Shanghai, historic architecture from the colonial era can be easily repackaged for today's consumer culture, while in Beijing, the centuries-old Chinese hutongs are harder to reinvent.

Some argue that Beijing's hutongs are too old to be renovated for modern living—many hutong neighborhoods are overcrowded and lack basic amenities. Some attribute the loss of hutongs to the weak enforcement of zoning laws by city authorities, who often prioritize real estate development over preservation. Yet others see the massive construction programs for the 2008 Olympics as the main factor accounting for the disappearance of hutongs. However, all these constraints faced by Beijing are also present in Shanghai. The physical condition of shikumen houses in Shanghai by the 1990s was as fragile as that of hutongs in Beijing. In Shanghai, the enforcement of zoning laws is far from sufficient, and private developers frequently "break through" zoning regulations to tear down the old and build the new. Also, Shanghai has its own mega-event, the 2010 World Expo, and the city has initiated a massive construction program across the Huangpu River to prepare for it. The scale of the construction for the World Expo is no less grand than that undertaken for the Beijing Olympics. Facing similar constraints, why has Shanghai been better able to "preserve" or utilize its historical buildings, while Beijing has had a hard time doing so?

The answer lies in the different kinds of historical buildings in these two cities and the different marketability associated with them. Historical preservation is always easier in Shanghai than in Beijing because Shanghai is modern and its "historic buildings" are mostly structures built in the early twentieth century. These buildings are mostly examples of Western architecture, such as the neoclassical buildings on the Bund, which can be easily framed as a symbol of Shanghai's cosmopolitan past. In contrast, hutongs and courtyard houses in Beijing have no Western linkages and cannot be marketed in the same fashion as the colonial architecture in Shanghai. In addition, hutongs are vernacular residential structures and cannot be compared to grand imperial architecture such as the Forbidden City, which is well protected. This in-between status of hutongs—neither Western enough nor imperial enough—has confounded municipal planners and officials in search of new ways to rebrand them. Government officials and private developers in Beijing for a long time could not see any possibility of making a profit by preserving hutongs, and as a result, most hutongs were "let go" during the urban renewal.

Only as the Olympics were approaching were the charms and "Chineseness" of hutongs and courtyard houses "rediscovered" by foreign expatriates seeking the authentic Beijing experience. Some courtyard houses have been converted into multimillion-dollar mansions, and hutong living, like the shikumen chic in Shanghai, has become popular among young and wealthy urbanites in Beijing.

Hutong Chic

In the 1980s, architect Wu Liangyong took his research team from Tsinghua University to Nanluoguxiang—an inner-city area near Drum Tower and Bell Tower with a large concentration of courtyards dating back to the Yuan dynasty—to experiment with the idea of "organic renewal." Wu's pilot preservation project in Ju'er Hutong is widely regarded as a success and won many prestigious international awards. Instead of clearing out the entire neighborhood, the architects saved what could be saved and built similar-looking buildings to replace those that were truly hopeless. But Wu and his team would not have predicted the state of the neighborhood twenty years later. The relatively well-protected hutongs and courtyard houses—already a rarity in Beijing—have turned Nanluoguxiang into an epicenter of gentrification. Private investors spend millions of dollars on renovating old courtyard houses and turning them into luxury residences, private clubs, galleries, and upscale restaurants. Western tourists stroll up and down the alleys in Nanluoguxiang trying to find traces of the authentic Beijing.

Just like loft living in the West, "hutong living" has become a new fashion statement among foreign expatriates and wealthy Chinese urbanites. Many foreigners have rented hutong houses without modern infrastructure to experience authentic hutong living. In spite of inconveniences such as poor heating and lack of privacy, some foreigners still prefer a hutong residence over fancy villas in Shunyi (an upscale suburb with many gated communities). Others with more capital have invested handsome amounts in buying and remodeling courtyard houses. Expat magazines in Beijing frequently feature articles on how to renovate courtyard houses and publish photos of completely remodeled ultramodern courtyard mansions with their proud new owners—mostly young couples working in the media, design, law, or other high-paid professions. In March 2007, a courtyard house of three thousand square meters in the popular Houhai area was sold to a Russian buyer for 110 million RMB, which is the largest courtyard purchase in Beijing to this day.

Realizing the increasing demand from foreigners for an authentic Beijing experience, a significant number of Chinese and foreign entrepreneurs have emerged to fill the need. They have bought and refurbished courtyard houses, turning them into boutique hotels catering to foreign tourists. A quick Internet search can instantly lead to dozens of links for hutong hotels in Beijing, most of them having appeared just a few months before the Olympics. Although the new interest in hutong living has helped to save hutong neighbourhoods from demolition and decay, gentrification has posed a new threat to the vanishing hutongs. As wealthy residents move into their hutong mansions with private garages, residential density declines, and streets become empty.

Hutong chic emerged at a unique juncture of time and space—the period right before the Olympics, as Beijing was going through a quick makeover, with massive construction of modern buildings, an increasing foreign population, and diminishing traditional urban forms. As high-rise gated communities quickly took over the city, the rarity of low-rise hutong houses became attractive to thrill-seeking, fashion-conscious Chinese and foreign urbanites in Beijing. Although the fetish of hutong in a way raised awareness of the cultural value of architectural heritage, the fast gentrification of hutong neighbourhoods has also redefined the meaning of the hutong, changing it from a common residential form in old Beijing to a symbol of taste, sophistication, and conspicuous consumption.

The New "Old" Chinese City

> Like the steam engine, preservation is an "invention," in fact it is part of the repertoire of inventions that define modernization. The past is only an issue when the future is being constructed. . . . Preservation is an integral part of modernization.[57]

Just as the concept of heritage (*patrimoine*) was invented in the aftermath of the French Revolution, urban preservation in China was invented in the traumatic period of demolition and urban renewal in the 1990s. Until then there was little effort at preservation, and old buildings were preserved either through lack of resources to demolish or through benign neglect. Beginning in the 1990s, as historic architecture and neighborhoods began to disappear during government-sponsored urban renewal, there emerged a strong preservation discourse lamenting the loss of history and cultural heritage.

However, as I have shown in this chapter, Chinese preservation quickly deviated from the goal of protecting cultural heritage per se and instead has become a modernist project of remaking a cosmopolitan urban landscape, driven primarily by political and economic interests. International architects, acting as symbolic analysts, are actively involved in many high-profile preservation-based property developments. The government used preservation legislation in order to pacify criticism of urban renewal and to regain legitimacy, while private businesses have rediscovered the economic value of old buildings and engaged in symbolic preservation as a means of redevelopment. As Ackbar Abbas commented, urban preservation in Shanghai is "motivated by anticipations of a new Shanghai that will rival the old rather than by tender feelings for the old."[58]

Urban preservation in post-1990s China has become a new strategy for city promotion. Unlike preservation that values social history and local culture, Chinese preservation commodifies history and wipes out preexisting place-based social networks. Unlike preservation that rejects development, Chinese preservation celebrates development and urban renewal. Unlike preservation that cherishes the past, Chinese preservation uses the past only to embrace the present and project the future. From colonial villas and shikumen houses in Shanghai, to courtyards and hutongs in Beijing, renovating old buildings into posh properties has become the next new thing for place making.

This chapter has analyzed how old shikumen houses that were lower-middle-class dwellings have been transformed by global and local actors into a modern space for conspicuous consumption. In the arena of preservation and redevelopment, the power relationship in the governing urban regime in Shanghai is far more complex than the "strong public—weak private—no community" model, as suggested by previous studies.[59] This chapter has shown that international architecture firms, the media, and local universities are all part of the growth machine. Among these actors, international architecture firms have played a crucial role in creating new hybrid spaces in postindustrial Shanghai. These firms have "educated" private developers on how to profit from historic buildings and how to create an urban spectacle by mixing the old with the new. Moreover, although private business has a limited impact on urban governance in general, a handful of business elites with strong connections to the local government can have a tremendous impact on the direction, pace, and magnitude of urban development. Private developers especially have great autonomy in determining the spatial design of their projects. Once a contract for development is signed, conjuring an image for the project is entirely left to the developers. Last, although residents are not yet formally organized to make an impact on urban governance, informal resistance has significantly changed the pace of urban development and forced the state to make more accommodating relocation policies. If there is a governing urban regime in the making in Shanghai, it might be best described as an informal project-based coalition of international and domestic business, governmental, professional, and cultural elites under constant challenge from community residents.

Triggered by Xintiandi's success, Shanghai's urban development policies have shifted from demolition to preservation. The policy shift is the result of multiple structural forces at the global, national, and urban levels working through the preexisting local built environment. At the global level, Shanghai has increasingly integrated itself into the world economy, and a large amount of investment capital from overseas is poured into the city's real estate sector. At the national level, the Open Door policy, housing reform, and land reform have provided institutional support for real estate development. The decentralization of power from the central government has provided great freedom for local governments to implement entrepreneurial development policies. At the urban level, business service functions take precedence over manufacturing, and inner-city Shanghai has entered into a postindustrial age. Historical preservation is a new strategy employed by local governments to stimulate tourism and consumption. The local specific factors in this case are the available stock of historic buildings that can be recycled as symbols of Shanghai's cosmopolitan past.

The comparison of Shanghai and Beijing illustrates that Western and colonial architecture is much easier to get preserved, because it is often interpreted as a symbol of globalism and cosmopolitanism, while non-Western vernacular architecture, such as hutongs, has been largely ignored and destroyed, as municipal planners, government officials, and private developers could not easily relate it to any globalist appeals. Only recently, as hutong living has become chic among the upper class and foreign expatriates in Beijing, have courtyard houses become objects for preservation. These motivations and operations of Chinese preservation show that historic architecture has to pay back in order to be worthy of preservation.

The past is a moving target. As Rem Koolhaas and his research team observed, the interval between the object and the moment of its preservation has shrunk from two millennia to mere decades.[60] It is only a matter of time before buildings from the more recent past, such as urban factories and workers' villages, will be "rediscovered" and will get "pre-served." Historian Jeffrey Wasserstrom also predicted, in his ten theses about twenty-first-century Shanghai, that the treaty port past would not be the only one that continued to shape Shanghai's future, and soon there would be nostalgic fascination with more recent pasts such as the Maoist 1950s or even the post-Maoist 1980s.[61] But for now, in the first decade of the twenty-first century, the past that clearly matters the most for urban pres-ervation in Shanghai is not the communist past but the colonial past. In Beijing, similarly, communist-era architecture and buildings have received little attention, and most preservation efforts have focused on the ancient dynastic Chinese past and the republican era of modernization. The prag-matic nature of urban preservation has led to a narrow interpretation of the past. History is simplified to serve a range of political and economic purposes. The creative reconstruction of a particular past, by international architects, developers, and government officials, plays a crucial role in the making of Chinese global cities by creating a hybrid, cosmopolitan urban landscape. Historical preservation plays the same role of creating an urban spectacle as the construction of architectural megaprojects designed by global architects, as in the cases of SOHO China and the Olympic Stadium.

In 2008, ten years after Xintiandi was conceived, the American archi-tect Ben Wood, who supervised the preservation there, was working with SOHO China to replicate the same concept of a Disneyfied historic down-town in the Qianmen area of Beijing, turning the century-old neighbor-hood into yet another commodified built environment of nostalgia and hyperconsumption. Historical preservation in China provides an intrigu-ing lens through which observe the hybrid blending of the past and the future, the old and the new, executed by public-private coalitions and in-ternational architects in the project of global city formation.

Olympic Spectacles, Critical Architecture, and New State Spaces

Architecture is a major vehicle with which to negotiate national identity and express national ambitions. In general, deciding upon the right architectural form for large-scale state projects, such as parliament buildings, national libraries, and museums, has always been a contested issue. In the past, national elites searched for a national form that incorporated indigenous architectural elements to express distinctive national identities.[1] In the age of globalization, however, state politicians and bureaucrats have increasingly adopted a global architectural language to rebrand their cities and nations. The National Stadium for the 2008 Beijing Olympics is an example of this. The National Stadium was the highest-profile architectural project among the thirty-one stadiums prepared for the Olympics. With eighty thousand permanent spectator seats and another eleven thousand temporary seats, the National Stadium was the center stage for the Olympic spectacle. Through an international competition, the central and city governments chose Swiss architects Jacques Herzog and Pierre de Meuron as the chief designers. The stadium design was dubbed the Bird's Nest, as its gridlike steel structures resemble a bird's nest with interwoven twigs (see fig. 5.1). The choice of two laureates of the Pritzker Prize, the most prestigious prize in architecture, reveals the ambitions among territorial elites to demonstrate China's rise as an eminent economic and political power on the world stage.

This chapter examines the relationship between the state and transnational architectural production by delving into the controversies surrounding the design and construction of the Bird's Nest. The year 2008 saw a surge of academic publications on the Beijing Olympics, addressing a

FIGURE 5.1. The Bird's Nest, Beijing, August 2008. Photograph by the author.

wide range of questions, from Olympic media, gender, sports, and politics to the variegated representations of and responses to the Games.[2] In addition, journalists' reports on the Beijing Games dominated the headlines of major world newspapers in the months before and after the Games, covering topics from human rights and the environment to city development and architecture. The Bird's Nest and the Water Cube (the National Swimming Center) have become familiar images through this saturated reporting on Olympic Beijing. Taking account of recent publications on the Beijing Olympics (2008–10), this chapter examines why the Chinese state chose global architecture to represent the nation and what the consequences of this rebranding are.

The decision to use Herzog and de Meuron's design was first challenged by local cultural conservatives who were highly critical of commissioning foreign architects to design major state projects. To gather popular support and gain legitimacy, the government responded to these criticisms by stopping construction and having the stadium's design revised to minimize the cost. However, the government was then severely criticized by cultural liberals who challenged the inconsistent and nontransparent decision-making process. The Bird's Nest debate, however, should not be interpreted only as a clash between conservatives and liberals. It is a debate with nationalistic elements, but at the same time it also raises questions about government accountability and undemocratic decision making. And ultimately, it is a debate about identity—that is, what it means to be contemporary Chinese. These themes will be examined in the first part of the chapter. In the second part of the chapter, I situate the Bird's Nest debate in the development of architectural criticism in China by examining how architectural debates have shifted from questioning the nationality of architects, budgets, and aesthetics to more central themes such as architectural criticality. Taken together, these investigations will present Olympic Beijing as a contested space produced by the fusion of Chinese state sponsorship and global architectural flows, and correct some of the biases in the current academic and journalistic narrative that either romanticizes or demonizes the Beijing Olympics.[3]

Olympic Beijing

On August 8, 2008, the day of the opening ceremony of the Beijing Olympics, the streets in Beijing were unusually quiet. The traffic in the most hectic section of the CBD was exceptionally smooth, owing to a new regulation that magically reduced the city's daily traffic by half (see fig. 5.2). Shops and department stores were almost empty of customers. Many college students and migrant workers, major components of the population of this metropolis of seventeen million, had left the city since the beginning of summer—some voluntarily and some not. Walking down the streets of Beijing on this symbolic day, one could hardly feel the celebratory atmosphere of a long-awaited mega-event. Instead, police vehicles, security guards, and surveillance cameras were placed on every street corner, bridge, and highway overpass. The surveillance and police presence were especially visible in sensitive hot spots such as Tiananmen Square, the Olympic venues, and the embassy area, with its large foreign population. After the botched torch relay and the Tibetan unrest earlier in the year, the Chinese authorities did not want to take any chances and were determined to stage a "safe" Olympics at any cost. The various security measures taken to ensure a successful opening ceremony significantly altered how the capital city looked and felt.

The "fortressification" of the city struck a sharp contrast to the hyper-production of Olympic programming in the national media. The Olympic

FIGURE 5.2. Jianguomen Boulevard, central business district, Beijing, August 2008. Photograph by the author.

programming filling the air around the clock testified that the Beijing Olympics were a media event, and among all the media extravaganzas, the most extravagant was the opening ceremony directed by Zhang Yimou. The government summoned this accomplished Chinese director to stage a spectacular, never-before-seen opening ceremony for one billion domestic viewers and a much larger global audience. With high-tech coordination of sounds, lights, and well-rehearsed movements by human-pixel performers, the few seconds at the beginning of the ceremony assured spectators that this would be a showcase of the manpower, wealth, and extravagance that China now could afford to deploy to impress the world. The ceremony continued with an innovative fireworks show titled "Historical Footprints," directed by Cai Quoqiang, a rising-star artist whose Guggenheim exhibition drew a record number of visitors in New York in 2008. Fireworks in the shape of human footprints illuminated historic architecture along Beijing's central axis—the Forbidden City, Tiananmen Square, Qianmen—and arrived above the Bird's Nest.

Zhang Yimou's production of the Olympic pageantry unfolded around one central theme—emphasizing the splendor of Chinese culture and downplaying messy politics. The performance began with a display of symbols of ancient Chinese civilization—the four great inventions of gun-powder, the compass, the printing press, and paper—and then continued with other Chinese cultural icons. The modern replaced the traditional as Lang Lang, the world-renowned young pianist, took the central stage. Lang Lang is a symbol of the new China, a country that is eager to be portrayed not only as an economic powerhouse but also as a cultural giant. As Lang Lang filled the stadium with his fluent, strong, and confident playing, thousands of performers dressed in futuristic green costumes formed a human Bird's Nest around him. The enormous scale of the performance, along with the combination of blinking lights and Lang Lang's piano playing, brought an ecstasy to the stadium. The opening ceremony staged in the Bird's Nest showed the extraordinary capacity of the Chinese state, which was determined to use this sociopolitical ritual to demonstrate the rise of China as a geopolitical and cultural power on the world stage.

What are the urban legacies left by the 2008 Beijing Games? One of the sites for such investigations is the numerous state-sponsored mega-structures built in the eight years (2001–8) before the Olympics, such as the new subway lines, expressways, national stadiums, museums, libraries, and airports. I call these state-sponsored infrastructure and building projects "new state spaces."[4] I emphasize the word "new" and differentiate these spaces from the previous structures accommodating state functions, such as the "Ten Great Buildings" of the 1950s. These Olympic megastructures are new spaces because they were designed and built at breakneck speed in the years leading up to 2008. But more important, these spaces embody a new kind of transnational flow—that of architectural and design expertise—which was not seen, at least not to the same degree, in the socialist years. Can these new state spaces—articulated in the architectural language of modernity, transparency, and openness—entail possibilities for real political change? Or will these spaces simply become "state crafts" for the Party to legitimate and solidify its power? The following sections will examine these questions about architecture, state, and political change generated by the fusion of Chinese state sponsorship and transnational architectural design.

A National Bid for the Olympics

The commercial success of the Los Angeles Olympics in 1984 turned the Olympics into a highly profitable mega-event.[5] Owing to the Games' enormous potential for urban regeneration and image building, more and more cities around the world are showing great enthusiasm for hosting them, hoping to solve urban problems and boost growth in a relatively short period of time.[6] Recently, the list of cities bidding for the Olympics has included not only struggling postindustrial cities but also leading global cities such as Paris (2008 and 2012 bids), New York, and London (2012 bid). These cities view the Olympics as an opportunity to finance infrastructure projects with international money, instead of their own resources. By hosting the Games, top-tier global cities can further widen the gap between themselves and the rest.[7]

It is tempting at first glance to characterize Beijing's bid for the 2008 Olympics as a strategy by the Beijing city government to better position the city in the intensified interurban competition. However, an analysis of Beijing's bid and its preparations for the Olympics reveals that the 2008 Olympics involved much higher stakes. In addition to the tangible economic benefits to urban growth, the symbolic significance of hosting the Olympics is what drove the central government to support Beijing's bid. Similar to the Tokyo and Seoul Olympics for Japan and Korea, the Beijing Olympics were a coming-of-age event for China. They represented to the world China's rise as a new global power, backed by the dynamic Chinese economy and consolidated under the rule of the Communist Party.

The central government strongly influences urban politics in Beijing. The bidding process and the preparations for the Olympics were initiated and tightly monitored by the central government. In the late 1980s, the city government of Beijing was ordered by the central government to submit an official application for the 2000 Games. Beijing came tantalizingly close to winning the bid in 1993, losing to Sydney by only two votes in the last ballot. The central government was determined to bring the Olympics to China. In 1998, Beijing bid again for the 2008 Games. The Beijing 2008 Olympic Games Bid Committee (BOBICO) was established in September 1999. Its members included not only municipal officials but also high-ranking politicians from the State Council and national government agencies in charge of cultural affairs, sports, and urban planning. In August 2000, the International Olympic Committee (IOC) officially announced Beijing as a candidate city, along with Osaka, Istanbul, Toronto, and Paris.[8]

The BOBICO mobilized a wide range of public support for the bid. Zhang Yimou was appointed to direct a short video clip to promote Beijing's bid. The BOBICO also promised the IOC that it would provide state-of-the-art stadiums for the Games. Hundreds of local architects and planners drafted designs for thirty-two Olympic venues. In Beijing's *Olympic Candidature File,* 235 out of the 596 pages were devoted to explanations of stadium design and construction. Hundreds of cultural events and programs were organized during the bidding process. In February 2001, a delegation from the IOC visited Beijing. The delegates were highly impressed by the advanced preparations and rated Beijing's bid as "excellent."[9] Although Beijing fell far behind its rival cities in environmental protection and infrastructure, the strong political endorsement from both the city and central governments convinced the IOC that Beijing would deliver on its promises. On July 13, 2001, IOC president Juan Antonio Samaranch announced in Moscow that the host city of the 2008 Olympic Games was Beijing.[10]

Hosting the Olympics gave a major boost to economic development and urban construction in Beijing. As the host city, Beijing was entitled to receive a substantial amount of sales revenue from broadcasting rights and corporate sponsorship. Large domestic banks and corporations lined up to provide the capital to finance infrastructure projects. Olympics-related investment quickly improved transportation and telecommunications infrastructure, which the city had been desperately trying to upgrade. It added public amenities that the city had lacked before, such as sports stadiums and parks. The event also pushed the city government to put more effort into environmental protection.[11] In addition to these tangible benefits, hosting the Olympics also helped to build a new image of Beijing as a modern and international metropolis. The saturating media coverage before, during, and after the event definitely put Beijing under the global media spotlight.[12] The government's determination to create a new image of Beijing was reflected in the first official slogan of the 2008 Games: "New Olympics—New Beijing." Some questioned calling it the "new" Olympics, saying there was nothing wrong with the "old" Olympics, and the BOBICO revised it later into "Great Olympics—New Beijing." The government hoped that the unfolding Olympic legacy could attract global business investment and tourists to the city in the years following the Games.

In spite of these positive economic prospects, it was evident that the Olympics presented a huge challenge for Beijing's real estate market and social stability. Millions of urban homes were demolished in order to make space for Olympics-related construction. Urban residents were relocated to remote suburbs with poor infrastructure.[13] The pre-Olympics construction rush led to speculation in the real estate sector. Together with the tightening of the land supply by the government, this made real estate prices in Beijing skyrocket, becoming the highest in the country. There were widespread concerns that the real estate market would crash in the post-Olympics years, and it did happen, albeit only briefly, in the midst of the global recession in 2008. Moreover, the location of the Olympic Park in the well-developed north side further widened spatial inequality within the city. Concentrated capital investment in Beijing also had an impact on the already unbalanced regional development in China, as Beijing pulled resources and investment from other regions. The central government's choice of Beijing as the host city sent a clear signal to Shanghai, the financial capital of China. Beijing's hosting of the Olympics has inevitably intensified the rivalry between the two cities. After Beijing's successful bid, Shanghai immediately secured the right to host the World Expo in 2010. The race between Beijing and Shanghai will further concentrate capital investment in these two cities, increasing the regional inequality between the two and the rest of the country.

The city government issued a series of strategic plans for the pre-Games preparations. In July 2002, the Beijing Organizing Committee for the Olympic Games (BOCOG) issued the *Olympic Action Plan.* The plan emphasized three themes—Green Olympics, High-Tech Olympics, and People's Olympics. According to the plan, the preparation period leading up to 2008 would be divided into three phases. The first phase, from December 2001 to June 2003, was for consolidation of supervisory organizations and preparation for facility construction. The second phase, from July 2003 to June 2006, would be the peak period of facility construction. In the third period, from June 2006 to July 2008, officials would reinspect facilities and make last-minute preparations for the Games. The plan also specified development goals in diverse fields such as environment, transportation, communication, and other types of civic infrastructure. The environmental improvement project was estimated to require an investment of $8.6 billion, in order to relocate manufacturing facilities outside the Fourth Ring Road, build gas pipes to reduce coal consumption, and construct three green belts around the city to improve air quality. The upgrading of the transportation infrastructure would require an investment of another $3.6 billion and would include the construction of the Sixth Ring Road, ten expressways, and seven subway lines, as well as the expansion of Beijing International Airport. To promote the "People's Olympics," historical preservation and the construction of cultural facilities were also proposed. Dozens of brand-new museums, libraries, and television station headquarters were built in the city. Twenty-five historical areas were identified as preservation zones. The total investment that would be required by all of the preparations was estimated to exceed $20 billion.[14]

The 2008 Olympics were no longer a sports event or even an urban regeneration effort. They were a national event and a symbolic showcase through which the central government of China intended to demonstrate to the world the country's economic achievements over the past three decades. Hosting a successful Olympics carried great weight for China as a whole. As Beijing was quickly building up momentum toward 2008 through various strategic plans and large-scale construction projects, the international design competition for the National Olympic Stadium took place.

Going for Global Architecture

In order to win the Olympic bid, the political elites associated with the BOCOG and the Beijing Municipal Planning Commission (BMPC) chose prime land on the north side of Beijing for the Olympic Park. The master plan was drafted by a prominent engineering firm—Sasaki & Associates from the United States. The Olympic Park is strategically located on the extension of the central axis of Beijing. The central axis is 7.8 kilometers in length, starting from Yongding Gate in the south and ending at Bell Tower in the north. All major landmarks of Beijing, such as the Forbidden City and Tiananmen Square, are located on this axis. In the new Olympic Green of 1,135 hectares, three major sports facilities—the National Stadium, the National Gymnasium, and the National Swimming Center—are separately located on either side of the axis.

From the start of the competition, the BMPC, the BOCOG, and the city government aimed for a prestigious international firm to design the stadium. In June 2002, the mayor of Beijing announced, "Beijing would gather the best architectural designs from the world for Olympic stadiums."[15] In October 2002, the city government and the BOCOG asked the BMPC to organize a competition of conceptual architectural designs for the stadium. The BMPC specified that the mission of the project was "constructing a large-scale stadium equal to the world's best practice" and that "the stadium design shall embody the new image of urban development in Beijing, and fully reflect the idea of Great Olympics—New Beijing."[16]

The overwhelming number of international design teams and jury members reflected the globalizing tendency of the political elites in the

BOCOG and the BMPC. The BMPC specified a set of prequalification requirements, such as prior experience in designing large-scale stadiums, such that only established international firms and a few large domestic design institutes could qualify to compete. The invited design firms included eight international firms, three joint ventures, and two Chinese design institutes. Among the thirteen jurors, six were international architects, including prominent figures such as Dominique Perrault, Rem Koolhaas, Jean Nouvel, and Kisho Kurosawa. The Chinese panel was composed of two officials from the BOCOG, one from the BMPC, and four senior engineering experts from the Chinese Academy of Sciences. None of the Chinese jurors were architects.

The BMPC listed few specific requirements for the conceptual design. However, it insisted that the stadium "shall have a retractable roof, with the configuration designed to fully reflect the characteristics of modern sports buildings."[17] The BMPC officials believed that "the stadium with a retractable roof will turn out to be a significant architectural legacy of the 2008 Olympics."[18] The retractable roof became the focus both for architects in their design process and for jurors in their evaluation. Specialist engineering firms were hired by architectural teams to design a safe and cost-effective roof. Experts carefully evaluated the feasibility of each team's roof design. However, all of these efforts turned out to be an exercise in futility, as the government later ordered the retractable roof removed to cut down the cost.

Although architectural competitions are still a new practice in China, the BMPC staged a professional international competition. The officials of the BMPC knew well that a widely publicized international design competition was no less important than the stadium itself in promoting the 2008 Olympics. On March 23–25, 2003, the thirteen-member international panel evaluated design proposals. The evaluation included a site visit, a presentation of technical details, a review of booklets, exhibition panels, and models, as well as discussions and analyses of the merits and demerits of each scheme. Herzog and de Meuron's design won eight votes out of thirteen, the highest among all proposals. The Bird's Nest was short-listed together with another two design schemes from the Beijing Institute of Architectural Design and Research (BIAD) and a joint venture of a Japanese design firm and the local Tsinghua University. As a largely symbolic gesture, the three short-listed design proposals went into a public exhibition for popular voting. Herzog and de Meuron's design had a thin margin of public votes over the other two.

Herzog and de Meuron's decision to enter China was triggered by Rem Koolhaas's winning of the CCTV project in Beijing in 2002. Herzog and de Meuron were also invited to the CCTV competition. However, they decided not to compete after learning about the poor protection of intellectual property rights and the unfair practices of design competitions in China.[19] In the winter of 2002, they received the news that Rem Koolhaas, their friend and rival, had won the design competition. They regretted the lost opportunity and believed that if they had participated, they would have won.[20]

For Herzog and de Meuron—two architects based in Basel, Switzerland—China was unfamiliar terrain. They sought advice from Uli Sigg, the former Swiss ambassador to China and a Chinese art collector. Uli Sigg recommended Ai Wei Wei as their local consultant. Ai Wei Wei is a well-established artist who returned to Beijing after a ten-year stay in New York. As the son of China's famous poet of the 1920s, Ai Qing, Ai Wei Wei had sufficient political capital to help Herzog and de Meuron navigate the complicated bureaucratic procedures and unpredictable domestic politics. Ai Wei Wei first found a local design partner for Herzog and de Meuron—the China Architecture and Design Group—to build a design consortium. He also turned out to be the most outspoken advocate for Herzog and de Meuron's design when the project was later caught in a culture war between liberals and conservatives. In April 2003, only six months after Herzog and de Meuron came to China, they were told that they had won the largest trophy—the commission to design the National Stadium.

Architect Stephan Marbach on Herzog and de Meuron's team, in an interview about his experience of working on the Bird's Nest, said,

> I participated from the beginning stage of the National Stadium. When we decided to bid, forty people back in Switzerland worked on the proposal. Then after we won the competition, the company sent three people to work in Beijing. I work in the Beijing office and fly back and forth between China and Switzerland. We now have about twenty staff here. Some are recruited locally in Beijing, but most are Germans and other Europeans, or graduates from Harvard and Yale. . . . In terms of profit, it's not a lot. We only get 6 percent as the design fee. But here in China you get big projects, and the scale and speed are amazing. A project that will take eighteen years in Switzerland takes eighteen months here to build. . . . Projects like this are not possible outside China. It's very difficult to build. It uses too much steel, and the price of steel is going up

now. Only in China it's possible to do work like this. . . . Now we also have four other projects in China, collaborating with Ai Wei Wei's studio.[21]

In the brief accompanying the conceptual design, Herzog and de Meuron described their design as "a collective vessel for the People's Olympics." They emphasized the pure shape of the stadium, with interwoven gridlike structures "producing dramatic effects." Referencing the Eiffel Tower, they claimed that the stadium would become "a unique historical landmark for the 2008 Olympics."[22] With an unusually exposed structure that mimics a bird's nest, the design delivered the most arresting visual impact of all the proposals, capturing the votes of both the international architects and the Chinese politicians on the jury. The BMPC praised the design highly, commenting that "the pure, simple and powerful building shape blends all into a harmonious whole" and that "the entire building gives a strong sense of dynamics and vigor."[23]

The proposed budget for the Bird's Nest was 3.89 billion RMB (roughly $550 million). Although this figure did not exceed the budget limit of 4 billion RMB set by the BMPC, it was well above the budget of the second-place design entry by BIAD, who proposed a modern stadium meeting all the Olympics' requirements for only 0.27 billion RMB, 7 percent of the budget proposed by Herzog and de Meuron. Obviously, compared with visual impact, the budget was only of secondary concern for the BMPC.

While the design competition was going on, another separate bidding process for ownership of the stadium took place. In August 2003, it was announced that a group of five firms led by CITIC (China International Trust and Investment Corporation), a large state bank, was the winner of the ownership tender. CITIC would invest 42 percent of the total construction cost, with the remaining 58 percent to be provided by the city government, represented by Beijing State-Owned Assets Management Corporation. The city government would also provide subsidies by reducing land-leasing fees and helping with demolition. CITIC and the city government registered the company—the National Stadium Ltd.—which has thirty years of usage rights to the stadium after the Olympic Games. The city government will not share profits for those thirty years, but then ownership of the stadium will revert to the city. In November 2003, a service agreement was signed between CITIC, the city government, and the Sino-Swiss design consortium. To keep up the momentum of the preparations for the Olympics, the BOCOG decided to start construction immediately.

In December 2003, while the architects were still working on preliminary design drawings, the construction of the National Stadium began.

The Bird's Nest Controversy

On July 30, 2004, in the Olympic Park in north Beijing, the construction site of the National Stadium was unusually quiet. Huge machines were lying on the ground. Workers had been ordered to take a two-month break. The construction of the stadium, which had started seven months earlier in December 2003, was suddenly stopped by order of the central government. The direct cause for stopping the construction was a petition submitted to the central government by a group of academicians from the Chinese Academy of Sciences. In the letter, the academicians criticized the stadium design for its "extravagance, huge costs, wasteful use of steel, engineering difficulty, and potential safety problems."[24] The central government responded to the petition by ordering a financial review of the project. The review's conclusion was that the design of the stadium would have to be revised in order to cut down construction costs.

In general, it is not uncommon to observe controversies regarding the form, function, and location of flagship architectural projects. The debates over the Bird's Nest, and a few previous state-sponsored projects in Beijing, however, are primarily centered on the nationality of the architects, along with aesthetics and cost.

Before going into analysis of these debates, it is also important to highlight the symbolic importance of Beijing. Shanghai predates Beijing in commissioning major public projects to international architects, such as the development of the Pudong financial district in the 1990s. But in Shanghai, commissioning high-profile public projects to foreign architects did not lead to controversies as seen in Beijing. The difference must be understood in relation to the status of the two cities within China, the interaction patterns between their municipal governments and the central government, the unique composition of the local intellectual community in each city, and the global penetration of the local architectural design markets. First, the status of Beijing as the capital of China significantly raises the stakes and symbolic importance of large-scale public projects in the city. Unlike the municipal projects in Shanghai, the national stadiums, museums, and libraries in Beijing are widely viewed as architectural icons symbolizing China in the twenty-first century and therefore can easily become subjects for debates and criticism. Second, in contrast to Shanghai, the decision-making process in Beijing is strongly influenced, regulated, and penetrated by the central government. In the case of the National Stadium, direct intervention from the central government became the target of criticism from cultural liberals. Third, there is a larger and more active intellectual community in Beijing than in Shanghai. The Chinese Academy of Sciences, major leading architectural journals, institutes, and publishing houses are all based in Beijing. The cultural elites affiliated with these institutions actively participated in the debates over the Bird's Nest. Last, the architectural design market in Beijing was less open to foreign competition than the market in Shanghai in the early 2000s, and therefore the decision to commission the National Stadium to foreign architects came as something of a shock to many local architects.

From 1998 to 2003, three large-scale public projects in Beijing were commissioned to international architects: the National Theater to Paul Andreu, the National Stadium to Herzog and de Meuron, and the CCTV building to Rem Koolhaas.[25] This led to a heated debate in the local architectural community. Wu Chen, the leading opponent and the son of architect Wu Liangyong of Tsinghua University, cynically called Beijing "the laboratory for foreign architects."[26] He saw the dominance of foreign architects in Chinese megaprojects as a new form of cultural colonialism. Wu Chen criticized the central government for providing too much political and financial support to foreign architects who use Chinese taxpayers' money for their avant-garde architectural experiments that could in no way be realized in their own countries. He argued that Chinese cities were losing their authentic character, becoming banal, homogenized cities similar to everywhere else in the world.[27] These opinions were widely shared among cultural conservatives, a group of Beijing-based architects and academics who strongly opposed commissioning state-sponsored projects to foreign architects. Many of the cultural conservatives are from an older generation of architects who designed many monumental state buildings in Beijing in the 1950s. They see the participation of international architects as a threat that endangers the development of modern Chinese architecture.

In July 2004, seven months after the stadium's groundbreaking, four senior members of the Chinese Academy of Sciences submitted a petition to Prime Minister Wen Jiabao. In the letter, the petitioners criticized the recent architectural trend in China for "ever bigger, newer, and foreign design," which they saw as leading to serious problems in safety and raising construction costs significantly. The petitioners criticized the design of the National Stadium, saying it "not only required an extraordinary use of steel, but also had potential problems in safety and stability." They wrote that such extravagant design was an unnecessary waste and risk and would damage the Olympic preparation efforts.[28] The central government accepted the petition promptly, called the construction to a halt, and requested a financial review of the stadium.

A similar petition, also by cultural conservatives, was submitted in 1998 protesting Paul Andreu's design of the National Theater.[29] Although that petition was on a much larger scale, mobilizing more than a hundred academy members, it was rejected by the central government. The central government saw the ultramodern design of the National Theater as a symbol showcasing China's progress, open-mindedness, and imagined political transparency. The project is also interpreted by critics as an attempt by Jiang Zemin (the Communist Party secretary until 2002) to leave a personal landmark in Tiananmen Square in the last year of his term.

However, the political climate in China has changed significantly since 1998. Domestic politics in 2004 were more favorable to cultural conservatives. Two major events happened around this time. In March 2003, Jiang Zemin stepped down as the general secretary of the Chinese Communist Party and was succeeded by two populist politicians—Hu Jintao as the president and Wen Jiabao as the prime minister. Compared with that of their predecessor, Hu and Wen's administration has expended more effort winning popular support, and they saw the Olympic preparations as a good political opportunity to mobilize such support. In July 2003, Wen Jiabao delivered a speech at a meeting of the State Council, declaring that Olympic preparations must avoid extravagance and pay more attention to cost saving. The city government of Beijing closely followed the new retrenchment policy. In July 2004, the mayor of Beijing announced three requirements guiding stadium construction: using existing stadiums and avoiding repetitive construction, reducing construction costs, and emphasizing post-Games usage.[30] The retrenchment policy provided a political opportunity for senior academicians to have their voices heard.

The second significant event that triggered the negative sentiments toward foreign architects was the collapse of a terminal at Charles de Gaulle International Airport in Paris in May 2004. In the accident, two Chinese passengers were killed. The airport terminal was designed by Paul Andreu, the same architect who designed the National Theater. The accident triggered a wide range of suspicions in Beijing regarding the safety of foreign-designed buildings, and it provided an immediate catalyst for the order to stop construction of the National Stadium.[31]

After a financial review by the central government, the original budget of $500 million was cut down to $325 million, and then to $290 million. According to an interview with Li Xinggang, the chief architect and local partner of Herzog and de Meuron, the budget cut was "like squeezing a wet towel—when the budget was reduced from $500 to $290 million, there's no water to squeeze anymore, and we had to cut features of the design."[32] A panel of domestic structural engineers made the final decision on the design change—removing the retractable roof. This saved an estimated fifteen thousand tons of steel and $50 million. Herzog and de Meuron were content with the design change, but they were not part of the decision-making process. Architect Stephan Marbach commented in an interview about their isolated position in the midst of the controversy:

> There were some meetings with the mayor and vice mayor of Beijing. Some Chinese experts were at the meetings. In the beginning, our revision was almost approved. But then the case was sent to the upper level, and more upper levels. In the end, we got the order that we need to take the ceiling off.

Herzog and de Meuron told a *New York Times* reporter later that the roof would have been an engineering triumph, but that without it, the overall form became more consistent and powerful.[33] CITIC initially complained about removing the roof, as it might affect the operation of the stadium in bad weather. However, CITIC did not insist on having the roof after the government adopted the new retrenchment policy. Although the government's decision did not spark strong opposition either from CITIC or from the architects, it became the focus of criticism from local cultural liberals who questioned the inconsistent and nontransparent decision-making process of the government.

The cultural liberals are a group of architects, artists, journalists, and academics in Beijing who embrace and collaborate with international architects. Many of them are from a younger generation, who have studied abroad and have extensive connections with international architecture firms, schools, and cultural institutions. They have played a crucial role in introducing international architects to China and helping them win design competitions. On August 20, 2004, approximately twenty prominent Beijing-based artists, art critics, and architects held a discussion forum about the new developments in the National Stadium project. The organizers intended the meeting to be a platform for this small circle of cultural elites to freely express their opinions on the government intervention in the construction of the National Stadium. Although the media were not present at the meeting, many of the opinions and speeches from the meeting were later widely circulated on the Internet and played an important role in guiding public opinion on the events surrounding the stadium's construction. The criticisms were mainly focused on three subjects: the unduly powerful lobby by senior academy members, the inconsistent and contradictory decision-making process of the central government, and the impact of that process on the development of contemporary Chinese architecture.

Some architects expressed concern over the negative impact the government's decision would have on China's architectural development. They saw the original retractable roof as an engineering triumph and a technological breakthrough. They compared it to early skyscrapers in New York and the Eiffel Tower in Paris. They argued that new architectural projects like the National Stadium "have posed new challenges to contemporary architectural development, and in the meantime are trying to offer possible solutions." They saw the revision of the design as a lost opportunity to experiment with new engineering technologies.

This professional concern was not shared by other cultural critics at the meeting, who were more aware of the larger issues that the government's intervention in the design revisions implied. For them, the event revealed the illegitimate dominance in urban planning by senior academicians. Some questioned the qualifications of the academicians who submitted the petition. Others called the act of the academicians "conservative, reactionary, backward-looking, and a kind of blind patriotism," and "not the proper way to get things done." For them, the petition was not about cost saving, technology, or the retractable roof but symbolized "the clash of old and new cultural forces." As critic Bao Pao said at the meeting,

> I was very excited when I heard the Bird's Nest won the competition. I wrote an article about it, calling it a "great historical moment." But when I read news that the construction was stopped, I felt this was a revival of old and evil forces, a very conservative force trying to kill the new culture. China is making a great leap that hasn't been seen since the Tang dynasty. The National Theater, the CCTV, and the National Stadium symbolize that China's architectural culture has become part of the international architectural movement, and it also shows the end of Big Roof, classical, and neoclassical architecture. But a few conservatives, the so-called "experts," are trying to block the new development.

The most frequently appearing theme in the discussion was the decision-making process of the government. Many saw the controversy as a result of the "system" (*tizhi*), namely, the current authoritarian decision-making process characterized by inconsistency and nontransparency. Some people questioned the government's act of cutting the costs of Olympic projects in order to gain popular support. As Ai Wei Wei argued, "If we only want to cut the costs, why bid for the Olympics and build the National Stadium at all? What the government is doing is quite self-contradicting." Others argued that "policy makers should be consistent and keep what they've promised." It was agreed by the group that "it is OK to cut costs, but it has to be based on scientific analyses, instead of ad hoc decisions." The various criticisms are well summarized in the following comment by Ai Wei Wei:

> The Bird's Nest is an event. I wonder why the decisions have to be made by a few academicians sending petitions to the central government. What happened in the process? Our society is not yet a democratic society. The decision-making process has many remnants from the feudal society. The petitioners do not reveal their names, and they don't tell the media what they wrote in the letter to the State Council. This is still the "black-box" way of doing things . . . when government officials make their decisions, what are the criteria, values, and standards? I think China must change the current decision-making process controlled by big powers instead of people.

For these liberal cultural elites, China cannot make progress without opening up. Economic reforms need to be accompanied by reform of the political system. Global competition and influences—both within architecture and beyond—can change ways of doing politics and redistribute power from the top down to the people.

The cultural liberals and conservatives held opposite positions regarding the use of foreign architects for the Olympic Stadium. But as anthropologist Susan Brownell noted, the debate over the Bird's Nest should not be reduced to a clear-cut conflict "between a conservative, nationalist old guard and innovative, open-minded future talent."[34] The analysis of the meeting memos and speeches above reveals the multifaceted themes in the Bird's Nest debate. From the side of the cultural conservatives, first, there was undoubtedly nationalistic resentment about letting foreign rather than Chinese architects design the Olympic Stadium. Most popular discussions in the mass media were framed along these lines, and the entry of international architects was often conceived as a threat. Second, there was also resentment about spending the state's revenue on Olympic projects that required huge budgets to build. Unlike other Olympics that mainly relied upon the private sector, the Beijing Olympics were primarily sponsored by the central and city governments. Critics called this a misuse of taxpayers' money and called for government accountability on spending. From the side of the cultural liberals, as represented by Ai Wei Wei, the revision of the design ordered from above by the government was another instance of unchallenged state power in contemporary China. What they were protesting against was not simply a stadium with or without a retractable roof. Rather, it was the "system" by which decisions were made in China. The fact that a petition, from a few experts, could stop construction exemplified the undemocratic nature of the Chinese polity. By questioning the legitimacy and expertise of the senior architects, and by embracing international design—no matter the cost—the cultural liberals were attacking the power structure and the status quo in architecture and beyond.

For both sides, the Bird's Nest debate also involved a questioning and discussion of what "contemporary Chinese architecture" or, more broadly, "contemporary Chinese" means. For some, Chinese people must be involved in the creation of anything contemporary Chinese, and in the case of the Bird's Nest, the architects should have been Chinese. Non-Chinese architects, no matter how articulate and sophisticated they are in their conceptual accommodation of Chinese cultural elements, cannot create a design that is essentially Chinese. But for others, contemporary "Chineseness" can be captured and achieved by non-Chinese, and very well. They believe that the work of international architects in China *is* contemporary Chinese architecture and should be a source of pride. By opening the door to international architects and having the best ones design the most important buildings, the cultural liberals believe that China has come to the center of global architectural production, and it is only a matter of time before local architects catch up and join the scene.

The debate over the Bird's Nest and other foreign-designed high-profile projects, which took place mostly between 1998 and 2004, served as a harbinger for the later development of architecture criticism. Since 2005, the debates over nationality and cost have quickly faded and given way to more reflexive subjects, such as the meaning of critical architecture and whether critical architecture is currently emerging in China. In spite of, or because of, the controversies, the works and practices of international architects have played a crucial role in jump-starting the previously nonexistent field of architectural criticism in China.

Critical Architecture: A Debate

In 2005, the *Journal of Architecture* published an essay by Zhu Jianfei, a Chinese architectural historian based at the University of Melbourne, titled "Criticality in between China and the West." In the essay, Zhu asserts that "while there has been a flow of influence from China (and Asia) through figures such as Rem Koolhaas who are supporting a post-critical argument in the West, there has also been a flow of ideas from the West through Chang Young Ho and Ma Qingyun that are facilitating a rise of criticality in the Chinese context."[35] Zhu argues that there is a symmetrical exchange of ideas and influences in architectural practices in recent years whereby transnational architects, represented by Koolhaas, Chang, and Ma, act as agents to introduce critical architecture from the West to China and market pragmatism from China to the West. Zhu's essay triggered a wide range of responses. The original essay and its responses were translated into Chinese and published by major architecture journals and websites in China, and a seminar on critical architecture was organized at Tongji University in Shanghai. The debate on criticality in architecture was a significant step in the development of architecture as a discipline and a profession in China. It took place in the midst of the rampant urban construction, continued the previous debates on foreign-designed megaprojects, and filled the vacuum of architectural criticism. The debate has provoked much-needed reflection on current architectural practices in China. This section does not intend to reproduce or summarize the debate but instead will highlight its key points and push it further by raising a number of new questions.[36]

To understand what "critical architecture" is, we need to first distinguish it from *theory*. In other words, beliefs and assumptions about critical architecture are geared toward architectural *practice,* instead of toward *theory* building. Though theory and practice are often intertwined, critical architecture is clearly oriented toward practice: it is about how to operate critical practices through various modes such as building, drawing, and writing. Having distinguished critical architecture (practice) from critical theory, we also need to acknowledge that much of the formulation of critical architecture draws from the lineage of critical theory, which can be traced back to early writings by Kant, Marx, and the more recent Frankfurt School. Based on a careful reading of the Frankfurt School, urban theorist Neil Brenner locates the "criticality" of critical theory in its reflexivity, its critique of instrumental reason, and its emphasis on the disjuncture between the actual and the possible. Criticality, therefore, involves both critiques of ideology and critiques of social inequalities and injustice.[37]

A similar understanding of criticality can be observed in architectural discourses as well. Critical architecture, as formulated by Michael Hays, involves resistance and opposition, imagination and construction of alternatives, and sustainment of autonomy.[38] Resistance, opposition, and transgression have been well examined and clearly understood as geared toward challenging power, knowledge, the market, and the status quo. But the concept of autonomy or autonomous architectural practice is never clearly defined. As Jane Rendell pointed out, what autonomy is and how it relates to the economy, to social and cultural relations, to aesthetics and to self-reflection, need further investigation.[39]

An emphasis on autonomy also forms a major element of Zhu Jianfei's articulation of the emerging criticality in new architecture in China, and the ambiguity of the concept has led to a number of confusions. The thrust of Zhu's argument is twofold. First, he argues that in recent years, especially since 2001, there has been a tendency in global architectural traffic to import critical architecture from the West to China, and to export market impetus (called the "postcritical") from China to the West. Second, the emerging critical architecture in China is exemplified in the purist, tectonic, modernist designs transgressing the mainstream and in the professional autonomy of the new generation of architects as enabled by market and state deregulation. Examples of the critical architects examined include Chang Young Ho, Liu Jiakun, and Ma Qingyun.

The above formulation of critical architecture is problematic in a number of aspects. First, as Michael Speaks and a number of others have pointed out, the clear-cut division between critical and postcritical on which Zhu's essay is based is misleading, because it reduces complex realities to static categories, and "what . . . unites all those identified as post-critical is nothing more than the belief that the critical project that dominated vanguard architecture in the West from the 1970s to the 1990s is bankrupt now."[40] According to Zhu, the postcritical impetus is largely equal to efficacy and market pragmatism. And if we follow this formulation, it is clear that it is not Koolhaas or any other global architect who exported market ideology from China to the West; rather, the market-oriented architectural practices in both China and the West are shaped by the same global capitalist forces.

Second, the criticality debate is largely formulated in a statecentric framework that embraces the world system theory and juxtaposes China—

a periphery or semiperiphery country—with the West, which forms the core. Zhu argues that as the Chinese economy grows, China is entering the core, and we now witness a "symmetrical" architectural flow between China and the West, which is different from the former one-way transplantation of architecture from the West to China.[41] The critiques of this statecentric perspective, as presented in chapter 2 above, apply to the architectural debate as well. By taking the nation-state as the basic scale of analysis, the discussion inevitably creates a false dichotomy of China versus the West and narrows the scope of the debate to what China has borrowed from the West and vice versa. This statist formulation ignores fragmented development patterns within each nation, and, more important, it obscures the multiscalar nature of architectural globalization. In short, the conceptualization of the debate on architectural exchange between China and the West, with the subsequent question of whether this exchange is symmetrical or not, is inadequate for analyzing the uneven development process of transnational architectural production and the roles of cities, particular agents, and global capitalism in that process.

Third, if we understand critical architecture as architectural practices that critique both ideology and social injustice, then we have not yet observed practices of this kind emerging from the Chinese context. Repeatedly in his writings, Zhu emphasizes the modern, purist, and tectonic approach to architecture, seen in works by Chang, Liu, and Ma, and he sees this as evidence of architectural criticality. As Michael Speaks rightly pointed out, what Zhu has identified as "criticality" in these architects is actually architectural intelligence based on conceptual thinking and research, instead of on a critique of ideology and injustice.

The emphasis on architectural intelligence can be seen in the architects' own articulations about their work. In his response to Zhu, Chang Young Ho, currently the dean of the School of Architecture and Planning at MIT, explained "what criticalities or the West meant" for him: criticalities meant design research and conceptual thinking. At the same time, he also acknowledged the necessity for architecture to offer a critique of capitalism and to take social responsibilities into consideration.[42] In a similar fashion, in "An Open Letter to Jianfei Zhu," architect Liu Jiakun candidly wrote about the urgency of problem solving: "real problems as a background of these designs were so great that they inevitably left behind their traces in my works."[43] In his mapping of design positions, Zhu categorizes Liu's work as "critical regionalism"—a concept first proposed by Kenneth Frampton—but as Michael Speaks points out, Liu Jiakun's work is better explained as "a practice driven by intelligence than by reference to Kenneth Frampton's ideological assertions of critical regionalism."[44] In short, architectural intelligence, conceptual thinking, and research-based design should not be mistaken for criticality. It is design intelligence, not critiques of ideology and social injustice, that constitutes the "self-conscious strategies that resist or transcend certain mainstream conventions" identified by Zhu.[45]

Having clarified what I see as the major confusions in the criticality debate, I proceed now to examine why a critique of ideology and social injustice is missing in the works of the new generation of Chinese architects. First, the lack of a critique of ideology—of both market and state—is related to how architects conceive their professional autonomy. As the participants in this debate have noted, the new generation of architects has obtained a high degree of professional autonomy as compared with the previous generation of architects in the socialist period. Under state socialism, private architecture firms were abolished, design contracts were assigned by government ministries, and architecture was highly politicized. Thus, the autonomous practice that has been made possible again since the 1990s entails a breakaway from the previously omnipresent state ideology and an embrace of design experimentation. This newly acquired professional autonomy, however, does not directly translate into a critique of the state ideology of authoritarianism, and it also does not form the basis for a critique of market neoliberalism. On the contrary, professional autonomy and market neoliberalism can be very much compatible, as seen in the current wild architectural experimentation enabled by the suddenly available commercial opportunities. This double silence, on the subject of both state and market ideology, characterizes the collective state of being of the new generation of architects. It has driven some of the leading architects, such as Chang Young Ho, to pursue a "third attitude," a middle path that pursues a purist, conceptual, and research-based design approach, but without completely rejecting the market. In short, what is identified as autonomous practice is in fact a voluntary choice on the part of the new generation of architects to avoid engaging in a critique of state and market.

The second missing element of criticality in new architecture in China is a critique of power, exploitation, and social injustice. This can be seen in the types of commissions undertaken by the leading architects. Some of the best works are part of "group designs," where local developers or governments commission a group of international and Chinese architects to design a collection of individual buildings, such as the Commune by the

Great Wall in Beijing, Ordos 100 in Inner Mongolia, the Architecture and Sculpture Garden in Jinhua (Zhejiang province), and the currently on-going CIPEA (China International Practice Exhibition of Architecture) in Nanjing. These are examples of place-promotion schemes initiated by private developers and local governments to brand their projects or cities by use of architecture. On these occasions, architects are given freedom and resources to be creative and turn their design concepts into reality, and some of the most interesting works in China have been born from these initiatives. However, questions of power, exploitation, and social injustice are carefully ignored when architects team up with and work for powerful clients. The upscale villas of the Commune in Beijing, with their cutting-edge design, offer a leisure space exclusively reserved for the economically privileged few. The CCTV headquarters, with its provocative design challenging the concept of skyscrapers, provides a state-of-the-art infrastructure for the smooth operation of the main state propaganda organization. As seen in these instances, when design intelligence from leading architects is mostly used to facilitate accumulation of wealth for the few, or to solidify state power, the questions of social justice and responsibilities are largely left unaddressed. Chinese cities are facing a plethora of problems, from shortages of affordable housing and lack of public space to segregation and environmental degradation. In what is identified as "critical architecture" in this debate, few genuine efforts can be found to tackle these problems.

Capitalist globalization has created conditions of possibility for the rise of the transnational mode of architectural production. The globalizing forces transforming architectural practices in the West and in China are the same, and therefore it is an exercise in futility to try to distinguish criticality in China from that in the West. In the current phase of capitalist globalization, critical architecture should engage in critiques of both ideology (market, state) and social injustice. The pure pursuit of design intelligence without challenging ideology and without questioning social inequality falls short of being critical.

While recognizing these universal tendencies, it is also important to acknowledge that to be critical also means to be reflexive about particular contexts. As examined in chapter 2 and throughout the book, the urban conditions in China entail numerous context-specific particularities. The field of architecture in China has gone through distinct phases from the nineteenth century to the present. The social, economic, cultural, and political conditions for architectural production in China differ greatly from those in other places. Therefore, an important question remains for the debate on architectural criticality: If critical architecture—understood as architectural responses that critique ideology and injustice—is possible in China, then what specific forms or approaches will it take?

Here I suggest two tentative answers, one pertaining to architectural criticism and the other to design and building practices. The fast-paced design and construction activities since the 1990s have not been accompanied by an equally vibrant scene of architectural criticism, in the sense of professional judgment of designs through writings and debates. High-profile works by international architects, such as the Bird's Nest, led to a heated debate that was nationalistic in tone. But the influx of international architects and their works has also helped to jump-start architectural criticism, as seen in Zhu Jianfei's essay on criticality and the wide range of responses and feedback it triggered. A group of architectural critics, such as Li Xiangning, Zhou Rong, and Peng Nu, is quickly emerging and providing a fresh injection of critiques on current practices. Overall, an engagement with critical architecture in China will require the development and maturation of architectural criticism through writings and debates.

With respect to practices, a possible approach to engaging in critical architecture is to explore building or project types other than monumental projects for the state and elitist projects for the wealthy. The rapid urbanization in China today offers a rich social laboratory for built environment professionals, by presenting both problems and opportunities. The not-so-glamorous commissions—such as migrant housing, social housing for the urban poor, energy-efficiency solutions in both cities and the countryside, safe construction in earthquake zones, rehabilitation of workers' housing blocks from the socialist era, and historical preservation of vernacular structures—embody great potential for challenging ideology and contributing to social justice. Some architecture firms have been moving in this direction, as seen in the examples of the *tulou* migrant housing project by Urbanus in Guangzhou and the rebuilding after the Wenchuan earthquake in May 2008. An alternative and more just urban future is possible through these critical architectural engagements by way of writings, designs, and buildings.

Architecture, State, and Political Change

By analyzing the controversies surrounding the National Stadium, this chapter has shown that national aspirations, along with the cultural ideology of global consumerism, drive the production of flagship architectural projects in Beijing. The design and construction process of the National Stadium reveals the rationale underlying the search for global architecture by state bureaucrats in China, as well as its mixed consequences for local cultural discourses. The debate on critical architecture, as analyzed in the previous section, has shown the progress in design intelligence and the development of architectural criticism. In this concluding section, I will tie these strands together by briefly reflecting on the relationship between state and transnational architectural production under conditions of globalization.

Although many have examined the economic imperatives and impact of flagship architectural projects, social scientists have just begun to explore the linkage between statehood, architecture, and political change under the conditions of globalization. Donald McNeill examines the impact of globalization on European territorial politics by analyzing the debates surrounding the opening of the Frank Gehry–designed Guggenheim Museum in Bilbao. He argues that the construction of the Guggenheim Museum was not only an economic initiative to revitalize Bilbao's deindustrialized urban economy but also part of a political maneuver by the ruling party in the Basque region to compete with other oppositional institutions and to enhance its relative strength within Spain.[46] In a study on the unbuilt Welsh Opera House in Cardiff Bay designed by Zaha Hadid, McNeill and Mark Tewdwr-Jones apply the concept of "banal nationalism" to describe how territorial elites use architectural projects as a form of symbolic intervention to rebrand their nations. They argue that the new architectural projects mushrooming in Europe can be seen as vehicles of such banal nationalism, promoted by nervous European political elites in an attempt to renarrate their nations at a time when sovereignty in Europe has been rebundled and reregulated.[47] Along these same lines of investigation, sociologist Leslie Sklair further connects the production, marketing, and consumption of iconic architecture to the agents of the transnational capitalist class.[48] According to Sklair, the transnational capitalist class in and around architecture includes multinational architectural firms with great delivery capacity, globalizing politicians and bureaucrats who commission and regulate architectural projects, and professionals in the engineering, finance, and real estate sectors, as well as merchants and the media, who are responsible for the marketing and consumption of architecture. Sklair particularly stresses the role of the state in sponsoring and regulating architectural projects.

In the Chinese context, the role of the state in facilitating transnational architectural production is even more evident. In contrast to Europe, where it is the uncertainty and anxiety over economic globalization that drive territorial elites to the construction of monumental architectural projects, in China it is robust economic growth and rising national ambitions that enable the state to construct architectural monuments that symbolize power and progress. The 2008 Beijing Olympics, which took place thirty years after the beginning of the market reform in 1978, presented a great opportunity for the Chinese state to demonstrate the country's achievements. Similar to other Olympics hosted by Asian countries, they were a coming-of-age event for China. In 1964, the Tokyo Olympics showed the world that postwar Japan had reemerged on the global scene in the form of a new economic power. In 1988, the Seoul Olympics represented South Korea as a prosperous and dynamic country on its way to political democracy. In a similar fashion, the Beijing Olympics were a much-anticipated opportunity for the Chinese state to demonstrate the remarkable progress achieved in the past three decades of market reform. But in contrast to Tokyo and Seoul, where the main Olympic stadiums were designed by local architects (Kenzo Tange and Soo Geun Kim, respectively), state politicians and bureaucrats in Beijing chose two prominent international architects to design the Olympic Stadium. The paradox between national ambitions and the impulse to embrace international architects illustrates the changing relationship of architecture and nation building under conditions of globalization—global architecture has become the form for national aspirations.

To return to the questions in the beginning part of the chapter: Can these new state spaces—such as the Bird's Nest, articulated in the architectural language of modernity, transparency, and openness—entail possibilities for real political change? Or will these spaces simply become "state crafts" for the Party to legitimate and solidify its power? The key to the answer lies in whether or not the new generation of architects has the capability and willingness to engage in critical architecture, to offer an architectural response to the state and market ideology, and to contribute to social justice. Without a critical stance on architectural practices, the current union of state sponsorship and transnational architectural production will remain a perpetual process of capital accumulation and lead to the deepening of social inequalities.

The Power of Symbols

O n one of my trips to Beijing, in the summer of 2006, Xu Yang, the vice president of SOHO China, informed me about a new book release from his company. Titled *The Power of Symbol,* the book compiles all major projects built by SOHO China over the past ten years (1996–2006). With more than three hundred pages of color photos and essays, it illustrates the company's long-term collaboration with international architects. The publication is obviously another media strategy characteristic of SOHO China's concept-driven real estate operation. In fact, the title of the book is a telling example of how the symbolic capital of architecture is deliberately and systematically used and exploited in the exercise of place making.

Symbolic Spaces

The production of symbols, and symbolic spaces, is the main theme running throughout *The Power of Symbol.* Local and transnational players all realize very well the power of symbolic spatial strategies in making Beijing and Shanghai into China's new global cities.

SOHO China is the archetype of the creative mixing of art, architecture, media, and real estate speculation. For its various SOHO projects in the CBD in Beijing, SOHO China replaced conventional means of marketing with panel discussions on art and architecture. Each project's property sales commenced with an opening ceremony that was staged as a media extravaganza centered on prominent international architects. By associating themselves with cutting-edge architecture and design, the developers successfully built a public image as sophisticated architecture patrons rather than profit-driven speculators. Combining this use of architecture with book publishing, blogging, and other media strategies, SOHO China has quickly built connections with local and international cultural elites who have tremendous power in influencing urban consumption trends. These meticulous promotional strategies have turned SOHO apartments and offices into symbols of modern urban living. With their minimalist and futuristic design, large, open floor plans, and flexible use of space, SOHO apartments have a strong appeal for members of China's wealthy urban middle class, who are eager to acquire such new symbols to showcase their privileged social status. Through its spatial strategies, SOHO China, a private firm with no prior government connections, has become a symbol of the thriving entrepreneurial class emerging from the new Chinese market economy. At the same time, through media strategies and backed by their newly accumulated wealth, this group of private entrepreneurs are exerting more and more influence on government policy making, and as shown in chapter 3, they can often resist government regulations and reverse the direction of policy to their advantage.

In Shanghai, historic architecture—old shikumen row houses from the 1930s—was recycled to mix with contemporary design at Xintiandi. Backed up by the Luwan district and municipal governments and with help from American architects, the Hong Kong–based investment company Shui On Group turned Xintiandi, a former "lower corner," into the most desirable address in Shanghai. In addition to huge economic profit, the symbolic capital created in this process of transnational architectural production was also transformed into social and political capital for both the investors and the architects. The renovated city blocks at Xintiandi are not merely another shopping district filled with international brands. Rather, by evoking memories of Old Shanghai as the "Paris of the Orient" of the 1930s, Xintiandi acts as a symbolic space that projects the city's global future by connecting to its cosmopolitan past. Chapter 4 argued that urban preservation, as practiced in today's Chinese cities, is an integral part of the larger modernization project. Preservation and modernization, instead of being opposites, make a compatible duo in the exercise of global city building in China. It is international architects as symbolic analysts who helped make the transition from demolition to preservation in urban policy making.

If Xintiandi and SOHO China are examples of symbolic spatial production undertaken by private developers driven by profits, then the National Olympic Stadium provides an example of how the Chinese state has become a major player in constructing symbolic architectural monuments to solidify its power and, by doing so, has become a key enabler of transnational architectural production. Here we observe an interesting fusion of national aspirations and global architecture: more and more government functions of the communist party-state are accommodated in foreign-designed, often cutting-edge structures. The Bird's Nest controversies revealed conflicts over the form and aesthetics of national representations as well as over government decision making and accountability, but essentially these were debates over the meaning of "contemporary Chinese." The conflicts and controversies surrounding the National Stadium reveal that symbolic spaces are subject to multiple and conflicting interpretations, and these debates and discussions can become catalysts for engendering critical architectural practices that challenge both the market and the state, and contribute to social justice.

Overall, the private and public architectural megaprojects examined in this book illustrate how Chinese cities have become increasingly embedded in the global network of architectural production. Chapter 2 provided a mapping of the geography of architectural globalization by focusing on the office locations of leading architectural firms. It found that powerful cities in this network of architectural production could be divided into two groups: the production cities and the consumption cities. Production cities are the sites where cutting-edge design and research are initially conducted, such as Basel, Rotterdam, many other smaller European cities, and Tokyo, whereas consumption cities have the attraction of large and active construction markets and are the places where architectural design, much of it conceived and produced elsewhere, is commissioned and put into building form. Beijing and Shanghai clearly belong to the category of consumption cities, where international design firms set up local offices (often on a project basis) in order to stay close to the market, have access to the local design labor market, and supervise construction. The increasing geographic separation between the globalized consumption and production of design has raised challenges but also possibilities for new architectural practices.

Symbolic Capital and Its Transformations

The production of symbolic spaces entails the transformation of symbolic capital, objectified in architectural design, into other forms of capital,

such as economic, political, and cultural capital. French sociologist Pierre
Bourdieu, in his classic essay *The Forms of Capital*, called for an inquiry
into how different forms of capital change into one another in specific
social contexts.[1] According to Bourdieu, capital can present itself in three
fundamental guises—as economic capital, cultural capital, and social capital. Economic capital takes the form of money, profit, or property rights.
Cultural capital can assume an embodied, objectified, or institutionalized
form (e.g., as assimilation of cultural customs, as cultural goods such as
books and movies, or as school diplomas and certifications, respectively).
Social capital is made up of social connections that carry certain advantages and resources. Bourdieu argues that each form of capital conceals
social power and is convertible into the other forms, because all forms
of capital are based on accumulated labor time. Bourdieu specifies that
symbolic capital is based on the recognition or misrecognition of honor
and prestige, and that other types of capital assume the form of symbolic
capital when they are recognized or misrecognized as legitimate.

The latter point on misrecognition is the key to understanding symbolic
capital and needs some further elaboration here. To borrow Bourdieu's
own example, when multiple bidders compete for a piece of land by offering higher and higher prices, the land takes on a symbolic value that is
disproportionate to its technical and economic qualities, and therefore
the symbolic capital of the land is a kind of misrecognition, an arbitrary
and inflated assessment of value.[2] Thus, symbolic capital is constituted by
both recognition and misrecognition of the qualities of individuals and
objects. Overall, symbolic capital is context-specific and is always defined
within the cultural system in which it is valued. Bourdieu's articulation
of symbolic capital and conversions among different forms of capital is
useful for understanding the operation of transnational architectural
production.

What are the special meanings accorded to a design by an international architect such as Riken Yamamoto (Jianwai SOHO), Herzog and
de Meuron (the Bird's Nest), and Ben Wood (Xintiandi) that constitute
its symbolic capital? I argue that the symbolic capital of designs by these
international architects is based first on the professional, market, and public recognition of their works. But equally important, the symbolic capital is also based on a *misrecognition,* understood as, in Bourdieu's words,
"according special meaning larger than the economic or technical use"
of the architectural design itself. And more specifically, this misrecognition is based on an "inflated assessment" of international architects' work
that derives from false distinctions between Chinese and foreign design,

Chinese and foreign architects. When China opened up in the 1980s, the lag in its economic development was painfully evident, and anything associated with the foreign was conceived as superior and better. In this transitional context of reform, local clients have also developed a misrecognition of the value of international design, one that is based on the belief that international design is better than domestic design. No matter the actual excellence of their design, international design firms are distinguished from domestic ones and associated with the modern, new, Western, urban, and cosmopolitan—versus the local, vernacular, and traditional. The symbolic capital objectified in the design of international architects is based on recognition and misrecognition of design excellence and prestige, and these perceptions are in turn defined and shaped within the contemporary Chinese society that is eager to catch up with the world after a long period of isolation and lack of development.

Throughout the book, I have traced the transformation of symbolic capital into other forms of capital. Local and transnational actors have deployed the symbolic capital of architectural design to open up other venues for the expansion and accumulation of economic, cultural, and social capital. In the case of SOHO China, the developers accumulated tremendous wealth from their design-intensive real estate speculation, turning SOHO China into one of the most powerful real estate firms in China. At the same time, the symbolic capital of architectural design has also been changed into cultural capital by the developers, by means of publications, lectures, blogging, and other self-promotional appearances in the media. The distinction derived from architectural design has also differentiated SOHO China from other developers and helped it to build connections with the government, as illustrated by the nomination of Pan Shiyi—the CEO of SOHO China—to the Beijing People's Congress in 2008. In the cases of Xintiandi and the Bird's Nest, similar conversions between different forms of capital can be observed as well.[3]

The ascending importance of symbolic spatial strategies reflects the shift of the Chinese urban economy from manufacturing to consumption and services, a postindustrial shift that entails uneven development and the repositioning of older power logics. The massive private and public investments in high-profile megaprojects indicate an extremely uneven pattern of wealth distribution. As powerful public and private players forge coalitions to speculate on property development, the majority of urban residents are further marginalized in the process. China's urban revolution is underlined by such repositioning of territorial elites and changes in power logics.

Symbolic Power: Repositioning of Territorial Elites

The magnitude of urban change narrated in this book reveals the rapidly changing urban class structure and the repositioning of territorial elites in contemporary China. Previous studies on urban China tended to overemphasize the impact of "outsiders" on China's urban transformation, such as overseas ethnic Chinese investors from Hong Kong, Taiwan, and Singapore and global multinational corporations providing foreign direct investment. In her discussion on post-Mao Beijing, Anne-Marie Broudehoux argues that the elite that engineered and benefited from urban image construction in Beijing is partly made up of overseas investors such as those from Hong Kong.[4] The analyses in this book present a more complex picture of social stratification and power realignment than the clear-cut polarization of outsiders versus locals. Although China's economic growth has been highly dependent on FDI and foreign investors have great bargaining power when negotiating with local partners, their success is not always guaranteed and they need to navigate in an uncertain political environment. In addition to the influx of foreign capital and investors, we also see the rise of other new power holders, such as private domestic entrepreneurs, the new property-owning class, globalizing state bureaucrats, and the emerging cultural elites. Below, I summarize five major trends in the repositioning of territorial elites that have been analyzed in the previous chapters.

First, there is an emerging domestic entrepreneurial class in and around the property development sector. During the 1990s, land and housing reforms enabled large-scale urban renewals, and the real estate sector quickly became one of the key industries driving China's spectacular economic growth. The number of registered real estate firms has increased from only a handful in the early 1980s to 37,123 in 2003. Foreign-owned companies made up a small percentage of this number (about 11 percent in 2003).[5] The majority were private or quasi-private enterprises led by domestic Chinese entrepreneurs, many of whom were former cadres from the state sector. They can often acquire land at deeply discounted prices owing to their strong government connections. The developers without such political capital need to acquire land at much higher prices through competitive bidding, and they need to explore other, and often creative, means to create their market niche, such as SOHO China's approach of using international architects and media. In spite of the variations in government connections, what is common throughout this entrepreneurial class is the financial power and resources accumulated through real estate speculation. As many of these entrepreneurs have made it onto the *Forbes* billionaire list, China has changed from one of the most egalitarian countries to one of the most unequal. The widening gap between the rich and the poor can largely be attributed to the vast accumulation of wealth in the hands of this entrepreneurial class in the sector of property development.

Along with business entrepreneurs, there is also a rapidly growing class of property owners. At the top of the pyramid in this class are those who have purchased high-end residential and commercial properties, mostly for investment purposes, in central locations in Beijing and Shanghai. The loft-style apartments at Jianwai SOHO and the luxury condos near Xintiandi, for example, both target this group of the extremely wealthy. The clientele of Jianwai SOHO illustrates the mixed composition of this group, ranging from sophisticated urban professionals and foreign expatriates to coal mine bosses and factory owners from the provinces. Lower in the hierarchy are the millions of urban families who have pulled together resources—savings, employer subsidies, and mortgages—to purchase a modern high-rise apartment within a moderate price range. The rise of this diverse class of property owners suggests the magnitude of China's housing reform, which is often described as the largest privatization effort in history. In less than three decades, from the early 1980s to 2005, the urban homeownership rate has jumped from nearly zero to more than 80 percent.[6] This property class forms the backbone of China's urban consumption, and various laws have been passed in recent years to protect its interests, such as the Property Rights Law of 2007. However, as sociologist Deborah Davis has pointed out, the privatization of urban housing has benefited different social strata unevenly.[7] Pensioners, laid-off workers, and millions of rural migrants have been excluded from participation in the new housing market. Rural migrants, especially, are denied rights to housing by the institutional barrier of *hukou*—China's household registration system that separates rural from urban population. In 2009, the homeownership rate of rural migrants in cities was less than one percent. The tension between property-owning and propertyless classes will certainly intensify unless the central government intervenes with new legal and administrative instruments for wealth redistribution and social welfare.

The third trend in power repositioning is the emerging stratum of globalizing state bureaucrats. Chapter 5 analyzed the active role played by the political elites associated with the BOCOG in staging an international design competition to choose the design for the National Stadium. An example is Huang Yan, the director of the Beijing Municipal Commission for Urban Planning, a Harvard-trained urban planner and the chief "choreographer" of the design competition. Like Ms. Huang, many of the high-ranking municipal officials in Beijing and Shanghai have postgraduate degrees and overseas experience. Well educated and globally oriented, they contrast sharply with their predecessors from the older generation of Chinese politicians. They are important players in forging growth coalitions and alliances with the private sector. As sociologist Leslie Sklair rightly pointed out, these globalizing bureaucrats constitute the state faction of the transnational capitalist class.[8] They exert critical influence on transnational architectural production as they sponsor, commission, and regulate the highest-profile megaprojects.

Fourth, foreign investors and companies play an important role in urban property development, but their relationship with the Chinese government, mostly at the city and district levels, is not always straightforward. The interaction between private investors and local governments is often more complex than what is depicted in the typical growth machine thesis, in which private investors form coalitions with local governments to benefit together from real estate development and urban renewal. Contrary to the previous studies that suggest a stable growth coalition of private investors and government, this book shows that the private-public partnership governing urban development in China is an informal and project-based relationship that constantly changes according to unpredictable domestic politics.

As chapter 4 showed, foreign investors become especially powerful when teamed up with local governments. Without political support from the district government, the Hong Kong–based developer of Xintiandi would not have been able to relocate residents in such a short time period. However, later, when the government shifted to a more protective stance toward residents, the project was substantially delayed by lengthy negotiations with squatting families. In 2007, after a scandal over misuse of pension funds in municipal construction that involved the top party secretary of Shanghai, Shui On Group immediately had to return the government subsidies it had received for its next project in Yangpu district.[9] The controversies over the National Stadium in Beijing suggest the same sort of fragile public-private partnership. The sponsorship of international architects on the part of the state is not unconditional and can often take a sudden turn upon leadership succession, as seen in the Olympic retrenchment policy after 2003, when Hu Jintao succeeded Jiang Zemin as chairman of the CCP. Even after Jacques Herzog and Pierre de Meuron were chosen as the architects for the National Stadium, the client and owner

of the stadium—a large state-owned enterprise funded by several powerful state banks—attempted to replace them with another architecture
firm. In the case of SOHO China, in spite of the fact that the company had
been painstakingly courting the local government over the years, the relationship soured over the recent Qianmen renewal project (2008–present).
After investing more than $50 million, SOHO China was asked by the city
government to withdraw from further involvement in the project, owing
to the public's concerns about a private developer's taking charge of (and
profiting from) the redevelopment of Qianmen—an area only a few hundred meters away from Tiananmen Square.[10]

The final trend in power repositioning is the rise of the globally mobile
cultural elites in facilitating transnational architectural production. They
are a younger generation of artists, architects, and academics with extensive overseas experience, familiar with both international trends and local
conditions in China. Acting as bridges between international architects
and local clients, they have introduced international architects to China
and helped them land prestigious commissions and understand how local
politics work. Behind all major projects commissioned to international
architects, there are always key figures from this cultural elite acting as
partners, advisors, and consultants. Architect Ma Qingyun helped Rem
Koolhaas to bid for the CCTV project. Wu Yaodong, on the architecture
faculty at Tsinghua University, worked with Paul Andreu on the National
Theater. Architect Chang Young Ho introduced a group of foreign architects to Pan Shiyi and Zhang Xin of SOHO China. Herzog and de
Meuron, after two failed projects in Moscow and Abu Dhabi—on account
of miscommunications and cultural misunderstandings—approached artist Ai Wei Wei, a central player in the contemporary Chinese art scene,
to help them navigate the unfamiliar Chinese terrain. The rise of the new
cultural elites has created conflicts with the long-standing locally embedded power holders, such as the senior architects affiliated with the Chinese
Academy of Sciences, who designed many of the monumental buildings in
the 1950s. The Bird's Nest controversy is a telling example of the changing power landscape within the cultural elite. Because of their advantaged
positions in the global network of cultural production, bridging between
China and the outside, the new cultural elites have quickly gained power
and status and become the main articulators of the contemporary Chinese
cultural scene.

These multifaceted trends of power repositioning demonstrate the
changing patterns of social stratification in contemporary urban Chinese

society. As the new economic, political, and cultural elites ascend to power, the dispossessed—migrant workers, the urban unemployed, and pensioners, to name just a few—form the new urban poor and further drift away to the margins of China's global-city-making enterprise. Transnational architectural production in China, therefore, presents a specific site in which to examine worldwide capital accumulation and uneven development.

An Urban Revolution, from Above and Below

This book is an exploration of the spatial strategies of global city formation in China. Among other aspiring cities, Beijing and Shanghai are rapidly ascending through the global urban hierarchy and have become major nodes in the global flows of capital, information, and talent. As revealed in this study, the strategy and practice of building global cities in China have been characterized by heavy investment in infrastructure, privatization and deregulation endorsed by the state, and the symbolic articulation of urban space by the elite. The policy priority placed on urban infrastructure investment has helped channel surplus capital accumulated in the manufacturing and export sectors to the built environment. Real estate construction and property development have become a major industry driving national GDP growth. Meanwhile, the spectacular urban growth could not have been achieved without the introduction of a series of new legal and administrative instruments by the state, including the legalization of land transactions, protection of private property, and the deregulation of foreign producer services firms. These legal measures have opened up, if only partially, the domestic property market to global investors and firms. The rise of a service-based urban economy, the official promotion system emphasizing "physical achievements," i.e., urban construction and property development, and the dual land market have made conditions ripe for the urban elite to pursue symbolic spatial strategies in the competitive race of urbanization. By examining the articulation of urban space in the process of global city formation, this book shows that urban space is not a container in which broader social processes take place, but a strategic terrain where symbolic spatial production leads to capital accumulation and where older power logics are rescaled to produce new dynamics.

How does the microhistory of Chinese urbanization fit into, or subvert, the macrohistory of global transformation? Transnational architectural production in Chinese cities offers a specific site in which to examine global transformations. Architectural globalization has been taking place and will continue to develop with or without the opening-up of the Chinese market. But the integration of China into the global economy is nevertheless a significant event in the history of global urban transformations, not only because the country offers new possibilities to build, experiment, and innovate, but also because the capitalist urbanization unfolding in China forces us to think about our collective urban future. As similar structural forces are shaping uneven development processes across the globe, it is no longer relevant to analyze capitalist urbanization within distinct national boundaries, as is done by setting China in opposition to the West. The Chinese urban future, with its problems and possibilities, has become part of the global urban future.

In 1968, when students and workers revolted in Paris, the Cultural Revolution was taking place in China under Mao. Having come to power through a mobilization of the rural masses, Chinese communist leaders developed a strong animosity toward everything associated with the urban. Mao envisioned a rural revolution that would resist imperialism and the urbanized core of the world system. In the same period, the French theorist Henri Lefebvre predicted the triumph of a completely urbanized society. Lefebvre saw an urban revolution unfolding, a process of "transformations that affect contemporary society, ranging from the period when questions of growth and industrialization predominate to the period when the urban problematic becomes predominant."[11] History proved Lefebvre right. The willful attempts at a rural revolution by Mao turned out to be no more than temporary reversals. Since China embarked on the road of market reform, the country has experienced a full-fledged urban revolution. China's urban revolution in the first three decades of reform has clearly exhibited a top-down pattern of decision making, as the political, economic, and cultural elites formulate key spatial strategies for global city formation. This book has examined both the efficacy and the fragility of this top-down model of city making, a model that has produced vast discontents and inequalities. The changing power balance among citizens, state, and global capital engenders possibilities for an urban revolution from below; later urban research will examine the critical and creative input of ordinary Chinese citizens in the making of our collective global urban future.

Appendix

A Methodological Note on Network Analysis

A social network is a set of actors (e.g., people, organizations, and cities) that may have relationships with one another (e.g., family ties and economic transactions). The purpose of social network analysis is to map the complex pattern of relationships between actors. The major network analysis technique used in chapter 2 is centrality analysis, which maps the power relationship of actors within a network. In the case of the network of cities constituted by branch offices of architecture firms, centrality analysis can help to identify the global urban hierarchy based on power scores of each city. The network approach considers power to be a function of patterns of relations. An actor has more power if it occupies a central position.

Three centrality measurements are used: degree, closeness, and betweenness centrality. Descriptive statistics of these three centrality measurements are shown in the table below. Degree and betweenness centrality measurements are highly skewed. The range of the degree centrality score is from 2 to 329, and the range of the betweenness score is from 0 to 4599. The standard deviations for the two measurements are 51.786 and 406.183, respectively. These statistics suggest that the population of cities is more heterogeneous and some cities have much more centrality and power than others in the network of architectural design.

TABLE A.1 **Correlations of different centrality measures**

	Degree centrality	Closeness centrality	Betweenness centrality
Maximum	329	76.062	4599.720
Minimum	2	31.774	0
Mean	43.465	49.664	104.657
Standard deviation	51.786	7.443	406.183

Note: N = 198 cities.

TABLE A.2 **Fifty largest architecture firms by country in the *BD* survey, 2007**

Rank	Firm	Country
1	Gensler	US
2	HOK	US
3	Nikken Sekkei	Japan
4	Aedas	UK
5	Foster & Partners	UK
6	Skidmore, Owings & Merrill	US
7	RMJM	UK
8	HKS	US
9	P&T Architects and Engineers	China (Hong Kong)
10	Wood Bagot	Australia
11	RTKL	US
12	Perkins Eastman	US
13	Smith Group	US
14	Capita Architecture	UK
15	NBBJ	US
16	Callison	US
17	Burt Hill	US
18	Nihon Sekkei	Japan
19	Cannon Design	US
20	Perkins & Will	US
21	Cox Architects & Planners	Australia
22	Leo A Daly	US
23	Broadway Malyan	UK
24	Woodhead	Australia
25	Kume Sekkei	Japan
26	Chapman Taylor	UK
27	Smallwood, Reynolds, Stewart, Stewart	US
28	White Arkitekter AB	Sweden
29	Zimmer Gunsul Frasca Architects	US
30	DLR Group	US
31	Hassell	Australia
32	SMC Group	UK
33	KlingStubbins	US
34	HBO+EMTB	Australia
35	WATG	US
36	KEO International Consultants	UAE

Rank	Firm	Country
37	Office for Metropolitan Architecture	The Netherlands
38	Benoy	UK
39	Leigh & Orange	China (Hong Kong)
40	Cooper Carry	US
41	Ankrom Moisan Associated Architects	US
42	Sasaki Associates	US
43	Thompson, Ventulett, Stainback	US
44	Valode & Pistre Architects	France
45	J.S.K Architects	Germany
46	Ellerbe Becket	US
47	PRP Architects	UK
48	Arkitektfirmaet C. F. Moller	Denmark
49	Aukett Fitzroy Robinson	UK
50	Sheppard Robson	UK

Note: *BD* magazine conducts an annual survey of the largest architecture firms worldwide, based on fee incomes and the number of fee-earning architects. Three firms that are within the top fifty of the original *BD* survey are not included in the table and the network analysis. These are BDP International (ranked no. 7), Atkins (ranked no. 10), and Hamilton Architects (ranked no. 38). The first two firms do not list architectural design as their main activity, and the third has only one office location and therefore cannot be used in the network analysis.

TABLE A.3 **Select list of fifty boutique architecture firms by city location**

Architect/firm	City location
SANAA	Tokyo
Fumihiko Maki	Tokyo
Go Hasegawa	Tokyo
Jun Aoki	Tokyo
Shigeru Ban	Tokyo
Sou Fujimoto	Tokyo
Takaharu + Yui Tezuka Architects	Tokyo
Terunobu Fujimori, Yoshio Uchida	Tokyo
Toyo Ito	Tokyo
Bernard Tschumi	New York
I. M. Pei	New York
Libeskind	New York
Philip Johnson	New York
Polshek Partnership	New York
Richard Meier	New York
Steven Holl	New York
Weiss/Manfredi	New York
Allford Hall Monaghan Morris	London
Foreign Office Architects	London
Jamie Fobert Architects	London
Norman Foster	London
Richard Rogers	London
Zaha Hadid	London
Barkow Leibinger	Berlin
David Chipperfield	Berlin

Architect/firm	City location
Die Baupiloten	Berlin
Alberto Campo Baeza	Madrid
Rafael Moneo	Madrid
Christian de Portzamparc	Paris
Jean Nouvel	Paris
Niels Trop	Oslo
Sverre Fehn	Oslo
Morphosis	Santa Monica
Thom Mayne	Santa Monica
UN Studio	Amsterdam
Herzog & de Meuron	Basel
Odos Architects	Dublin
Renzo Piano	Geneva
Peter Zumthor	Haldenstein
FAR: Frohn & Rojas	Cologne
Alvaro Siza	Lisbon
OFIS	Ljubljana
Baumschlager & Eberle	Lochau
Frank Gehry	Los Angeles
Studio Mumbai Architects	Mumbai
Tadao Ando	Osaka
Robert Venturi	Philadelphia
Rem Koolhaas/OMA	Rotterdam
Paulo Mendes da Rocha	São Paulo
Hertl Architekten	Steyr
Glenn Murcutt	Sydney
Studio Tamassociati	Venice
COOP HIMMELB(L)AU	Vienna

Note: This list is compiled of firms or architects that have been reviewed at least twice in *Domus* and *Architectural Review* in 2007 and 2008, together with the living Pritzker Architecture Prize winners from 1990 to 2008.

TABLE A.4 **OMA's global architectural team working on the CCTV project, Beijing**

Category	Collaborators
Associate architects and engineers	East China Architecture & Design Institute, Shanghai
Structure, services, fire, security	Arup, London/Hong Kong/Beijing Project Principal: Cecil Balmond Project Director: Rory McGowan Project Director Beijing: Michael Kwok Project Manager Beijing: Craig Gibbons CCTV Structure—Lead: Chris Carroll Technical Adviser Beijing: Goman Ho Project Manager: Alexis Lee TVCC Structure—Lead: Stuart Smith

Category	Collaborators
Architectural team	Carolina Bartram, Paul Cross, Mimmy Dino, Richard Lawson, Zhao-Fan Li, Peng Liu, Andrew Luong, John MacArthur, Hamish Nevile, Dan Pook, Chas Pope, Andrew Smith, Terence Yip, with Abdul Ahmed, Wayne Chan, Dean Clabrough, Omar Diallo, Sam Hatch, Jonathan Kerry, Ronald Li, Man-kit Luk, Steve Peet, Fei Tong, Paul Tonkin, Ben Urick, William Whitby, Robin Wilkinson, Baiqian Wan, Yihua Wang, Michelle Wong, Stella Wong, Eric Wu, Angela Yeung, George Zhao.
	Services—Directors: Alistair Guthrie, Stephen Jolly, Iain Lyall.
	Mechanical—Lead: Clodagh Ryan; Lead Beijing: Lewis Shiu; Team: John Allcock, Olly Base, Graham Beadle, Peter Brickell, Kenneth Chong, Judy Coleman, Eddie Scuffell, Jodh Singh, William Zhang, with Annie Chen, Rachel Harris, Alex Hart, Tai Hollingsbee, Paul Lander, Martin Walton, William Wong, G. B. Wang.
	Electrical—Lead: John Pullen; Lead HK/Beijing: Kenneth Sin; Team: Chi Wing Chow, Chai Kok Eow, Dane Green, Sabrina Wong, with Geoff Balrow, Tony Campbell, Stephen Chan, Mike Evans, Nathan Hattersley, Bob Jones, Tony Monroe, David Seager, Olumayowa Soluade, Sam Wise, Alba Xu, Kai-sing Yung.
	Public Health—Lead: David George; Team: Graham Humphreys, Bob Lau, Adam Martin, Glen Swinney, with James Cheung, Jun Chen, Yang Ming, De-Ming Wen.
	Security: David Hadden, Simon Brimble, with Philip Barker, Jeff Green, John Haddon, Ryan Sukhram, Andrew Webster.
	Geotechnics: Mark Choi, Jack Pappin, with Gary Ge, Dominic Holt, James Lui.
	ATG: Xiaonian Duan, with Colin Ho, Yang Wang; Control: David Pritchard; Wind: Roy Denoon, Alex To, with Andrew Minson.
	Fire—Lead: Mingchun Luo, Longde Zhao; Team: Angela Chan, Barbara Lane, Susan Lamont, with Shi Bibo, Dagang Guo, Gene Kwan, Kang Li, He Wei, Kelvin Wong.
Facade engineering and design consultancy	Front Inc, New York
	Partner, project leader: Marc Simmons
	Partners: Bruce Nichol, Martin Riese
	Director of engineering: Philip Khalil
	Senior engineer: Chen Zhan
	Facade consultant: Brian Guerrero
Broadcast consultancy	Sandy Brown Associates LLP, London
	Consultant: David Lamberty
Lighting	Lighting Planners Associates
	Tokyo principal: Kaoru Mende
	Directors: Yutaka Inaba, Mari Kubota, Hideto Mori, Ryuichi Sawada, Kentato Tanaka
	Senior associate: Mari Kubota
	Associates: Ken Okamoto, Chika Tanaka
	Planners: Aki Hayakawa, Junko Inomoto, Momoko Muraoka, Akiko Okunaka, Natsuko Ueda
Acoustics consultancy	DHV Building and Industry, Eindhoven
	Principal consultant: L.C.J. van Luxemburg
	Senior consultant: Theo M.J. Raijmakers
	Senior consultant: B. H. M. Kok
	Consultant: Stephan J. W. Nabbe
	Consultants: Nicole A. H. M. van Hout, Marly L. C. Kole, Bertie W. M. van den Braak

Category	Collaborators
Theater consultancy	Ducks Scéno, France
	Scenographer: Michel Cova
	Lighting and audiovisual designers: Aldo de Sousa, Jean-François Mathais
	Stage equipment designers and engineers: Stefan Abromeit, Clément Dreano
Vertical transportation consultants	Lerch, Bates & Associates, London
	Project director: Adrian Godwin
	Project engineers: Chris Manning, Peter Noon
	Design engineers: Les Gilbey, Thet Khin
High-rise consultant	DMJMH+N, Los Angeles
	Principal: Michael Mann
	Project architect: Bruce Toman
	Senior architect: John Hess
	Architect: Jane Chen
Food service consulting and planning	Romano Gatland, New York
	Principal for programming; Principal in Charge: Christopher C. Brady
	CCTV principal for Design CCTV, project manager: Mark V. Romano
	TVCC principal for Design TVCC: Russ Pizzuto
	Principal for programming: Gary Nokes
	Team: David Cutrone, Stanley D. Gatland, Matthew Gatland, Matthew Klein, W. Michael Kell, John LoBianco, James Pizzuto, Shirley Heng Romano
Landscape	Inside/Outside, Amsterdam
	Principal designer: Petra Blaisse
	Architect: Mathias Lehner
	Landscape architect: Rosetta Elkin
	Architectural assistant: Yukiko Nezu
	Consultant: Marieke van den Heuvel
Buildability	Stephen Scanlon, San Diego
Strategic advisor	Qingyun Ma, Shanghai

Source: http://www.oma.com.

TABLE A.5 **List of participating architects for Ordos 100 project, Inner Mongolia, China**

Phase and parcel number	Company name	City, country
Phase 1:		
29	Bill Price Inc.	Houston, US
11	blacklinesonwhitepaper	Johannesburg, South Africa
27	Christophe Hutin Architecture	Bordeaux, France
19	Coll-Leclerc, Arquitectos SL	Barcelona, Spain
14	Dellekamp Arquitectura, SA de CV	Condesa, Mexico
10	Encore heureux + G Studio	Paris, France
9	Estudio Barozzi Veiga SL	Barcelona, Spain
1	Jan De Vylder architecten	Ghent, Belgium
22	John Palmesino / Palmesino Rönnskog— Territorial Agency	Basel, Switzerland
7	Leon de Lima	Lima, Peru
5	Luca Selva Architekten ETH BSA SIA AG	Basel, Switzerland
7	Lyn Rice Architects	New York, US
25	Manuel Herz Architecture	Basel, Switzerland
23	Matharoo Associates	Ahmedabad, India
20	MIMARLAR YAPI TASARIM MÜHENDISLIK ve DANISMANLIK HIZMETLERI LTD. STI.	Istanbul, Turkey
6	MOS	Cambridge, US
24	Multiplicities	New York, US
13	NL Architects	Amsterdam, The Netherlands
28	NU architectuuratelier	Ghent, Belgium
16	OBRA Architects	New York, US
21	Pedrocchi Meier Architects	Basel, Switzerland
2	PRODUCTORA	Condesa, Mexico
26	R&Sie(n), architect-Paris-NY	Paris, France
3	Rafi Segal Architect Princeton	Princeton, UK
18	Senan Architects	Jerusalem, Israel
4	Shadi Rahbaran/studio-sr	Switzerland/Germany
8	Testbedstudio Architects	Stockholm, Sweden
12	Tham & Videgård Hansson Arkitekter AB	Stockholm, Sweden
Phase 2:		
84	AndreasThiele.Architekten / Ines Geisler Weizman Architecture	Berlin, Germany / London, UK
39	Ann-Sofi Rönnskog / Palmesino Rönnskog—Territorial Agency	Basel, Switzerland
32	Aravena, Alejandro	Santiago, Chile
48	at103 Pardo, Francisco and Amezcua, Julio	Cuauhtémoc, Mexico
30	Atelier Bow Wow, Yoshiharu Tsukamoto, Momoyo Tsukamoto	Tokyo, Japan
90	Babel Architects—Sharon Rotbard, Dan Hasson,Yuval Yasky	Tel Aviv, Israel
60	Bachelard Wagner Architekten ETH SIA, Anne Marie Wagner	Basel, Switzerland
33	Barker, Alexandra	New York, NY
52	Bilbao, Tatiana	Mexico City, Mexico
42	Bottega + Ehrhardt Architekten GmbH	Stuttgart, Germany

Phase and parcel number	Company name	City, country
Phase 2:		
54	Buchner Bründler AG, Andras Brundler	Basel, Switzerland
58	Christ + Gantenbein	Basel, Switzerland
59	Colboc & Franzen	Paris, France
56	Dieguez Fridman	Buenos Aires, Argentina
69	DRDH Architects Daniel Rosbottom, David Howarth	London, UK
45	Efrat-Kowalsky Architects	Tel Aviv, Israel
49	Escobedo, Frida	Mexico
61	F451arquitectura	Cambridge, US
35	FRENTEarquitectura, Juan Pablo Maza	Condesa, Mexico
70	Fujimoto, Sou	Tokyo, Japan
98	HA: SKA, Mia Hagg+Sunkoo Kang+Jennifer Schmachtenberg	Paris, France
73	Heiermann Architekten, Bernadette und Severin Heiermann	Cologne, Germany
51	HHF	Basel, Switzerland
55	Ikstudio, Mariana Ibanez+Simon Kim	Cambridge, US
53	ines huber architektin eth sia	Basel, Switzerland
80	Ingeborg Rocker, Rocker-Lange Architects	Cambridge, US
43	Iwamoto, Lisa and Scott, Craig > IWAMOTOSCOTT	San Francisco, US
74	JDS architects—Julien De Smedt	Copenhagen, Denmark
41	Jean-Frédéric Luscher Architect	Basel, Switzerland
86	JS^a(formerly Higuera + Sánchez), Javier Sánchez	Mexico City, Mexico
88	JSA @ Norway—Jensen Skodvin Arch., Jan Olav Jensen	Norway
50	Jun Igarashi Architects Inc.	Hokkaido, Japan
38	Keller Easterling	New York, US
15	Könz Molo Architects—KOENZ Jachen, MOLO KOENZ Ludovica	Lugano, Switzerland
40	L'Atelier Provisoire	Bordeaux, France
77	Larnaudie Jean & Luc	Toulouse, France
46	Lee, Mark > Johnston Mark Lee architects	Los Angeles, US
81	Lekker Design, Ker-Shing Ong & Josh Comaroff	Singapore
99	Ligia Nobre + Eduardo de Oliveira Rosa	Brazil/Switzerland
79	Lost Architekten > Dietrich Lohmann	Basel, Switzerland
93	LTL Architects, Paul Lewis+Marc Tsurumaki+David Lewis	New York, US
91	weberbuess Architekten	Basel, Switzerland
83	Makeka Designs Mokena Makeka	Cape Town, South Africa
82	Mazzapokora, Daniel Pokora, Gabriela Mazza	Zurich, Switzerland
65	Michelle Howard, constructconcept	Berlin, Germany
100	Mierta & Kurt Lazzarini Architects	Samedan, Switzerland
72	Milica Topalovic—Bas Princen— Paul Gerretsen	Basel, Switzerland
95	Miller Maranta Architekten	Basel, Switzerland

Phase and parcel number	Company name	City, country
Phase 2:		
57	Minsuk Cho Mass Studies	Seoul, Korea
64	Mori, Toshiko	New York, US
89	n Architects: Eric Bunge, AIA. Mimi Hoang, NCARB	New York, US
44	OFFICE Kersten Geers David Van Severen	Belgium
34	Oyler Wu Collaborative	Los Angeles, US
66	PAD	Toronto, Canada
63	Polaris Architects	Luxembourg-Belair, Luxembourg
47	Preston Scott Cohen	Cambridge, US
87	Puga, Cecilia	Santiago, Chile
78	Purnomo, Adi	Indonesia
36	Radic Clarke, Similian	Santiago, Chile
85	Rintala Eggertsson Architects, Sami Rintala + Dagur Eggertsson	Oslo, Norway
71	Rodriquez, Pako	San Juan, Puerto Rico
67	Rojkind Arquitectos, Michel Rojkind	Mexico City, Mexico
76	Sami arquitectos	Setubal, Portugal
68	Sanaksenaho, Matti	Finland
75	Simon Conder associates, Nile Street studios	London, UK
31	Slade Architecture: James Slade and Hayes Slade	New York, US
62	Srdjan Jovanovic Weiss / NAO	Philadelphia, US
92	SSD: Jinhee Park, John Hong	Cambridge, New York, US
97	Taller Territorial de Mexico Arturo Ortiz Struck	Mexico City, Mexico
37	UNI: Chaewon Kim, Beat Schenk	Cambridge, US
96	WORK: Dan Wood and Amale Andraos	New York, US
94	Zenin, Adrian	Jakarta, Indonesia

Source: http://www.ordos100.com.

Notes

Preface

1. See more photos and reports on the CCTV fire at http://www.chinasmack .com, accessed on October 20, 2009.

Chapter One

1. For the literature on urban regeneration and interurban competition, see King (1990), Sudjic (1992), Hubbard (1996), Loftman and Nevin (1996), Fainstein (2001), Evans (2003), Marshall (2003), McNeill and Tewdwr-Jones (2003), Greenberg (2003), Lehrer (2002), and del Cerro (2007).

2. Tombesi (2002).

3. Ibid.

4. See Castells (1996), Sassen (1996), Graham and Marvin (1996), Tombesi, Dave, and Scriver (2003), and Latham and Sassen (2005) on digitization and globalization.

5. Harvey (1989), Soja (1989), Zukin (1991, 1995), Dear (1991), Sassen (1991), Clark (2004).

6. See Baudrillard (1981) and Zukin (1982, 1991, 1995).

7. See Brenner and Theodore (2002) and Brenner (2004).

8. See Ren and Weinstein (2008) on state rescaling processes in China and India.

9. The concept of "world cities" is first discussed in Friedmann and Wolff (1982) and Friedmann (1986). The "global cities" model was originally proposed by Sassen (1984, 1991).

10. Friedmann (1986), Friedmann and Wolff (1982), Sassen (1991).

11. Sassen (1984, 1991, 2001).

12. See Sassen (1991), Haila (1998, 1999), Lo and Yeung (1996, 1998), Abu-Lughod (1999), Machimura (2000), Meyer (2000), Scott (2001), Lo and Marcotullio

(2001), Marcuse and Van Kempen (2000, 2002), Sassen (2002), Grant and Short (2002), Brenner and Theodore (2002), Boschken (2003), Alderson and Beckfield (2004), Diane Davis (2005), and Chen (2009).

13. The CAJ database provides access to more than 3,300 Chinese academic journals in the humanities and social sciences published in mainland China. The first phase covers until 1993, and the second phase covers from 1994 to the present. The subjects covered include literature, history, and philosophy; economics, politics, and law; and education and social science.

14. Yan (1994).

15. Gu and Sun (1999).

16. Tu and Yang (2003).

17. Gu and Sun (1999).

18. For example, see the most up-to-date research articles in Wu Fulong, Xu, and Yeh (2007), Wu Fulong (2006), and Laurence Ma and Wu (2005).

19. Previously published monographs on Shanghai's global transformation include Hook (1998), Olds (2001), and Gamble (2003). Edited volumes on Shanghai include Gandelsonas (2002), Logan (2002), Kuan and Rowe (2004), Laurence Ma and Wu (2005), Chen (2009), and Gil (2008). Articles and book chapters include Olds (1995, 1997, 1999), Haila (1998, 1999), Wu Fulong (2000a, 2000b), Zhang Tingwei (2002), Gu and Tang (2002), He and Wu (2005), Wu Jiaping and Radbone (2005), Wai (2006), and Chen (2007).

20. For journal articles and monographs published on urban transformations in Beijing, see Gaubatz (1995), Zhang Jie (1997), Lv (1997), King and Kusno (2000), Abramson (2001, 2007), Zhang Yan and Fang (2004), Broudehoux (2004, 2007a, 2007b), and Zhao and Bell (2005). The English-language scholarship on other major Chinese cities, such as Guangzhou, Shenzhen, Tianjin, and Chongqing, is even more limited. See Cartier (2002) on Shenzhen; Zhou and Logan (1996) and Xu Jiang and Yeh (2005) on Guangzhou.

Chapter Two

1. *Domus,* May 2008.

2. Wallerstein (1974).

3. Taylor et al. (2007).

4. Witlox and Derudder (2007:38).

5. Friedmann (1986).

6. Sassen (1991, 2001).

7. Short et al. (1996).

8. Sassen (1991, 2001).

9. Taylor (2006).

10. Beaverstock, Smith, and Taylor (1999).

11. Taylor (2004).

12. Alderson and Beckfield (2004).

13. See Cattan (1995), Shin and Timberlake (2000), Smith (2001), and Smith and Timberlake (1995a, 1995b, 2002).

14. Smith and Timberlake (1995a, 1995b, 2002).

15. Tulacz (2008).

16. Buckley (2008).

17. Ibid.

18. *BD* magazine conducts an annual survey of the largest architecture firms worldwide, based on fee incomes and the number of fee-earning architects. The survey provides a comprehensive source on the largest architecture firms. See the list of the fifty largest firms in table A.2.

19. In design revenue and number of employees, large Chinese design institutes are comparable to the top hundred firms, but they did not participate in the survey. Some of these are state-owned, and they are often affiliated with government ministries.

20. Borgatti, Everett, and Freeman (2002).

21. Cuff (1992), Larson (1993), Sklair (2005, 2006), McNeill (2005).

22. McNeill (2005).

23. The list includes firms that appeared at least twice in *Domus* and *Architectural Review* in 2007 and 2008.

24. Japanese architects Kazuyo Seijima and Ryue Nishizawa of SANAA won the prestigious Pritzker Architecture Prize in 2010.

25. Koolhaas et al. (1998:369).

26. Koolhaas (2004:494–95).

27. See Rowe and Kuan (2002), Cody (2003, 2004), and Xue (2006).

28. The 1850s marked the first influx of Western architecture with the opening of treaty ports, although earlier examples of Western buildings can also be found, such as the neo-baroque Catholic South Church built in Beijing in 1657.

29. King (2004).

30. Lou and Xue (2004:55).

31. Lou and Xue (2004).

32. Rujivacharakul (2007).

33. Wu Jiang (2001).

34. Cody (2003).

35. Lou and Xue (2004).

36. Rowe and Kuan (2002).

37. Cody (2003:xvii).

38. Cody (2004).

39. Lai (2007).

40. Rowe and Kuan (2002).

41. Quoted from Mars and Hornsby (2009:96).

42. Rowe and Kuan (2002).

43. Czepczynski (2008).

44. Lin (2001).

45. Wang Jing (1996:235).

46. Xue (2006).

47. Ibid.

48. Wang Jing (1996:234).

49. Ma Qingyun (2001).

50. Jiang (2008).

51. Ma Qingyun (2001).

52. Class-A design institutes can work on large-scale commissions of any kind in any city. Design institutes in classes B, C, and D can undertake only smaller-scale projects in limited locations.

53. Jiang (2008).

54. Ibid.

55. Ibid., 357.

56. Blackwell (forthcoming).

57. "Urban villages" (*cheng zhong cun*) refer to the migrant settlements often found in inner cities, where farmland was swamped by urban sprawl and farmers turned themselves into landlords by constructing (often illegal) substandard dormitory housing for renting to migrants.

58. Examples include the Dynamic City Foundation, run by Dutch architect Neville Mars, and the Moving Cities Project, by Belgian architect and writer Bert de Muynck and Portuguese architect Monica Carrico.

59. Project statement, from http://www.ordos100.com.

60. From de Muynck (2008), Ordos 100: Avant-garde Architecture in the Desert, available at http://www.movingcities.org, accessed in April 2008.

Chapter Three

1. *Jianwai* is the name of the area on the outer side of Jian'guomen Boulevard where the project is located.

2. http://www.sohochina.com, accessed on May 3, 2009.

3. Beijing has been called by different names in Chinese. It was first called Ji as the small center of the Warring States Kingdom of Yan, and then Youzhou in the medieval period, Dadu in the Yuan dynasty, and Jingshi in the Ming and Qing periods. It was renamed Beijing in 1912 by the Nationalist Party, changed to Beiping in 1928, and back to Beijing again in 1949 by the communist government. Although Beijing has been used as the official name since 1949, the name Peking was widely used in the Western media until the 1980s. *Beijing* and *Peking* are different romanizations of the same Chinese word, 北京. See details on the name changes in Naquin (2000).

4. The five imperial dynasties are Liao (938–1122), Jin (1122–1215), Yuan (1267–1367), Ming (1368–1643), and Qing (1644–1911). Since 1949, Beijing has been the capital of the People's Republic of China.

5. I follow historians such as Susan Naquin and define the early modern period of the Ming and Qing dynasties as the imperial period. In 1403, the Emperor Yongle of the Ming dynasty relocated the capital from Nanking to Peking. The fall of the Qing dynasty in 1911 is widely agreed upon as the beginning year of the republican era. The year 1978 is the year of Reform and Opening and is usually taken as the turning point of China's transition from a socialist to a market economy.

6. Naquin (2000).

7. The Ming emperor Yongle rebuilt Yuan Dadu into Peking in the 1500s. The basic spatial layout of Peking under the rule of Yongle has remained for five centuries, through today.

8. Such subcenters include, for example, the areas of Drum Tower and Bell Tower, Xisi, Dongsi, Xidan, Dongdan, Di'an Gate, Chongwen Gate, and Dashilar.

9. Dong (2003).

10. Naquin (2000).

11. Dong (2003).

12. The name Wangfujing means "Well of Princely Mansion." The presence of Manchu nobility within the Inner City during the Qing period was physically marked by their conspicuously grand mansions (*wangfu*). According to Broudehoux (2004), by the middle of the eighteenth century more than thirty such princely mansions occupied substantial portions of the urban real estate in the Inner City. Wangfujing was the residence of the highest-ranking princes and nobles dating back to the time of Ming emperor Yongle (1403–24).

13. Broudehoux (2004).

14. Xidan was another commercial center that emerged in the republican period, characterized by new styles of specialty shops. It was smaller in scale than Wangfujing. See Dong (2003).

15. Whyte and Parish (1984).

16. Ibid.

17. Wu Hung (2005).

18. Beijing City Government (1993).

19. Beijing City Government (1998).

20. From the CBD Administration Committee, see http://www.bjcbd.gov.cn, accessed on August 1, 2005.

21. Olds (1997, 2001).

22. The eight firms were Skidmore, Owings & Merrill, Johnson Fain & Partners, and NBBJ from the United States, GMP from Germany, Urban Environment and Research Institute from Japan, Kuipercom & Pangnons from Holland, and two Chinese firms—Beijing Planning and Design Institute and Shanghai Urban Planning and Design Institute.

23. From http://www.bjcbd.gov.cn, accessed on August 1, 2005.

24. Ibid.

25. In the preface of Pan Shiyi (2000), *SOHO NewTown Files.*

26. From "Simply a Game of Numbers" in the epilogue of Pan Shiyi (2000).

27. Interview with Pan Shiyi, April 4, 2005.

28. From an interview with Zhang Xin in the *Sunday Morning Post,* by Clifford Coonan, posted on http://www.sohochina.com, accessed on October 14, 2004.

29. Burdett (2003).

30. Zhang Xin (2000).

31. Ren (2008d).

32. Interview with Pan Shiyi, April 4, 2005.

33. Interview with architect Sako, March 25, 2005.

34. *Hutong* refers to narrow alleys lined with one-story courtyard houses on both sides.

35. Part of the forum conversation is reprinted in Pan Shiyi and Zhang (2006: 318–19).

36. Interview with architect Sako, March 25, 2005.

37. Zha (2005).

38. Interview with artist Yun Hao, April 26, 2005.

39. SOHO Xiaobao (2003, 2005a, 2005b, 2006).

40. From http://www.news.xinhuanet.com, retrieved on February 14, 2008.

41. Friday BBS discussion, retrieved on September 8, 2004, at www.sohochina .com.

42. Pan Shiyi (2008:57).

43. Su (2005:112).

44. Su (2005).

45. Zhang Jingping (2004:244).

46. Su (2005:112).

47. Zhang Jingping (2004:245).

48. From http://www.house.sina.com, retrieved on September 3, 2003.

49. Ibid.

50. Zhang Jingping (2004:241).

51. From *SOHO Xiaobao,* April 2004.

52. Mu and Wan (2004).

53. Ibid., 47.

54. Ibid., 70.

55. Ibid., 72.

56. Ibid., 78.

57. Interview with Yang Dongli, March 5, 2005.

58. Mu and Wan (2004:69).

59. The elected members of the Jianwai SOHO Property Owners Committee included a lawyer working for a US law firm, an IT executive, a business consultant,

and a high-ranking manager of a national chain of coffee shops, all of whom have postgraduate degrees. See www.sohochina.com, data retrieved on April 1, 2006.

60. Pan Shiyi (2000:89).

61. Zukin (1982:147).

Chapter Four

1. A team from Tsinghua University, led by architect Wu Liangyong, experimented with the concept of "organic renewal" in the Ju'er Hutong neighborhood in Beijing in the 1980s. Architects worked with the government and developers to relocate some residents, on a voluntary basis, in order to reduce residential density and mixed new structures with rehabilitated old courtyards. The experiment was a success but it was never replicated in other neighborhoods, because it was much more profitable for developers and local governments to raze everything and build high-rises. See Wu Liangyong (1999).

2. For example, the Beijing Cultural Heritage Protection Center is a leading nonprofit active in urban preservation. There are also a number of websites devoted to preservation issues, such as www.memoryofchina.org (founded in 2006, with 14,000 registered members across the country) and www.oldbeijing.org.

3. Wang Jun (2003).

4. Examples include Michael Meyer's nonfiction *The Last Days of Old Beijing* (2008); Greg Girard's photo essay book *Phantom Shanghai* (2007) and Rong Rong and Inri's photo exhibition "Tui-transfiguration" in the 798 art district in 2005; Ou Ning and Zhang Jinli's 2006 documentary *Meishi Street* on urban renewal in the Qianmen area of Beijing—the film portrays the fight of a restaurant owner, Zhang Jinli, with the government for fair compensation for his demolished hutong house.

5. See He and Wu (2005) on the property market; Zhang Yan and Fang (2004) on growth machines and public-private coalitions; Fang (2001), Zhang Jie (1997), and Lv (1997) on property rights; Zhao Xudong and Bell (2005) on a debate about the culture of *chai* and destruction; and Zhang Yue (2008) on fragmented government authorities.

6. Girard (2007).

7. Barthel (1989).

8. *Li* means neighborhoods, *long* means lanes. *Lilong* houses, also called *longtang*, are one- or two-story row houses arranged on both sides of a lane. See Luo and Wu (1997).

9. Wang Yaping and Murie (1996).

10. Zhang Tingwei (2002).

11. Xu Mingqian (2004).

12. Ibid.

13. Ibid.

14. From http://www.uuufun.com, May 21, 2009, accessed on June 4, 2009.

15. Shanghai City Government (2009).

16. Shanghai City Government (2003a). In 2009, Tongji University urban planning professor Ruan Yisan proposed to the government to add another four preservation areas.

17. Xia (2005).

18. Ibid.

19. Wai (2006).

20. Architectural historians often distinguish old *shikumen lilong* houses from new ones. Old shikumen houses were constructed between the 1870s and the 1910s, are bigger and more spacious in layout, and have more features of southern Chinese architectural traditions. New shikumen houses were constructed between the 1920s and 1940s. They are smaller in size owing to the higher land prices and changes in family sizes in the '20s and '30s. Also, new shikumen houses have more Western architectural features than the old ones. The two blocks of shikumen at Xintiandi are mostly the new sort, dating back to the '20s and '30s. See Luo and Wu (1997).

21. Shanghai Statistics Bureau (1990).

22. Luo (2002).

23. Interview with Vincent Lo, July 25, 2005.

24. He and Wu (2005).

25. Interview with Vincent Lo, July 25, 2005.

26. Interview with a district official, August 3, 2005.

27. Shanghai City Government (2003b).

28. Interview with Ben Wood, August 15, 2005.

29. Lu (2002:170).

30. Pan Tianshu (2005).

31. *People's Daily,* September 28, 2001.

32. *Los Angeles Times,* October 19, 2001.

33. "Building the Country," *Economist,* March 10, 2005.

34. *Xin Min Weekly,* October 22, 2001.

35. Luo (2002).

36. Luo (2002:74).

37. Farrer (2010).

38. Xintiandi newsletter, August 2005.

39. Zukin (1982).

40. From an interview with Zheng Shiling, May 12, 2005.

41. Brown-Saracino (2004).

42. Zhang Jun (2005).

43. Girard (2007:186).

44. State Council (1991).

45. Shanghai City Government (1991, articles 5 and 17).

46. State Council (2001).

47. Interview with a Luwan district official, August 3, 2005.

48. Ibid.

49. See details in Ren (2008a).

50. For a discussion on housing rights in China and India, see Weinstein and Ren (2009).

51. O'Brien and Li (2006).

52. State Council (2003).

53. State Council (2004).

54. From http://news.boxun.com, accessed on May 7, 2008.

55. Shanghai City Government (2009).

56. These estimates are provided by the Beijing Urban Planning Association.

57. Koolhaas (2004:458–59).

58. Abbas (2002:38).

59. Zhu Jieming (1999), Fu (2002), Zhang Tingwei (2002), Zhang Yan and Fang (2004), He and Wu (2005).

60. Koolhaas (2004).

61. Wasserstrom (2009).

Chapter Five

1. Lane (1985), Bozdogan (2001), Xue (2006).

2. See recent works on the Beijing Olympics such as Brownell (2008), Price and Dayan (2008), Caffrey (2008, 2009), Ren (2009), Mangan and Dong (2008), and two special issues of the *International Journal of the History of Sport* in 2008 (vol. 25, no. 7) and 2009 (vol. 26, no. 8), edited by J. A. Mangan and Kevin Caffrey.

3. Wasserstrom (2008) discusses the long history of binary perspectives on China in the West. He argues that the current narratives and counternarratives surrounding the 2008 Olympics continue patterns of demonization and romanticization that can be traced back to the nineteenth century, if not earlier.

4. Brenner (2004) uses the term "new state spaces" to refer to the key institutional sites, such as urban regions, where the rescaling of state power in Western Europe has been taking place since the 1970s.

5. Whitelegg (2000), Burbank, Andranovich, and Heying (2001), Preuss (2004).

6. Hall (1987), Essex and Chalkley (1998), Hiller (2000), Roche (2000).

7. Shoval (2002).

8. Ong (2004).

9. From http://en.beijing2008.cn.

10. According to Polumbaum (2003), Beijing's winning of the 2008 Games came at a time when the legitimacy of the IOC was in crisis after the Salt Lake City

bidding scandal. By choosing Beijing, a non-Western city in a developing country, the IOC attempted to build a new Olympic image by emphasizing diversity, transparency, and multiculturalism.

11. From *Olympic Action Plan* (2002), available from http://www.beijing-2008 .org.

12. Polumbaum (2003).

13. The site of the Olympic Park was previously occupied by 33 state enterprises, 721 collectives, and 5,700 households. The demolition started in August 2002. It took only four months to relocate all the households and enterprises. A total of 2.19 million square meters of existing structures were demolished. These statistics were released by the Beijing Municipal Bureau of State Land and Resources in November 2002. See http://www.bjgtj.gov.cn.

14. From *Olympic Action Plan* (2002).

15. From Wu Chenguang (2004).

16. From Beijing Municipal City Planning Commission (2004:9).

17. Ibid., 21.

18. Ibid., 37.

19. After a design competition, local clients often take the winning design from international firms and have local firms continue the work to minimize costs.

20. Interview with Ai Wei Wei, August 12, 2006.

21. Interview with Stephan Marbach, August 12, 2006.

22. From Beijing Municipal City Planning Commission (2004:57).

23. Ibid., 53.

24. Wu Chenguang (2004).

25. Ren (2006, 2008b).

26. From Wu Chen (2005).

27. Ibid.

28. From Wu Chenguang (2004).

29. Peng (2000).

30. The speech was delivered at the seventh plenary session of the Ninth Beijing Committee of the Communist Party of China, July 24–25, 2004, Beijing. The document can be retrieved at http://news.xinhuanet.com/newscenter/2004/08/03/content_1695377.htm.

31. The new retrenchment policy had repercussions on other Olympic stadium projects. The number of stadiums to be newly built was reduced from nineteen to eleven. The number of stadiums to be renovated was reduced from thirteen to eleven. All other facilities were temporary structures.

32. From the meeting memo of *Forum on Olympic Architecture and Mega Projects in Beijing,* held on August 24, 2004. The author was not present at the meeting but secured the complete meeting memo (37,145 words) from a participant at the meeting. Later the author interviewed other participants. Other quotations in this section are from the same document.

33. Lubow (2006).

34. Brownell (2008:92).

35. Zhu Jianfei (2009:129).

36. The original essay by Zhu and the various responses it triggered were republished in Zhu Jianfei (2009: chaps. 6 and 7).

37. Brenner (2009).

38. Hays (1981).

39. Rendell (2007).

40. Zhu Jianfei (2009:154).

41. Zhu Jianfei (2009).

42. Ibid.

43. Ibid., 153.

44. Ibid., 157.

45. Ibid., 129.

46. McNeill (2000).

47. McNeill and Tewdwr-Jones (2003); Billig (1995) suggests that in affluent societies, nationalism is observed in less visible forms. He uses the term "banal nationalism" to describe a presence of nationalism in everyday, mundane situations.

48. Sklair (2005, 2006).

Chapter Six

1. Bourdieu (1986).

2. Ibid.

3. Ren (2008c).

4. Broudehoux (2004).

5. China Statistics Bureau (2005).

6. Wu Fulong, Xu, and Yeh (2007).

7. Deborah Davis (2003).

8. Sklair (2006).

9. Areddy (2007).

10. Interview with Xu Yang, August 9, 2008.

11. Lefebvre (2003:5).

Bibliography

Abbas, Ackbar. 2002. "Play It Again Shanghai: Urban Preservation in the Global Era." In *Shanghai Reflections: Architecture, Urbanism and the Search for an Alternative Modernity,* ed. Mario Gandelsonas, 36–55. Princeton: Princeton Architectural Press.

Abramson, Daniel Benjamin. 2001. "Beijing's Preservation Policy and the Fate of the Siheyuan." *Traditional Dwellings and Settlements Review* 13 (1): 7–22.

———. 2007. "The Aesthetics of City-Scale Preservation Policy in Beijing." *Planning Perspectives* 22 (2): 129–66.

Abu-Lughod, Janet L. 1999. *New York, Chicago, Los Angeles: America's Global Cities.* Minneapolis: University of Minnesota Press.

Alderson, Arthur S., and Jason Beckfield. 2004. "Power and Position in the World City System." *American Journal of Sociology* 109 (4): 811–51.

Architecture & Design. 2005.

Areddy, James T. 2007. "Corruption Crackdown Targets Shanghai Inc." *Wall Street Journal,* February 7.

Barthel, Diane. 1989. "Historic Preservation: A Comparative Analysis." *Sociological Forum* 4 (1): 87–105.

Baudrillard, Jean. 1981. *For a Critique of the Political Economy of the Sign.* St. Louis: Telos Press.

Beaverstock, J. V., R. G. Smith, and P. J. Taylor. 1999. "The Long Arm of the Law: London's Law Firms in a Globalizing World-Economy." *Environment and Planning A* 31 (10): 1857–76.

Beijing City Government. 1993. *Beijing General City Plan.*

———. 1998. *Specific Controlling Plan.* N.p.: Beijing City Government.

———. 2002. *Olympic Action Plan.* N.p.: Beijing City Government. http://www.beijing-2008.org.

Beijing Municipal City Planning Commission. 2004. *The National Stadium.* Beijing: China Architecture & Building Press.

Billig, M. 1995. *Banal Nationalism.* Thousand Oaks: Sage.

Blackwell, Adrian. Forthcoming. *Detour.* Beijing: Timezone 8.

Borgatti, Steven P., Martin G. Everett, and Linton C. Freeman. 2002. *UCINET for Windows: Software for Social Network Analysis*. Cambridge: Harvard Analytic Technologies.

Boschken, Herman L. 2003. "Global Cities, Systemic Power, and Upper-Middle Class Influence." *Urban Affairs Review* 38 (6): 808–30.

Bourdieu, Pierre. 1986. "The Forms of Capital." In *Handbook of Theory and Research for the Sociology of Education*, ed. J. Richardson, 241–58. New York: Greenwood.

Bozdogan, Sibel. 2001. *Modernism and Nation Building: Turkish Architectural Culture in the Early Republic*. Seattle: University of Washington Press.

Brenner, Neil. 2004. *New State Spaces: Urban Governance and the Rescaling of Statehood*. New York: Oxford University Press.

———. 2009. "What Is Critical Urban Theory?" *City* 13 (2–3): 195–204.

Brenner, Neil, and Nik Theodore. 2002. *Space of Neoliberalism: Urban Restructuring in North America and West Europe*. Oxford: Blackwell.

Broudehoux, Anne-Marie. 2004. *The Making and Selling of Post-Mao Beijing*. New York: Routledge.

———. 2007a. "Spectacular Beijing: The Conspicuous Construction of an Olympic Metropolis." *Journal of Urban Affairs* 29 (4): 383–99.

———. 2007b. "Delirious Beijing: Euphoria and Despair in the Olympic Metropolis." In *Evil Paradises: Dreamworlds of Neoliberalism*, ed. Mike Davis and Daniel Monk, 87–101. New York: New Press.

Brownell, Susan. 2008. *Beijing's Games: What the Olympics Mean to China*. Lanham: Rowman & Littlefield.

Brown-Saracino, Japonica. 2004. "Social Preservationists and the Quest for Authentic Community." *City and Community* 3 (2): 125–56.

Buckley, Bruce. 2008. "Uncertain Economy Pushes Design Firms to Diversify Their Portfolios." *Engineering News Record (Sourcebook):* 33–38.

Burbank, Matthew, Gregory Andranovich, and Charles H. Heying. 2001. *Olympic Dreams: The Impact of Mega-events on Local Politics*. Boulder: Lynne Rienner.

Burdett, Ricky. 2003. "The Great Leap Forward." In *Commune by the Great Wall*, ed. Jian Shi, 28–30. Tianjin: Tianjin Academy of Social Sciences Press.

Caffrey, Kevin. 2008. "Olympian Politics in Beijing: Games but Not Just Games." *International Journal of the History of Sports* 25 (7): 807–25.

———. 2009. "The Beijing Olympics as Indicator of a Chinese Competitive Ethic." *International Journal of the History of Sports* 26 (8): 1122–45.

Cartier, Carolyn. 2002. "Transnational Urbanism in the Reform-Era Chinese City: Landscape from Shenzhen." *Urban Studies* 39 (9): 1513–32.

Castells, Manuel. 1996. *The Rise of the Network Society*. Oxford: Blackwell.

Cattan, Nadine. 1995. "Attractivity and Internationalisation of Major European Cities: The Example of Air Traffic." *Urban Studies* 32: 303–12.

Chen, Xiangming. 2007. "A Tale of Two Regions in China: Rapid Economic

Development and Slow Industrial Upgrading in the Pearl River and the Yangtze River Deltas." *International Journal of Comparative Sociology* 48 (2–3): 167–201.

———, ed. 2009. *Shanghai Rising: State Power and Local Transformations in a Global Megacity.* Minneapolis: University of Minnesota Press.

China Statistics Bureau. 2005. *China Statistics Yearbook 2004.*

Clark, Terry N. 2004. *The City as an Entertainment Machine.* Amsterdam: Elsevier—JAI Press.

Cody, Jeffrey W. 2003. *Exporting American Architecture, 1870–2000.* New York: Routledge.

———. 2004. "Making History (Pay) in Shanghai: Architectural Dialogues about Space, Place, and Face." In *Shanghai: Architecture and Urbanism for Modern China,* ed. Seng Kuan and Peter G. Rowe, 128–45. Munich: Prestel.

Cuff, Dana. 1992. *Architecture: The Story of Practice.* Cambridge: MIT Press.

Czepczynski, Mariusz. 2008. *Cultural Landscapes of Post-socialist Cities: Representation of Powers and Needs.* Aldershot: Ashgate.

Davis, Deborah. 2003. "From Welfare Benefit to Capitalized Asset: The Recommodification of Residential Space in Urban China." In *Chinese Urban Housing Reform,* ed. Richard Forrest and James Lee, 183–96. New York: Routledge.

Davis, Diane. 2005. "Cities in Global Context: A Brief Intellectual History." *International Journal of Urban and Regional Research* 29 (1): 92–109.

Dear, Michael. 1991. "The Premature Demise of Postmodern Urbanism." *Cultural Anthropology* 6 (4): 538–52.

Del Cerro, Gerardo. 2007. *Bilbao: Basque Pathways to Globalization.* London: Elsevier.

De Muynck, Bert. 2008. "Ordos 100: Avant-garde Architecture in the Desert." Retrieved on April 30, 2008. http://www.movingcities.org.

Dong, Madeleine Yue. 2003. *Republican Beijing: The City and Its Histories.* Berkeley: University of California Press.

Essex, S., and B. Chalkley. 1998. "Olympic Games: Catalyst of Urban Change." *Leisure Studies* 17 (3): 187–206.

Evans, Graeme. 2003. "Hard-Branding the Cultural City: From Prado to Prada." *International Journal of Urban and Regional Research* 27 (2): 417–40.

Fainstein, Susan S. 2001. *The City Builders: Property Development in New York and London, 1980–2000.* 2nd ed. Lawrence: University Press of Kansas.

Fang, Ke. 2001. *Dangdai Beijing Jiucheng Gengxin: Diaocha, Yanjiu, Tansuo* [Contemporary Redevelopment in the Inner City of Beijing: Survey, Analysis, and Investigation]. Beijing: China Architecture & Building Press.

Farrer, James. 2010. "Shanghai Bars: Patchwork Globalization and Flexible Cosmopolitanism in Reform-Era Urban Leisure Spaces." *Chinese Sociology and Anthropology* 2 (2).

Friedmann, John. 1986. "The World City Hypothesis." *Development and Change* 17 (1): 69–83.

———. 1995. "Where We Stand: A Decade of World City Research." In *World Cities in a World System*, ed. P. L. Knox and P. J. Taylor, 21–47. Cambridge: Cambridge University Press.

Friedmann, John, and G. Wolff. 1982. "World City Formation: An Agenda for Research and Action." *International Journal of Urban and Regional Research* 6 (3): 309–44.

Fu, Zhengji. 2002. "The State, Capital and Urban Restructuring in Post-reform Shanghai." In *The New Chinese City: Globalization and Market Reform*, ed. John Logan, 106–20. Oxford: Blackwell.

Gamble, Jos. 2003. *Shanghai in Transition: Changing Perspectives and Social Contours of a Chinese Metropolis*. New York: Routledge Curzon.

Gandelsonas, Mario. 2002. "Shanghai Reflections." In *Shanghai Reflections: Architecture, Urbanism and the Search for an Alternative Modernity*, ed. Gandelsonas, 21–35. Princeton: Princeton Architectural Press.

Gaubatz, Piper. 1995. "Changing Beijing." *Geographical Review* 85 (1): 79–96.

Gil, Iker, ed. 2008. *Shanghai Transforming*. New York: Actar D.

Girard, Greg. 2007. *Phantom Shanghai*. Toronto: Magenta Foundation.

Graham, Stephen, and Simon Marvin. 1996. *Telecommunications and the City: Electronic Spaces, Urban Places*. New York: Routledge.

Grant, Richard, and John R. Short, eds. 2002. *Globalization and the Margins*. New York: Palgrave Macmillan.

Greenberg, Miriam. 2003. "The Limits of Branding: The World Trade Center, Fiscal Crisis and the Marketing of Recovery." *International Journal of Urban and Regional Research* 27 (2): 386–416.

Gu, Chaolin, and Ying Sun. 1999. "Jingji Quanqiuhua yu Zhongguo Guojixing Chengshi Jianshe" [Economic Globalization and Building China's International Metropolises]. *Urban Planning Forum* 1999 (3): 1–6.

Gu, Felicity Rose, and Zilai Tang. 2002. "Shanghai: Reconnecting to the Global Economy." In *Global Networks, Linked Cities*, ed. Saskia Sassen, 273–308. New York: Routledge.

Haila, Anne. 1998. "The Neglected Builder of Global Cities." In *Cities in Transformation: Social and Symbolic Change of Urban Space*, ed. O. Kalltrop, I. Elander, O. Ericsson, and M. Franzen, 51–64. Aldershot: Ashgate.

———. 1999. "Why Is Shanghai Building a Giant Speculative Property Bubble?" *International Journal of Urban and Regional Research* 23 (3): 583–88.

Hall, Colin Michael. 1987. "The Effects of Hallmark Events on Cities." *Journal of Travel Research* 26 (2): 44–45.

Harvey, David. 1989. "From Managerialism to Entrepreneurialism: The Transformation of Governance in Late Capitalism." *Geografiska Annaler* 71B: 3–17.

Hays, Michael. 1981. "Critical Architecture: Between Culture and Form." *Perspecta* (21): 14–29.

He, Shenjing, and Fulong Wu. 2005. "Property-Led Redevelopment in Post-reform

China: A Case Study of Xintiandi Redevelopment Project in Shanghai." *Journal of Urban Affairs* 27 (1): 1–23.

Hiller, Harry. 2000. "Mega-events, Urban Boosterism and Growth Strategies: An Analysis of Objectives and Legitimations of the Cape Town 2004 Olympic Bid." *International Journal of Urban and Regional Research* 24 (2): 439–58.

Hook, Brian. 1998. *Shanghai and the Yangtze Delta: A City Reborn.* New York: Oxford University Press.

Hubbard, Phil. 1996. "Urban Design and City Regeneration: Social Representation of Entrepreneurial Landscapes." *Urban Studies* 33 (8): 1441–61.

Jiang, Jun. 2008. "Why MAD Is Mad?" In *MAD dinner,* ed. Brendan McGetrick, Shuyu Chen, and M. A. D. Ltd., 349–64. New York: Actar.

King, Anthony. 1990. "Architecture, Capital and Globalization." *Theory, Culture & Society* 7 (2–3): 397–411.

———. 2004. *Spaces of Global Cultures: Architecture, Urbanism, Identity.* New York: Routledge.

King, Anthony, and Abidin Kusno. 2000. "On Bei(ji)ng in the World: Globalization, Postmodernism and the Making of Transnational Space in China." In *Postmodernism and China,* ed. Arif Dirlik and Xudong Zhang, 41–67. Durham: Duke University Press.

Koolhaas, Rem. 2004. *Content.* Cologne: Taschen.

Koolhaas, Rem, Bruce Mau, Jennifer Sigler, and Hans Werlemann. 1998. *Small, Medium, Large, Extra-large.* 2nd ed. New York: Monacelli Press.

Kuan, Seng, and Peter G. Rowe, eds. 2004. *Shanghai: Architecture and Urbanism for Modern China.* Munich: Prestel Verlag.

Lai, Delin. 2007. "Chinese Modern: Sun Yat-sen's Mausoleum as a Crucible for Defining Modern Chinese Architecture, 1925–32." Ph.D. diss., University of Chicago.

Lane, Barbara Miller. 1985. *Architecture and Politics in Germany, 1918–1945.* 2nd ed. Cambridge: Harvard University Press.

Larson, Magali Sarfatti. 1993. *Behind the Postmodern Facade: Architectural Change in Late Twentieth-Century America.* Berkeley: University of California Press.

Latham, Robert, and Saskia Sassen. 2005. *Digital Formations: IT and New Architectures in the Global Realm.* Princeton: Princeton University Press.

Lefebvre, Henri. 2003. *The Urban Revolution.* Minneapolis: University of Minnesota Press.

Lehrer, Ute. 2002. "Image Production and Globalization: City-Building Processes at Potsdamer Platz." Ph.D. diss., University of California, Los Angeles.

Lin, Nancy. 2001. "Architecture Shenzhen." In *Great Leap Forward,* ed. Chuihua Judy Chung and Bernard Chang, 158–61. Cologne: Taschen.

Lo, Fu-Chen, and Peter Marcotullio. 2001. *Globalization and the Sustainability of Cities in the Asia Pacific Region.* Tokyo: United Nations University Press.

Lo, Fu-Chen, and Yue-Man Yeung. 1996. *Emerging World Cities in Pacific Asia.* Tokyo: United Nations University Press.

————. 1998. *Globalization and the World of Large Cities*. Tokyo: United Nations University Press.

Loftman, Patrick, and Brendan Nevin. 1996. "Going for Growth: Prestige Projects in Three British Cities." *Urban Studies* 33 (6): 991–1019.

Logan, John R., ed. 2002. *The New Chinese City: Globalization and Market Reform*. Oxford: Blackwell.

Lou, Chenghao, and Shunsheng Xue. 2004. *Lao Shanghai Yingzaoye ji Jianzhushi* [Builders and Architects in Old Shanghai]. Shanghai: Tongji University Press.

Lu, Hanchao. 2002. "Nostalgia for the Future: The Resurgence of an Alienated Culture in China." *Pacific Affairs* 75 (2): 169–86.

Lubow, Arthur. 2006. "The China Syndrome." *New York Times,* May 21.

Luo, Xiaowei. 2002. *Shanghai Xintiandi*. Shanghai: Southeast University Press.

Luo, Xiaowei, and Jiang Wu. 1997. *Shanghai Longtang*. Shanghai: Shanghai Renmin Meishu Chubanshe.

Lv, Junhua. 1997. "Beijing's Old and Dilapidated Housing Renewal." *Cities* 14 (2): 59–69.

Ma, Laurence J. C., and Fulong Wu, eds. 2005. *Restructuring the Chinese City: Changing Society, Economy and Space*. New York: Routledge.

Ma, Qingyun. 2001. "Project Commentary on Mihai Craciun's 'Ideology: Shenzhen.'" In *Great Leap Forward,* ed. Chuihua Judy Chung and Bernard Chang, 53. Cologne: Taschen.

Machimura, Takashi. 2000. "Symbolic Use of Globalization in Urban Politics in Tokyo." *International Journal of Urban and Regional Research* 22 (2): 183–94.

Mangan, J. A., and Jinxia Dong, eds. 2008. *Beijing 2008: Preparing for Glory: Chinese Challenge in the "Chinese Century."* New York: Routledge.

Marcuse, Peter, and Ronald Van Kempen. 2000. *Globalizing Cities: A New Spatial Order?* Oxford: Blackwell.

————. 2002. *Of States and Cities: The Partitioning of Urban Space*. New York: Oxford University Press.

Mars, Neville, and Adrian Hornsby. 2009. *The Chinese Dream*. Rotterdam: NAi.

Marshall, Richard. 2003. *Emerging Urbanity: Global Urban Projects in the Asia Pacific Rim*. New York: Spon Press.

McNeill, Donald. 2000. "McGuggenisation? National Identity and Globalization in the Basque Country." *Political Geography* 19 (4): 473–94.

————. 2005. "In Search of the Global Architect: The Case of Norman Foster (and Partners)." *International Journal of Urban and Regional Research* 29 (3): 501–15.

McNeill, Donald, and Mark Tewdwr-Jones. 2003. "Architecture, Banal Nationalism and Re-territorialization." *International Journal of Urban and Regional Research* 27 (3): 738–43.

Meyer, David R. 2000. *Hong Kong as a Global Metropolis*. New York: Cambridge University Press.

Meyer, Michael J. 2008. *The Last Days of Old Beijing: Life in the Vanishing Backstreets of a City Transformed.* New York: Walker.

Mu, Mu, and Jing Wan, eds. 2004. *Xingcunzhe de Youxi* [Game of Survival]. Beijing: Xinxing Chubanshe.

Naquin, Susan. 2000. *Peking: Temples and City Life, 1400–1900.* Berkeley: University of California Press.

O'Brien, Kevin J., and Lianjiang Li. 2006. *Rightful Resistance in Rural China.* New York: Cambridge University Press.

Olds, Kris. 1995. "Globalization and the Production of New Urban Spaces: Pacific Rim Megaprojects in the Late Twentieth Century." *Environment and Planning A* 27 (11): 1713–43.

———. 1997. "Globalizing Shanghai: The 'Global Intelligence Corps' and the Building of Pudong." *Cities* 14 (2): 109–23.

———. 1999. *Globalisation and the Asia-Pacific: Contested Territories.* New York: Routledge.

———. 2001. *Globalization and Urban Change: Capital, Culture, and Pacific Rim Mega-projects.* New York: Oxford University Press.

Ong, R. 2004. "New Beijing, Great Olympics: Beijing and Its Unfolding Olympic Legacy." *Stanford Journal of East Asian Affairs* 4 (2): 35–49.

Pan, Shiyi, ed. 2000. *SOHO New Town Files.* Tianjin: Tianjin Academy of Social Sciences Press.

———. 2008. "The Chinese Economy Is a Whole." *SOHO Xiaobao* (91): 57.

Pan, Shiyi, and Xin Zhang, eds. 2006. *The Power of Symbol: SOHO China, Ten Years of Pioneering.* Beijing: Tsinghua University Press.

Pan, Tianshu. 2005. "Historical Memory, Community-Building and Place-Making in Neighborhood Shanghai." In *Restructuring the Chinese City: Changing Society, Economy and Space,* ed. Laurence J. C. Ma and Fulong Wu, 122–37. New York: Routledge.

Peng, Alfred Peigen. 2000. "Why Do We Strongly Oppose the French Architect's Scheme of Grand National Theatre?" *Architectural Journal* (11): 11–12.

Polumbaum, Judy. 2003. "Capturing the Flame: Aspirations and Representations of Beijing's 2008 Olympics." In *Chinese Media, Global Contexts,* ed. Chin-Chuan Lee, 57–75. New York: Routledge Cruzon.

Preuss, Holger. 2004. *The Economics of Staging the Olympics: A Comparison of the Games, 1972–2008.* Northampton, UK: Edward Elgar.

Price, Monroe Edwin, and Daniel Dayan. 2008. *Owning the Olympics: Narratives of the New China.* Ann Arbor: University of Michigan Press.

Ren, Xuefei. 2006. "La ville chinoise et ses 'grands projets' urbains: l'architecture internationale en question." *La Vie des Idées* (12): 77–83.

———. 2008a. "Forward to the Past: Historical Preservation in Globalizing Shanghai." *City & Community* 7 (1): 23–43.

———. 2008b. "Architecture and Nation Building in the Age of Globalization:

Construction of the National Stadium of Beijing 2008 Olympic Games." *Journal of Urban Affairs* 30 (2): 175–90.

———. 2008c. "Architecture and China's Urban Revolution." *City* 12 (2): 217–25.

———. 2008d. "Architecture as Branding: Mega Project Developments in Beijing." *Built Environment* 34 (4): 517–31.

———. 2009. "Olympic Beijing: Reflections on Urban Space and Global Connectivity." *International Journal of the History of Sports* 26 (8): 1011–39.

Ren, Xuefei, and Liza Weinstein. 2008. "Scalar Transformations and Mega-project Development in China and India." Paper presented to the American Sociological Association, Boston.

Rendell, Jane, ed. 2007. *Critical Architecture*. New York: Routledge.

Roche, Maurice. 2000. *Mega-events and Modernity: Olympics and Expos in the Growth of Global Culture*. New York: Routledge.

Rowe, Peter G., and Seng Kuan. 2002. *Architectural Encounters with Essence and Form in Modern China*. Cambridge: MIT Press.

Rujivacharakul, Vimalin. 2007. "Architects as Cultural Heroes: The Rise of Architectural Profession in China, 1840s–1949." In *Cities in Motion*, ed. Sherman Cochran and David Strand, 133–53. Berkeley: University of California Press.

Sassen, Saskia. 1984. "The New Labor Demand in Global Cities." In *Cities in Transformation: Class, Capital, and the State*, ed. M. P. Smith, 139–71. Thousand Oaks: Sage.

———. 1991. *The Global City: New York, London, Tokyo*. Princeton: Princeton University Press.

———. 1996. *Losing Control? Sovereignty in an Age of Globalization*. New York: Columbia University Press.

———. 2001. "Global Cities and Global City-Regions: A Comparison." In *Global City-Regions: Trends, Theory, Policy*, ed. Allen J. Scott, 78–95. New York: Oxford University Press.

———, ed. 2002. *Global Networks, Linked Cities*. New York: Routledge.

Scott, Allen John, ed. 2001. *Global City-Regions: Trends, Theory, Policy*. New York: Oxford University Press.

Shanghai City Government. 1991. *Implementation Guidelines for Shanghai Urban Housing Demolition Regulation*.

———. 2003a. *Regulation on Historic Cultural Districts and Excellent Historic Architecture Protection*.

———. 2003b. *Regulation on Preservation of Shanghai's Historical and Cultural Districts and Historical Architecture*.

———. 2009. *Some Suggestions on How to Advance Urban Neighborhood Renewal*.

Shanghai Statistics Bureau. 1990. *Shanghai Statistics Yearbook 1989*. Shanghai: Shanghai Statistics Bureau.

Shin, Kyoung-Ho, and Michael Timberlake. 2000. "World Cities in Asia: Cliques, Centrality and Connectedness." *Urban Studies* 37 (12): 2257–85.

Short, J. R., Y. Kim, M. Kuus, and H. Wells. 1996. "The Dirty Little Secret of World Cities Research: Data Problems in Comparative Analysis." *International Journal of Urban and Regional Research* 20 (4): 697–717.

Shoval, Noam. 2002. "A New Phase in the Competition for Olympic Gold: The London and New York Bids for 2012 Games." *Journal of Urban Affairs* 24 (5): 583–99.

Sklair, Leslie. 2005. "The Transnational Capitalist Class and Contemporary Architecture in Globalizing Cities." *International Journal of Urban and Regional Research* 29 (3): 485–500.

———. 2006. "Iconic Architecture and Capitalist Globalization." *City* 10 (1): 21–47.

Smith, David A. 2001. "World City Networks and Hierarchies, 1977–1997." *American Behavioral Scientist* 44 (10): 1656–78.

Smith, David A., and Michael Timberlake. 1995a. "Cities in Global Matrices: Toward Mapping the World-System's City-System." In *World Cities in a World System*, ed. Paul L. Knox and Peter J. Taylor, 79–97. New York: Cambridge University Press.

———. 1995b. "Conceptualising and Mapping the Structure of the World System's City System." *Urban Studies* 32: 287–302.

———. 2002. "Hierarchies of Dominance among World Cities: A Network Approach." In *Global Networks, Linked Cities*, ed. Saskia Sassen, 117–41. New York: Routledge.

SOHO Xiaobao, ed. 2003. *Na Yi Nian* [That Year]. Nanchang: Jiangxi Renmin Chubanshe.

———, ed. 2005a. *Quan Zi* [Urban Circles]. Wuhan: Changjiang Wenyi Chubanshe.

———, ed. 2005b. *Za Sui* [Fragments]. Beijing: Zhongguo Qingnian Chubanshe.

———, ed. 2006. *Chaoliu yu Fanchaoliu* [Fashion and Antifashion]. Wuhan: Changjiang Wenyi Chubanshe.

Soja, Edward W. 1989. *Postmodern Geographies: The Reassertion of Space in Critical Social Theory*. New York: Verso.

State Council. 1991. *Urban Housing Demolition Regulation*.

———. 2001. *Urban Housing Demolition Regulation*.

———. 2003. *Urgent Notice on Managing Urban Housing Demolition and Maintaining Social Stability*.

———. 2004. *Notice on Controlling Urban Housing Demolition and Strengthening Demolition Management*.

Su, Wen. 2005. *Pan Shiyi Yongyuan Buzuo Daduoshu*. Beijing: Renmin Wenxue Chubanshe.

Sudjic, Deyan. 1992. *Hundred Mile City*. San Diego: Harcourt Brace.

Taylor, Peter J. 2004. *World City Network: A Global Urban Analysis*. New York: Routledge.

———. 2006. "Parallel Paths to Understanding Global Intercity Relations." *American Journal of Sociology* 112 (3): 881–94.

Taylor, Peter J., Ben Derudder, Pieter Saey, and Frank Witlox, eds. 2007. *Cities in Globalization: Practices, Policies and Theories.* New York: Routledge.

Tombesi, Paolo. 2002. "Involving the Industry: Gehry's Use of Packages." *Architectural Research Quarterly* 6 (1): 77–87.

Tombesi, Paolo, Bharat Dave, and Peter Scriver. 2003. "Routine Production or Symbolic Analysis? India and the Globalisation of Architectural Services." *Journal of Architecture* 8 (1): 63.

Tu, Qiyu, and Yaqin Yang. 2003. "Jingji Quanqiuhua yu Suzao Shijie Chengshi" [Economic Globalization and the Making of Global Cities]. *World Economic Research* (7): 4–10.

Tulacz, Gary J. 2008. "The Top 500 Design Firms." *Engineering News Record:* 38–50.

Wai, Albert Wing Tai. 2006. "Place Promotion and Iconography in Shanghai's Xintiandi." *Habitat International* 30 (2): 245–60.

Wallerstein, Immanuel M. 1974. *The Modern World-System: Capitalist Agriculture and the Origins of the European World-Economy in the Sixteenth Century.* New York: Academic Press.

Wang, Jing. 1996. *High Culture Fever: Politics, Aesthetics, and Ideology in Deng's China.* Berkeley: University of California Press.

Wang, Jun. 2003. *Cheng Ji* [Beijing Record]. Beijing: Sanlian Chubanshe.

Wang, Yaping, and Alan Murie. 1996. "The Process of Commercialization of Urban Housing in China." *Urban Studies* 33 (6): 971–89.

Wasserstrom, Jeffrey N. 2008. "Dreams and Nightmares: History and U.S. Visions of the Beijing Games." In *Owning the Olympics: Narratives of the New China,* ed. Monroe E. Price and Daniel Dayan, 163–84. Ann Arbor: University of Michigan Press.

———. 2009. *Global Shanghai, 1850–2010: A History in Fragments.* New York: Routledge.

Weinstein, Liza, and Xuefei Ren. 2009. "The Changing Right to the City: Urban Renewal and Housing Rights in Globalizing Shanghai and Mumbai." *City and Community* 8 (4): 407–32.

Whitelegg, Drew. 2000. "Going for Gold: Atlanta's Bid for Fame." *International Journal of Urban and Regional Research* 24 (4): 801–17.

Whyte, Martin King, and William L. Parish. 1984. *Urban Life in Contemporary China.* Chicago: University of Chicago Press.

Witlox, Frank, and Ben Derudder. 2007. "Airline Passenger Flows through Cities." In *Cities in Globalization: Practices, Policies and Theories,* ed. Peter J. Taylor, Ben Derudder, Pieter Saey, and Frank Witlox, 37–51. New York: Routledge.

Wu, Chen. 2005. "Beijing: Waiguo Jianzhushi de Shiyanchang" [Beijing: A Laboratory for Foreign Architects]. *South China Weekly,* May 25.

Wu, Chenguang. 2004. "Beijing Aoyun Shoushen Diaocha" [Beijing Olympics "Diet" Report]. *Nanfang Daily,* August 12.

Wu, Fulong. 2000a. "The Global and Local Dimensions of Place-Making: Remaking Shanghai as a World City." *Urban Studies* 37 (8): 1359–77.

———. 2000b. "Place Promotion in Shanghai, PRC." *Cities* 17 (5): 349–61.

———, ed. 2006. *Globalization and the Chinese City.* New York: Routledge.

Wu, Fulong, Jiang Xu, and Anthony Gar-On Yeh. 2007. *Urban Development in Post-reform China: State, Market and Space.* New York: Routledge.

Wu, Hung. 2005. *Remaking Beijing: Tiananmen Square and the Creation of a Political Space.* Chicago: University of Chicago Press.

Wu, Jiang. 2001. *Shanghai Bainian Jianzhushi 1840–1949* [The History of Shanghai Architecture]. Shanghai: Tongji University Press.

Wu, Jiaping, and Ian Radbone. 2005. "Global Integration and the Intra-urban Determinants of Foreign Direct Investment in Shanghai." *Cities* 22 (4): 275–86.

Wu, Liangyong. 1999. *Rehabilitating the Old City of Beijing: A Project in the Ju'er Hutong Neighborhood.* Vancouver: UBC Press.

Xia, Jinting. 2005. "The Reuse of Old Buildings: The War of Space." *Architecture & Design,* August, 29–33.

Xu, Jiang, and Anthony G. O. Yeh. 2005. "City Repositioning and Competitiveness Building in Regional Development: New Development Strategies in Guangzhou, China." *International Journal of Urban and Regional Research* 29 (2): 283–308.

Xu, Mingqian. 2004. *Shanghai Zhongxincheng Jiuzhuqu Fazhan Fangshi Xinlun* [Redevelopment of Old Neighborhoods in Inner City Shanghai]. Shanghai: Xuelin Chubanshe.

Xue, Charlie Q. L. 2006. *Building a Revolution: Chinese Architecture since 1980.* Hong Kong: Hong Kong University Press.

Yan, Xiaopei. 1994. "Jinlai Woguo Chengshi Dilixue Zhuyao Yanjiu Lingyu de Xinjinzhan" (New Progress in China's Urban Geography). *ACTA Geographica Sinica* 49 (6): 533–42.

Zha, Jianying. 2005. "The Turtles: The Star Couple of Chinese Real Estate." *New Yorker,* July 11 and 18.

Zhang, Jie. 1997. "Informal Construction in Beijing's Old Neighborhoods." *Cities* 14 (2): 85–94.

Zhang, Jingping. 2004. *Crossroads.* Beijing: Xinshijie Chubanshe.

Zhang, Jun. 2005. "Creek Bank to Be Lined with Refit Shikumen." *Shanghai Daily,* December 7.

Zhang, Tingwei. 2002. "Urban Development and a Socialist Pro-growth Coalition in Shanghai." *Urban Affairs Review* 37 (4): 475–99.

Zhang, Xin. 2000. "How to Advance the Art of Architecture." In *SOHO New Town Files,* ed. Shiyi Pan, 18–19. Tianjin: Tianjin Academy of Social Sciences Press.

Zhang, Yan, and Ke Fang. 2004. "Is History Repeating Itself? From Urban Renewal in the United States to Inner-City Redevelopment in China." *Journal of Planning Education and Research* 23 (3): 286–98.

Zhang, Yue. 2008. "Steering toward Growth: Symbolic Urban Preservation in Beijing, 1990–2005." *Town Planning Review* 79 (2–3): 187–208.

Zhao, Xudong, and Duran Bell. 2005. "Destroying the Remembered and Recovering the Forgotten in Chai: Between Traditionalism and Modernity in Beijing." *China Information* 19 (3): 489–503.

Zhou, Min, and John R. Logan. 1996. "Market Transition and the Commodification of Housing." *International Journal of Urban and Regional Research* 20 (3): 400–421.

Zhu, Jianfei. 2009. *Architecture of Modern China: A Historical Critique.* New York: Routledge.

Zhu, Jieming. 1999. "Local Growth Coalition: The Context and Implications of China's Gradualist Urban Land Reforms." *International Journal of Urban and Regional Research* 23 (3): 534–48.

Zukin, Sharon. 1982. *Loft Living.* Baltimore: Johns Hopkins University Press.

———. 1991. *Landscapes of Power: From Detroit to Disney World.* Berkeley: University of California Press.

———. 1995. *The Cultures of Cities.* Oxford: Blackwell.

Index

administrative boundaries, 10
affordable housing, 12, 122
Ai, Wei Wei, xi, xiv, 21, 58, 73, 150–151,
    157–158, 175
American Institute of Architecture, 24, 41
Andreu, Paul, 2, 4, 153–154, 175
antiurban bias, 65, 66, 102
architectural criticism, 18, 158–159, 164–165
art deco, 41, 60, 109, 119
artist villages, 81
ARUP, 36, 54, 182
Asian financial crisis, 11, 12
authenticity, 117

Ban, Shigeru, 74, 181
banal nationalism, 165, 199
Bank of China, 52, 88–91
Basel, 16, 20, 32, 35, 37, 150, 169, 182, 185–186
Beaux Arts, 42
Becker, H., 41
Beijing: Beijing International Airport, 2,
    147; Catholic South Church, 191; CCTV,
    xi–xii, 2, 8, 35, 36, 70, 81, 150, 153, 156,
    163, 175, 182, 184, 189; Commune by the
    Great Wall, xii, 1–2, 74; Financial Street,
    66; Forbidden City, 62, 103, 134, 143, 148;
    Fragrant Hill Hotel, 49; Houhai, 135;
    Jian'Guo Hotel, 49; Ju'er hutong, 135, 195;
    Nanluoguxiang, 135; National Olympic
    Stadium, 2, 14, 17, 148, 168; National
    Swimming Center, 53, 141, 148; National
    Theater, 53, 153–154, 156, 175; Old Bei-
    jing, 103, 135, 195; Olympic Park, 15,
    147–148, 152, 198; Peking Union Medi-
    cal College, 43; Qianmen, 62–65, 69, 97,
139, 143, 175, 195; Oriental Plaza, 133;
    Shunyi, 135; Tiananmen Square, 66, 142–
    143, 148, 154, 175; Ten Great Buildings,
    16, 44, 144; Wangfujing, 64–66, 69, 97,
    193; Xidan, 65, 193; Yongding Gate, 103,
    148; Zhongguancun, 52, 66
Beijing Architectural Design Institute, 44
Beijing city government, 12, 68, 145, 193
Beijing Cultural Heritage Protection
    Center, 99, 195
Beijing Institute of Architectural Design
    and Research, 149
Beijing Municipal Planning Commission, 148
Beijing Organizing Committee for the
    Olympic Games, 147
big roof style, 44
Bilbao, 5, 8, 78, 165, 185
Bourdieu, Pierre, 170
Boxer Rebellion, 40
branch offices, 15, 19, 23–28, 33–34, 38, 41,
    119, 179
branding, 5, 17–18, 73–74, 81, 94, 96, 141
Brenner, Neil, 159
Brownell, Susan, 157
built environment, 12–14, 18–19, 37, 40, 46,
    59, 98, 100–102, 133, 138–139, 164, 176

capital: capital accumulation, 8, 14, 18, 98,
    166, 176; cultural capital, 6, 17–18, 61, 69,
    79, 83, 170–171; economic capital, 79, 91,
    95, 119, 170; political capital, 98, 114, 119,
    150, 168, 172; symbolic capital, 6, 9, 17–
    18, 55, 61, 79, 91, 95, 98, 102, 167–171
chai, 100, 104, 126–127, 174
Chang, Young Ho, 74, 159–162, 175

China Architecture and Design Group, 150
China International Trust and Investment
    Corp, 151
Chinese Academy of Sciences, 149, 152–153,
    175
Chinese architects, 40, 42–46, 49, 51, 54–57,
    71, 73, 77,157–158, 162
Chinese artists, 73
Chinese central government, 10
Chinese Communist Party, xi, 3, 46, 154
Chinese garden, 149, 152–153, 175
Chinese intellectuals, 47–48
Chinese middle class, 61
Chinese state, 4, 10, 17–18, 21, 39–40, 42, 51,
    58, 141–142, 144, 166, 168
Chongqing, 119–120, 190
city promotion, 137
Cody, Jeffery, 42, 191
colonial style, 41
Communist Youth League, 114
compensation, 99, 101, 124–131
connectivity, 8, 21–23, 33
consumerism, 64, 165
cosmopolitanism, 99–139
critical architecture, 18, 140–166
critical regionalism, 161–162
cultural colonialism, 153
cultural conservatives, 141, 153–154, 157
cultural elites, 83, 85–86, 120, 138, 153, 156–
    157, 168, 172, 175–176
cultural heritage, 69, 99
cultural liberals, 18, 141, 153, 155, 157–158
cultural professionals, 18
Cultural Revolution, xvi, 40, 45, 47, 102, 177

Davidson, Peter, 1, 3, 52, 75, 78,
de Meuron, Pierre, 2, 20–21, 34, 53, 58, 140–
    141, 149–151, 153, 155, 170, 174–175
deindustrialization, 9
demolition: demolition companies, 127, 131;
    demolition lawsuits, 130; demolition
    regulations, 130–131, 134, 142, 160, 168,
    176; forced demolition, 125–131
Deng, Xiaoping, 46, 50, 104
deregulation, 7, 51, 54, 58, 160, 176
design: conceptual design, 8, 149, 151; de-
    sign concepts, 15, 20, 37–38, 55, 57, 124,
    163; design firms, 4, 7, 20–21, 24–25, 27,
    33–35, 37, 51, 54, 56–57, 61–62, 68–69, 73,
    116, 149, 169, 171; design innovation, 20;
    design institutes, 15, 20–21, 45–46, 49,

51, 54–55, 57, 73–74, 149, 191–192; de-
    sign intelligence, 162–163, 165; design
    labor, 7, 37, 39, 51, 169; design work-
    force, 7–8
digitization, 8, 189
dingzihu, 130
displacement, 10, 99–101, 103, 120, 123–131
Dynamic City Foundation, 192

East Asia, xiii, xiv, 24, 32, 41
East China Architecture and Design Insti-
    tute, 182
entrepreneurs, 17–18, 136, 168, 172–173
expatriates, 1, 118, 121–122, 135, 138, 173
extraterritorial jurisdictions, 39

Farrer, James, xv, 121, 196
flexible production, 8
Fordist production, 9
foreign concessions, 16, 39–43, 46, 58, 110–
    111, 113
foreign direct investment, 7, 21, 172
formalism, 44–45
Foster, Norman, 2, 181
Four Socialist Modernizations, 46
Frampton, Kenneth, 161–162
free-trade zones, 21
Friedmann, John, 10, 22
Fujian Province, 56
Fuzhou, 40

Gansu Province, 83
gateway cities, 23
GaWC, 22–23
Gehry, Frank, 8, 165, 182
General Agreement for Trade in Services, 7
gentrification, 102, 121–123, 135–136
global architects, 33, 139
global cities, 1–18, 22–25, 32, 61, 69, 96, 98,
    120, 139, 145, 167, 176, 189
global economy, 6, 10, 118, 122, 177
global urban hierarchy, 11, 32, 176, 179
globalizing state bureaucrats, 18, 172–173
government officials, 9, 11–12, 15, 69, 89–90,
    110, 113, 134, 138–139, 157
Graves, Michael, 109
Guangzhou, 9, 40, 51, 56, 164, 190
guanxi, 113

Hainan Province, 90
Hakka communities, 56

Hangzhou, 119–120
harmonious society, 131
Heihe, 12
Herzog, Jacques, 2, 20–21, 34, 53, 58, 140–141, 149–151, 153, 155, 170, 174–175, 182
Hong Kong, xv, 23, 26–30, 32–36, 41, 47, 49–50, 74, 85, 113, 119, 168, 172, 174, 180–182
housing prices, 81, 83, 87
housing rights activism, 129
Hussey, Henry, 42–43
hutong, 77, 103, 133–138, 194–195

iconic architecture, xi, 17, 101, 165
infrastructure, 8, 12–13, 20, 24, 38, 47, 56, 69–70, 97, 129, 131, 135, 144–147, 163, 176
Inner Mongolia, 21, 58, 163
intergovernmental relations, 10
international architects, 2–5, 8–9, 14–18, 21, 39, 46–50, 54–55, 57, 59–60, 69, 74–77, 95, 98, 101–102, 104, 110, 123, 137, 139, 149, 151–153, 155, 157–158, 164–168, 170–172, 174–175
international design competitions, 69, 124
international metropolises, 11
International Olympic Committee, 145
International style, 41–42, 76
interurban competition, 9, 145, 189
investors, 4–5, 13, 15, 18, 47, 49, 75, 79, 85, 89, 91–96, 101, 105, 110, 124, 135, 168, 172, 174, 176
Isozaki, Arata, 75

Jameson, Fredric, 48
Jencks, Charles, 48
Jiang, Jun, 55–56
Jiang, Zemin, 154, 174
Jinhua Architecture Park, 54

Khrushchev, N., 44
King, Anthony, xiii
Koolhaas, Rem, 36, 138, 149–150, 153–154, 160, 175, 182
Kuan, Seng, 44, 190–192
Kuma, Kengo, 74–75

Lai, Delin, 43
land: land reform, 47, 87, 105, 125, 138; land transactions, 87–88, 176; land use fees,
47, 106; land use rights, 87, 105–106, 126; Ministry of Land, 83; public auctions of land, 87; public ownership of land, 126
large cities, 11, 20, 43, 56
Lefebvre, Henri, 177, 199
liberalization, 6, 7
lilong, 103–104, 106, 195–196
Liu, Suola, 83
Lo, Vincent, 113, 120, 129, 196
Logan, John, 190
London, 22–23, 25, 27–29, 32–34, 36–38, 61, 69, 74, 96, 145
loushu, 84
Luo, Xiaowei, 195–196
Lv, Yanzhi, 42–43

Ma, Laurence J., 190
Ma, Qingyun, 55
Ma, Yansong, 55–56
Macao, 47
manufacturing, 9, 11–12, 68, 94, 97, 138, 147, 171, 176
Manzhouli, 12
Mao, Zedong, 115
market economy, 17, 90–91, 168, 193
market ideology, 160, 162, 166
market reform, 7, 21, 47, 61, 66, 102, 104, 166, 177
master plans, 9, 68
medium- and small-sized cities, 11
megacity, 9
megaprojects, 4, 7, 9–10, 13, 15, 17, 21, 25, 35, 40, 51, 54, 58, 64, 139, 153, 159, 169, 171, 174
Melbourne, 1, 159
migrant housing, 164
migrants, 18, 22, 56, 111–112, 173, 192
Ming dynasty, 193
Ministry of Construction, 51
misrecognition, 170–171
modernism, 39, 44–45
modernity, 14, 56, 64, 69, 144, 166
modernization, 11, 46, 101, 103, 119, 136, 139, 168
monumentality, 43–45
Murphy, Henry, 41–43

Nanjing: Jin'Ling Hotel, 49; Mausoleum for Sun Yat-Sen, 43
Nanjing Treaty, 40
Naquin, Susan, 64, 192–193

nation building, 17, 166
national banking system, 88, 90
national form, 48, 140
national style, 40, 43–44
neoclassical style, 41
neoliberal reform, 14
network analysis, 23, 27, 29, 33, 179–188
networks, 5–6, 15, 21–23, 62, 74, 81, 84, 86, 137
new international division of labor, 8
new power elites, 18
new state spaces, 140–166
Ningbo, 40
nostalgia, 117–119, 139

Olympics: Beijing Olympics, 134, 140–143, 145, 158, 166, 197; Los Angeles Olympics, 144; Seoul Olympics, 145, 166; Tokyo Olympics, 166
OMA, 2, 8, 20, 34–37
Open Door Policy, 16, 46–47, 49–50, 138
Opium War, 40, 64, 110
Ordos, 21, 54, 58–59, 163, 192
organic renewal, 135, 195

Pan, Shiyi, 1, 71–75, 81–83, 86–90, 92, 171, 175, 194–195
Parish, William, 66, 193
Pearl River Delta, 47
Pei, I. M., 49
Peking University, 48–49
penghuqu, 113
People's Commune, 1
People's Court, 125–126, 130
People's Daily, 120
periphery, 21, 23, 113, 132, 161
petition, 130–131, 152–154, 156–158
planned economy, 89–91
policy making, 17, 86–91, 98, 110, 168
port cities, 16, 39–40, 42–43
Portman, John, 49
post-Fordist production, 9
postcolonial, 27
postindustrial cities, 6, 9, 145
postmodernism, 47–48
presales, 73, 78, 84, 88
preservation: creative preservation, 117; historical preservation, 17, 107, 110, 119, 123, 129, 132–134, 138–139, 147, 164; preservation discourse, 99, 101, 136; pres-

ervation laws, 99, 103, 107; preservation practices, 101; reconstruction, 103, 118, 139; remodeling, 103–104; social preservation, 123–124; symbolic preservation, 103–104, 137; urban acupuncture, 103; urban preservation, 99–103, 132–133, 136–137, 139–168, 195
Pritzker Prize, 140
private developers, 3, 14, 17–18, 69, 87, 105–106, 123–124, 134, 137–138, 163, 168
private-public coalition, 174
producer services, 11, 22–23, 32, 176
professional autonomy, 160, 162
property development, 13, 28, 47, 71, 88, 137, 171–174, 176
Property Rights Law, 131, 173
public housing, 125–126
public projects, 2, 152–153

Qing dynasty, 64

real estate speculation, 17, 60–98, 167, 171
relocation, 101, 107, 117, 121–131, 138
Ren, Zhiqiang, 89–90
repositioning of territorial elites, 18, 171–175
resettlement plans, 128
revivalist style, 41
rights to housing, 101, 173
Rotterdam, 16, 20, 37, 169
Rowe, Peter, 44
Royal Institute of British Architects, 41

SANAA, 20, 34, 181, 191
Sassen, Saskia, 10–11, 22
Scale: national scale, 10; rescaling 6, 9–10, 189; transnational scale, 7–8; urban scale, 10, 22
Schumacher, Patrick, 77
Seng, H. Seung, 75
Shanghai: Bund, 41, 103, 107, 109, 121, 124, 134; Chongming Island, 54; French Concession, 107, 110–111, 113; Historical and Cultural Heritage Areas, 107; HSBC building, 41; Huangpu River, 107, 123–124, 134; International Settlement, 107, 110; Jinmao Tower, 54; Old Shanghai, 103, 118–119, 168; Pudong, 107, 109; St. Petersburg Russo-Asiatic Bank, 41; Tianzifang, 123; Tongji University, 110,

119–120, 123–124, 159, 196; Shanghai
 Center, 49; Suzhou Creek, 109, 123–124;
 Xintiandi, 14, 17, 101, 103–104, 109–129,
 138–139, 168, 170–171, 173–174, 176;
 Zhujiajiao, 119
Shanghai city government, 105, 107, 112,
 126, 131
Shanghai Cultural Heritage Bureau, 107
Shanghai Gallery of Art, 109
Shanghai Municipal Planning Commission,
 110
Shanghai Urban Planning and Design
 Institute, 123
shangzhijiao, 113
Shantou, 47
Shanxi Province, 94–95
Shenzhen, 11, 47, 51, 55–56
shikumen, 17, 42–43, 109–129, 134–136, 168
Shui On Group, 112–113, 119, 168, 174
signature buildings, 8, 12, 69
Sklair, Leslie, 165, 174
slums, 46, 113, 118
socialist realist style, 39
Society of Chinese Architects, 42
SOHO China, 1–3, 17, 52, 60–61, 70–73, 75–
 98, 103, 167–168, 171–173
SOHO Xiaobao, 84–91
SOM, 19
Soviet Union: Moscow School of
 Architecture, 43; Soviet Exhibition Hall,
 44; Soviet monumental style, 39, 43
spatial segregation, 11
spatial strategies, 167–171, 176–177
Special Economic Zones, 47
spectacles, 61, 71, 79–84, 140–163
state ideology, 162
state power: configuration of, 10; rescaling
 of, 6, 197
state-owned enterprises, 13, 105
Sun Yat-Sen University, 11
symbolic economy, 6
symbolic interpretation, 103
symbolic power, 98, 172–175
symbolic space, 167–169

Taiping Rebellion, 111
Taiwan, 47, 74, 85
Tange, Kenzo, 166
Taylor, Peter, 23
Tianjin, 64, 119

tizhi, 157
Tokyo, 16, 20, 22–23, 32, 34–35, 37, 69, 78,
 120, 145, 166, 169
Tong, Jun, 48
tourism, 9, 16, 49–50, 61, 102, 138
townships, 10
Toyo, Ito, 77–78
Tsinghua Design Institute, 73
Tsinghua University, 135, 149, 153, 175
tulou, 56, 164
typology of cities, 37

uneven development, 161, 171, 176–177
University of Southern California, 36
Urban China magazine, 55
urban China studies, 13–14
urban destruction, 99, 125, 132
urban development, 10, 13, 101–102, 119,
 137–138, 148, 174
urban economy, 12, 14, 65–66,165, 171, 176
urban elites, 4–5, 14, 86
urban forms, 9, 136
urban fringes, 61, 97
urban glamour zones, 61
urban governance, 10, 137–138
urban planning, 14, 39, 42, 51, 120, 123–124,
 145, 156, 173
urban poor, 18, 131, 164, 176
urban regeneration, 145, 148
urban registration, 125
urban renewal, 10, 51, 99, 101–103, 105–107,
 122, 125–126, 129, 132, 134, 136–137, 162,
 164
urban revitalization, 9
urban revolution, 6, 171, 176–178
urban space, 5, 8–9, 14, 66, 95, 176
urban villages, 56
urbanism, 65
urbanization, 7, 18, 59, 105, 164, 176–177
Urbanus, 55–57, 164

Venice Biennale, 74

Wallerstein, Immanuel, 21
Wang, Jing, 47–48
Wang, Jun, 100, 195
Wang, Shi, 87
Wasserstrom, Jeffery, 139
welfare state, 9
Wen, Jiabao, 130–131, 153–154

Wenchuan earthquake, 164
Whyte, Martin, 66
Wood, Ben, 115
work units, 105, 113–114, 128
workers' villages, 103, 139
world city system, 22, 33
World Expo, 7, 99, 134
world system perspective, 21–22
World Trade Organization, 7
Wu, Fulong, 190
Wu, Liangyong, 135, 153, 195

Xiamen, 40, 47
xiazhijiao, 113
Xu, Yang, 80, 82, 85, 167
Xue, Charlie, 191

Yamamoto, Riken, 75–78, 170
Yan, Xiaopei, 11
Yellow River plateau, 83
Yim, Rocco, 75

Zha, Jianying, 83
Zhang, Tingwei, 190, 194–195, 197
Zhang, Xin, 71–74, 96, 175, 194
Zhang, Yimou, 83, 143, 145
Zheng, Enchong, 130
Zheng, Shiling, 123
Zhu, Jianfei, 18, 159–161, 164
Zhu, Pei, 77
Zhu, Qi, 79, 81
Zhuhai, 47
Zukin, Sharon, 98, 122